Teach... ...nic
...ng

Teaching
Academic
Writing

Edited by

Patricia Friedrich

continuum

Continuum International Publishing Group
The Tower Building   80 Maiden Lane, Suite 704
11 York Road   New York
London SE1 7NK   NY 10038

British Library of Cataloguing-in-Publication Data
A catalogue record for this book is available from the British Library.

ISBN: 978-08264-95327 (hardback)
       978-08264-95334 (paperback)

Library of Congress Cataloguing-in-Publication Data
Teaching academic writing/edited by Patricia Friedrich.
    p. cm.
    ISBN 978-0-8264-9532-7
    ISBN 978-0-8264-9533-4 (pbk.)
    1. English language—Rhetoric—Study and teaching. 2. Report writing—
    Study and teaching. I. Friedrich, Patricia. II. Title.

    PE1404.T369 2007
    808'.0420711—dc22

                                                        2007030181

Typeset by Newgen Imaging Systems Pvt Ltd, Chennai, India
Printed and bound in Great Britain by Antony Rowe, Eastbourne, East Sussex

For Roberto Ventura (in memoriam) and Margie Berns,
the best mentors one could ever wish for

Contents

Acknowledgments

I would like to thank the very talented scholars who agreed to contribute chapters to this collection. To be able to display my work alongside theirs is a privilege. I would also like to acknowledge the many instructors who so generously employ their time teaching students to write—from the kindergarten teachers who send their little ones on the path of writing discovery to the PhD dissertation advisors who manage to convince their advisees to stay on track when the writing gets tough. We are all potential writers in our own right, but it is thanks to these writing teachers that we learn to claim membership in a community of writers.

Contributors

Akua Duku Anokye is Associate Professor of Africana Language, Literature and Culture at the West Campus of Arizona State University. She earned her PhD in linguistics from the City University of New York Graduate School and University Center specializing in orality, literacy, and discourse analysis of language in the African American community. She is co-editor of a collection of essays *Get it Together: Reading in African American Life* published by Pearson and is currently researching the lives of African American community mothers of the civil rights movement. Dr. Anokye is director of the First-Year Composition program on the West Campus and is Chair of Conference on College Composition and Communication.

Shawn Casey is a doctoral student in the Rhetoric, Composition and Literacy program at the Ohio State University.

Jennifer Courtney is an Assistant Professor of Writing Arts at Rowan University. In addition to teaching first-year writing, she teaches writing in a team-taught course with the College of Engineering that integrates project-based engineering design and technical writing. She also teaches a capstone course on writing assessment. Her research interests include writing in the disciplines, writing program administration, and gender studies.

Siân Etherington is currently a lecturer in TESOL in the University of Salford, UK. She is program leader for the MA TEFL and Applied Linguistics programs in addition to co-coordinating in-sessional English for Academic Purposes teaching across the university. She has recently completed a small research project on the teaching and assessment of academic writing on pre-sessional programs and is now working on a project which centers on the learning of Academic Cultures by international students. She is an active member of BALEAP (British Association for Lecturers in English for Academic Purposes).

Dana Ferris is a Professor of English at California State University, Sacramento, where she teaches MA TESOL, applied linguistics, and multilingual composition courses and coordinates the multilingual writing program. She has published her research on second language writing in journals such as *TESOL Quarterly*, *Journal of Second Language Writing*, and *Research in the Teaching of English*. Her books include *Teaching ESL Composition* (with John Hedgcock, Erlbaum, 1998/2005), *Response to Student Writing* (Erlbaum, 2003), and Treatment of Error in Second Language Writing Classes (Michigan, 2002), and she is currently at work on a book called *Teaching Second Language Readers* (with John Hedgcock, Taylor & Francis, forthcoming).

Patricia Friedrich is Assistant Professor of English at Arizona State University where she also coordinates the Writing Certificate Program. She teaches a variety of courses in academic writing, sociolinguistics, cross-cultural communication and applied linguistics. She is a world Englishes scholar and the author of *Language, Peace and Negotiation* (Continuum, 2007). She has also guest co-edited a special issue of the journal *World Englishes* about English in South America (2003) and has published her work in such journals as *International Journal of Applied Linguistics*, *Harvard Business Review*, *Management Research* and *English Today*. She is a member of the editorial board of the *International Multilingual Research Journal*.

A. Abby Knoblauch is a doctoral candidate in composition studies at the University of New Hampshire, where she has served as Assistant Director of undergraduate composition. She has taught a variety of undergraduate writing courses, including first-year writing, creative nonfiction writing, and persuasive writing. Abby has co-edited a collection of essays entitled *What to Expect When You're Expected to Teach: The Anxious Craft of Teaching Composition*, published by Boynton/Cook in 2002.

Paul Kei Matsuda is Associate Professor of English at Arizona State University, where he teaches in the PhD program in Rhetoric, Composition and Linguistics. He has taught a variety of writing courses as well as graduate courses in rhetoric, composition and applied linguistics. His articles on the history of composition have appeared in journals such as *College Composition and Communication*, *College English*, *Journal of Basic Writing* and *Journal of Second Language Writing* as well as in edited collections such as *Linking Literacies* (2001), *Exploring the Dynamics of Second Language Writing*

(2003) and *Second Language Writing Research* (2005). URL: http://matsuda. jslw.org/.

John Morley works in the University Language Centre at Manchester University where he is Director of the Academic Support Programmes. He has an MEd (Hons) from the University of New England, Australia, and has previously worked in universities and schools in Australia, Singapore, Spain and Indonesia. His current research interest is the measurement of language gain during study abroad and factors affecting this. John is a Fellow of the UK Higher Education Academy.

Diane Pecorari is a Senior Lecturer in English applied linguistics and coordinator of the English Studies program at Mälardalen University in Sweden. She holds a BA and an MA from the Ohio State University and a PhD in English from Birmingham University. Her research interests include writing in the disciplines, discourse analysis and formulaic language. She teaches across the linguistics curriculum, including courses on discourse analysis and research writing for postgraduate students. She is a member of the editorial board of *English for Specific Purposes*.

Cynthia L. Selfe is Humanities Distinguished Professor in the Department of English at The Ohio State University, and the co-editor, with Gail Hawisher, of *Computers and Composition: An International Journal*. In 1996, Selfe was recognized as an EDUCOM Medal award winner for innovative computer use in higher education—the first woman and the first English teacher ever to receive this award. In 2000, Selfe, along with long-time collaborator Gail Hawisher, was presented with the Outstanding Technology Innovator award by the CCCC Committee on Computers. Selfe has served as the Chair of the Conference on College Composition and Communication and the Chair of the College Section of the National Council of Teachers of English.

Michael Stancliff is Assistant Professor of Rhetoric and Composition at Arizona State University where he teaches courses in writing, rhetoric, and literature. He is author, with Sharon Crowley, of *Critical Situations: A Rhetoric with Workshops*, as well as author of articles on pedagogy and politics. He is working on a book about race, emotion, and the politics of the Reconstruction era in the United States.

Christine Tardy is Assistant Professor at DePaul University in Chicago, where she teaches writing and the teaching of writing and ESL to undergraduate and graduate students. She has taught in the US, Europe, and Asia, in both academic and professional contexts. Her research interests include writing in the disciplines, writing in international contexts, and second language writing. She has published in *Written Communication*, *Journal of Second Language Writing*, *Journal of English for Academic Purposes*, and *English for Specific Purposes*.

Introduction
Teaching Academic Writing:
How Do We Do It?

Patricia Friedrich

Writing is hard work. Teaching writing is even harder work. When it comes to teaching academic writing, so many are the possible paths and pedagogical venues that the newcomer may feel overwhelmed and intimidated. Not only are his or her decisions going to affect the pedagogical outcome of classes, but such choices can also give away the instructor's views of the world and influence the students for years to come. When it comes to the large number of adjunct faculty, teaching assistants and graduate students who teach academic writing, the decisions involved may be of an even more complex nature. Many times choices are made by academic departments or department chairs and communicated to these constituencies; as a result, part-time faculty can be left out of important academic discussions which affect their teaching and the academic lives of their students.

It was thinking of these important decisions and the possible lack of opportunity for these individuals to engage in as much discussion about academic writing as they may desire and require, that we, directors and instructors of academic writing programs, have put together this collection of essays. Our goal is to establish a dialogue with those interested in the teaching of academic writing, and especially those who may feel they have limited access to academic discussions or yet who believe they are only partially ready to face the challenges ahead of them. We have tried hard to base our chapters on practical, useful and already-tried ideas which may facilitate the process of teaching academic writing. We have strived to be realistic about the time and work constraints of writing instructors and the need to balance out such constraints by providing students with sound writing instruction and useful feedback.

To that end, we have based our chapters on what we consider to be important aspects and background information for classroom instruction. The first chapter, written by A. Abby Knoblauch and Paul Matsuda, focuses on the evolution of composition studies, mainly in the United States, and the reasons why we came to teach academic writing the way(s) we do today. Chapter 2, by Siân Etherington, discusses writing and the disciplines, this time mainly in the United Kingdom, and the challenges of discipline-specific contexts. A list of useful resources is provided.

The third chapter, written by Akua Duku Anokye, provides that director of first-year composition's perspective on pedagogical aspects affecting the teaching of academic writing. Complementarily, Christine Tardy and Jennifer Courtney's Chapter 4 focuses on examples of pedagogical tasks to fulfill different teaching objectives. Once writing tasks have been completed, Dana Ferris, in Chapter 5, provides us with ideas of how to give feedback to the students in a manner that will truly impact their future writing.

In Chapter 6, John Morley provides us with a case study that illustrates the different approaches and writing support initiatives which can be made available to different students (e.g. undergraduates, graduate students and international students) in an attempt to increase their chances of success. Shawn Casey and Cynthia Selfe in Chapter 7 discuss the different ways in which technology can be an ally in the academic writing classroom.

In Chapter 8, I discuss diversity issues with a twist; I am interested in the ways monolingual users of English understand and perceive diversity and what can be done to make them sympathize and relate to the struggles of second and foreign language users. Still dealing with matters of perceptions and attitudes, Michael Stancliff, in Chapter 9, explains to us how community based approaches to teaching academic writing can not only enhance the outcomes in the composition classroom but also make more conscientious citizens of our students. Finally, Diane Pecorari in Chapter 10 brings to our attention another aspect with educational and moral ramification—the matter of plagiarism and academic integrity (and patchwriting) and how to best address these issues in our classroom.

The reader will notice that, in an attempt to preserve the voice and authenticity of the individual chapters, as well as to revere the multiplicity of Englishes available to writers, the original varieties of English chosen (instinctively or deliberately) by contributors were maintained. It is our hope that the aspects discussed in these ten chapters are of interest to our readers and that through the process of engaging in these discussions we all become better teachers to our students and better members of our academic communities. Writing these chapters for this collection has certainly already had this effect on us.

Patricia Friedrich, PhD
Peoria, Arizona, June 2007

First-Year Composition in Twentieth-Century US Higher Education: A Historical Overview

A. Abby Knoblauch and Paul Kei Matsuda

History of composition in US higher education is a complex subject, due in part to the multiplicity of stories. Take, for example, the beginning of the field, which has long been a contested issue among historians of composition (Connors, 1991; North, 1987; Young and Goggin, 1993). One could trace the teaching of rhetoric, broadly defined as purposeful language use, back to ancient times. It has been a common practice among Western academics to trace the history of rhetoric and writing instruction—along with most other contemporary academic disciplines—to fifth century BCE Greece (e.g. Bizzell and Herzberg, 2001; Murphy, 2001), although rhetoric is not unique to the so-called Western civilization nor were the ancient Greeks the first to come up with the idea (Kennedy, 1998; Mao, 2007).[i]

Another popular starting point is the institutionalization of the first-year composition course in US higher education during the late nineteenth century (Brereton, 1995; Connors, 1997; Crowley, 1998), although historians differ on exactly which event marks the beginning. It is also possible to imagine the history of composition as remarkably short, by starting the narrative from the mid-twentieth century, when composition began to emerge as an academic discipline in its own right (Berlin, 1987; Connors, 1999; Harris, 1997; Lauer, 1993; North, 1987; Nystrand, Greene and Wiemelt, 1993). Again, historians of composition have marked the beginning of the discipline at various points during this period.

This presence of multiple starting points is emblematic of the complexity of the history of composition. As Young and Goggin (1993) have pointed out, however, all of these perspectives have some merit, serving different purposes. For the purpose of this introductory overview, we will begin with the birth of the composition course itself at Harvard in the late nineteenth century, which we feel marks the first inkling of the course that many of the readers of this chapter are—or will be—teaching. But first, in order to provide a better sense of the historical context, we will take a brief look at the shape of writing instruction in early nineteenth-century US higher education.[ii]

Writing instruction in early US colleges

US higher education in the early part of the nineteenth century was greatly influenced by the British tradition (Berlin, 1984; Brereton, 1995). Most colleges at this time were small institutions catering to a population of students who were training for careers in law, medicine, or the church. All students were put through the same four-year course of study, taking the same classes from the same instructors. The needs of the time were perceived to be such that no majors, and very few electives, were offered. Most instructors—who were not trained academics but respected members of various professions—focused on the classics and math, and sometimes science. In contrast to the system that we see today, US higher education in the first half of the nineteenth century was less about training students in any particular domain of knowledge and more about building character and developing proper "taste" (Brereton, 1995: 3).

The education of these young men—and we do mean *men* in reference to the early nineteenth century—relied heavily on composition in the rhetorical tradition. Composition was "one of the oldest college courses" in the United States (Crowley, 1998: 49); in fact, it existed long before the English department became a commonplace or English literature became a legitimate subject of study in college (Berlin, 1984; Connors, 1997). In the early years, however, the emphasis was on oral performance, a practice borrowed from classical rhetoric. Students learned the art of rhetoric by two primary methods: transcription and recitation. Charged with memorizing a text (most often in Latin), a student would then be called upon to recite that text on demand. Such recitations were critiqued by the student's instructor and sometimes by other students. Students might also be asked to *declaim*—or defend a thesis—in the common hall. Such declamations were usually attended by the entire college population and were often followed by public criticism.

As Brereton (1995) is quick to point out, however, the emphasis on orality did not preclude written literacy in early US colleges. For example, students were often required to submit a written copy of their declamations after delivering them orally. Students were also asked to write themes (short compositions) on political, religious, or personal matters, and to keep a common book where they took copious lecture notes. Writing was considered so crucial to higher education that students received instruction in writing, rhetoric, and speaking, throughout the four years of their education.

By the last third of the nineteenth century, writing instruction had replaced speech as the primary concern of composition courses (Berlin, 1984; Connors, 1997; S. M. Halloran 1982). Wright and Halloran (2001) attribute the shift to three developments that are somewhat related to one another: the popularity of belletristic writing, which shifted the emphasis from text production (eloquence) to consumption (taste); the advancement of writing technology, such as improved writing instruments (e.g. pens, pencils); and the availability of relatively cheap papers; and the rise of the middle class and the quest for upward mobility through college education.

The changing shape of US higher education

Another reason that writing came to the fore as an integral part of US higher education was the growth and diversification of the student population due in part to several important changes. The first was the Morrill Act. First passed by Congress in 1862, the Morrill Act offered land for erecting institutions that included agricultural, mechanical, and engineering instruction in their curriculum (Connors, 1997; Crowley, 1998; Matsuda and Matsuda, in press). The second Morrill Act, passed in 1890, further increased the number of land-grant institutions. The Morrill Acts expanded the curricular possibilities of US higher education: A greater number of students, including women, might now attend college for reasons other than preparation for law, medicine, or the church. It also facilitated the creation of many historically Black colleges (Royster and Williams, 1999). The Morrill Acts also helped to create *more* colleges, increasing the number of options available to those with the desire and means to attend higher education.

With societal changes came greater German influence (Brereton, 1995; Connors, 1997; Crowley, 1998). The German model of education valued specialization over breadth, and stressed the creation of knowledge—research—rather than the transmission of traditional values. This focus on specialization necessitated a restructuring of US higher education institutions. Students and faculty would need something to specialize *in*; in other words, students would need majors. Within this context, US universities began to organize themselves by academic disciplines. The impact of the German model of education should not be underestimated. In the mere 30 years between 1870 and 1900, the majority of US institutions of higher education shifted from a series of smaller, more exclusive colleges with prescribed classical curricula to larger universities that prepared students for a broad range of specializations.

Changes in enrollment also contributed to major transformations in early US higher education. Enrollments in colleges and universities rose steadily after the Civil War, prompting modifications in pedagogical and assessment practices. Shifting enrollments meant that not every entering student could be assumed to have the kind of linguistic background and experience that traditional native speakers of privileged varieties of English had (Matsuda, 2006). In order to maintain the "purity of the language," and the standards of education, an entrance exam was created (Brereton, 1995; Crowley, 1998). The mandatory writing entrance exam, which asked students to write essays in response to a literary prompt, was first introduced by Adams Sherman Hill at Harvard in 1874. Other universities soon followed Harvard's lead and instituted similar entrance exams.

Hill and his contemporaries were shocked by what they saw as students' inability to write; half of the students who took the exam in 1897 failed it (Crowley, 1998). It is important to keep in mind, however, that the scope of the exam was rather limited; questions were based on literary works that students may or may not have read. Students were asked, for example, to write on a particular work by Thackeray or literary history, with no prior knowledge of the subject areas to be covered. It might have been that students *could* write, but just not in the ways—or on the topics—that were by valued by institutions at the time.

Still, given what were seen as deplorable results on the written entrance exam, colleges and universities had to decide what to do with students who, in every other way, seemed prepared for admission. In order to deal with this situation, Harvard developed a composition course to be taken during the sophomore year. But the college found itself in the uncomfortable position of requiring an entrance exam in a subject that was not offered until the second year of study. So in 1885, the course, called English A, was moved to the first year. Again, most schools followed Harvard's lead and, by 1900, the first-year writing course had become a staple of US higher education.

The emergence of a discipline

While the Harvard course led to the creation of first-year writing courses across the nation, composition did not begin to move toward a disciplinary status until well into the twentieth century. One of the early catalysts for the move was World War II. Convinced that the war was the result of a lack of communication both within and between nations, and certain that communication would be central to a victory in war, the US government set up training facilities at university campuses across the nation. Here, enlisted men were educated not only in medicine and science, but also a "basic" curriculum, designed by academics and military personnel, to "promote clarity and efficiency of communication" (Crowley, 1998: 157). These basic communications courses emphasized oral and written communication, what we might now call technical or professional writing (reports, memos, etc.), and an attention to popular media and forms of propaganda (Berlin, 1987).

By focusing on popular media, speech, and genres such as field reports, the communication movement changed the purpose and form of first-year courses at over 200 institutions. It also affected the field of composition in yet another way: Because so many of the graduate students assigned to teach the first-year course had been trained in literature and not composition or communication, many writing program directors were faced with a workforce prepared to teach the wrong course. Feeling the need to talk to others in the same boat, almost one hundred people attended a meeting of the National Council of Teachers of English (NCTE) on the first-year program. The meeting was met with a great enthusiasm, and John C. Gerber suggested another meeting in the spring to discuss composition and communication in first-year writing programs, which attracted 500 participants (Crowley, 1998: 182). The year

1949, then, saw the first meeting of the Conference on College Composition and Communication (CCCC), now the field's major national conference with Gerber as the first Chair.

The first CCCC convention did not, in itself, lead directly to disciplinary status for the field of composition. Unlike its counterparts at National Society of Speech Communication, CCCC members in early years were more interested in teaching rather than research—*sine qua non* of an academic discipline (D. George and Trimbur, 1999). While the founding of CCCC was accompanied by the creation of *College Composition and Communication* (*CCC*)—now a major flagship journal in the field—it did not evolve into a rigorous research journal until the 1960s.[iii] Composition was also without a sense of its own history; although Albert Kitzhaber (1953/1990) produced the first dissertation-length history of composition in the US in the early 1950s, it was not until two decades later that underground copies of the work became widely circulated (Connors, 1999).

The interest in communication, or the "fourth C" waned over the next decade—partly because of the lack of solid disciplinary footing as well as composition teachers' anxiety over the rise of the new media (Berlin, 1987; Crowley, 1998; D. George and Trimbur, 1999; Russell, 1991). By 1960, the communication component had all but disappeared from the organization. With the triumphs of composition over communication in what some have characterized as the "communication battle" (D. George and Trimbur, 1999: 682), composition began to move toward a more research-oriented discipline in the 1960s. In the meantime, various related disciplines—literature, linguistics, rhetoric—began to compete for attention as the intellectual bases on which to build the composition course, with rhetoric emerging as the dominant disciplinary influence (Berlin, 1987). Composition researchers also began to borrow theories and research methodologies from other related fields, including psychology, linguistics, education and sociology, among others, making it a "multimodal discipline" (Lauer, 1993: 44).

Historians of composition have identified various events that have stimulated composition's move toward disciplinary status: the launching of *Sputnik* in 1957 and the subsequent creation of funding opportunities through the National Defense Education Act (Berlin, 1987); the influential 1963 *CCCC* convention (North, 1987); the 1966 Dartmouth Seminar (Harris, 1997); the creation of research-oriented journals since the mid-1960s (Connors, 1984; Goggin, 2000); and the rise of historical consciousness and the proliferation of modes of disciplinary reproduction—i.e. doctoral programs—in the 1970s

(Brown, Jackson and Enos, 2000; Connors, 1999). With these changes, composition journals began to publish more theoretically grounded, research-based articles than those articles in which the primary goal was the sharing of teaching ideas or program descriptions (Goggin, 2000). The proliferation of scholarly journals in the latter half of the twentieth century encouraged pedagogical discussions and change that were grounded in theory and research. Teacher-scholars were able to hear from others like them across the country, comparing approaches and theoretical bases. In the next section, we present an overview of some of the major pedagogical approaches, starting with characterizations of writing courses in the late nineteenth and early twentieth centuries.

Major pedagogical conversations since the late twentieth century

While pedagogical changes might sometimes seem to follow a sort of cause-and-effect chronology—a reaction to one pedagogical approach sparks a new movement—there are dangers in relying too heavily on such a narrative. Such a simplistic view results in what Silva (1990) has dubbed as the "merry-go-round of approaches" that generates "more heat than light" (p. 18). To present pedagogical movements as paradigmatic shifts relies on a number of problematic assumptions (Matsuda, 2003): that pedagogical approaches have easily demarcated beginnings and endings, and that one simply leaves the old strategy behind and walks confidently toward a new approach, never looking back. Door closed. Old approach over. This, of course, is not the case. Yet, it is useful for newcomers to the field to know the conventional narrative of the field—if only to help them join the efforts to critique it. What follows, then, is not an attempt to delineate approaches as if they are mutually exclusive; instead, we offer a brief overview—a place to begin—which we hope will help the readers identify and contextualize existing teaching practices.

"Current-traditional rhetoric"

The first sixty years of writing instruction, beginning with the proliferation of first-year writing courses at the end of the nineteenth century and the early twentieth century, is often considered to be the "Dark Ages" of composition (Connors, 1986: 189). Marked by what has come to be known as "current-traditional rhetoric," the required first-year course during this period is often given as an example of all that is wrong with the way we "used to" teach writing. The term "current traditional rhetoric" (without a hyphen) was originally coined by Daniel Fogarty (1959), who sought to capture what he considered to be the then-traditional principles of writing and rhetoric as portrayed in textbooks. Two decades later, Richard Young (1978) adopted the term "current-traditional rhetoric" to point out the lack of attention to invention in composition research. Historians of composition such as Berlin (1984; Berlin and Inkster, 1980) and Crowley (1990) have documented in detail the development of current-traditional rhetoric as well as its theoretical underpinnings (Berlin, 1984; Berlin and Inkster, 1980; Crowley, 1990).

Current-traditional rhetoric has been characterized as an approach that values mechanical correctness above all, focusing more on proper comma placement than on content, thought, or expression. Young's (1978) most influential characterization of current-traditional rhetoric highlights "the emphasis on the composed product rather than the composing process; the analysis of discourse into words, sentences, and paragraphs; the strong concern with usage (syntax, spelling, punctuation) and with style (economy, clarity, emphasis); and so on" (p. 31). The focus on sentence and paragraph level concerns was one hallmark of current-traditional rhetoric; another was the structuring of writing around a particular conception of modes of discourse rooted in the late eighteenth-century faculty psychology: description, narration, exposition, and argumentation (see Crowley, 1990; Connors, 1997).

While there is some truth to the characterization of current-traditional rhetoric, such a depiction is ultimately an oversimplification—a discursively constructed caricature (Matsuda, 2003). Composition pedagogy in the mid-twentieth century was not as monolithic as is commonly thought. James Berlin (1987), for example, identified three alternative approaches that existed during the first half of the twentieth century: the rhetoric of liberal culture, a transactional rhetoric for democracy, and the ideas approach. Tirabassi (2007) has also problematized the simplistic periodization that conflates a dominant pedagogical practice with a historical era, and documented pedagogical innovations at the University of New Hampshire during the so-called "current-traditional era".

Furthermore, it is important to understand the historical context in which the pedagogical practices associated with current-traditional rhetoric were functioning—although we do not necessarily mean to defend those practices. The new university was populated more than ever by members of the emergent middle class; many of these students wanted instruction in proper grammar and structure, given that attention to such detail was, as the popular narrative goes, expected in the new business economy. While the focus on "proper" English may have served a gate-keeping function, acquisition of such discourse may have also assisted students in their quest for social mobility.

Additionally, the influx of students, coupled with the required first-year course, resulted in what might now seem like an impossible amount of student writing on which to comment. Connors (1986) reminds us that most writing instructors of the late nineteenth and early twentieth centuries taught large courses. Barrett Wendell at Harvard may have read upwards of twenty-two thousand brief (approximately one-page) student themes a year; Fred Newton Scott remarked that he had read at least three thousand student essays in a single year at the University of Michigan (Connors, 1986: 83). While many historians have lamented what they have seen as an unproductive focus on mechanical correctness during this time, Connors (1986) suggests that such an approach may have been little short of a survival technique— just as the notion of process was in its earlier manifestation in the 1950s (Mills, 1953).

The process movement

As the story goes, the process movement began in the late 1960s and early 1970s as a response to current-traditional rhetoric, and while scholars have begun to challenge the cause-and-effect chronology of the process narrative (a challenge that we will return to momentarily), there certainly was something in the composition air at this time. Scholars were beginning to question the usefulness of focusing only on the final written products, arguing that dissecting a students' final draft does little to help the student become a better writer. Instead, process proponents attempted to find ways to intervene in the process of writing. Some of these techniques included encouraging students to write multiple drafts, incorporating peer feedback, providing teacher feedback before students submit their final draft for evaluation, and even having students develop portfolios to highlight their processes of writing as well as their development as writers. "Teach writing as a process, not a product"— taken from the title of a 1972 newsletter article by process practitioner Donald Murray—became the motto of the burgeoning process movement, creating the false impression that to teach process was to abandon all concerns about product.

The process movement was seen by many as revolutionary; it has even been called a disciplinary paradigm shift by some (Hairston, 1982). Yet, many now acknowledge that process was not invented in the 1960s and 1970s

(Crowley, 1998; Tobin, 2001). Even in those early Harvard classes, some instructors were using strategies that are associated with process pedagogy— including "writing conferences, the use of student writing as the primary texts of the course, peer critiquing, [and] analytic evaluation tools" (Newkirk, 1994: 119). Some of the first sustained discussions of the writing process began in the early twentieth century (Matsuda, 2003). The paradigm shift narrative also functions as if there is singular entity or practice that we might call process or process pedagogy. But of course there are multiple versions of process and process pedagogies. As Berlin (1982) has noted, "everyone teaches the process of writing, but everyone does not teach the *same* process. The test of one's competence as a composition instructor [...] resides in being able to recognize and justify the version of the process being taught" (p. 777). It is to these different versions of process that we now turn.

In the early years of the process movement, composition scholars from different disciplinary orientations were united against a common enemy— current-traditional rhetoric. During the 1980s, composition scholars began to identify distinct categories within the larger process movement. In the concluding section of *Writing Instruction in Nineteenth-century American Colleges,* Berlin (1984) delineated "three contemporary approaches to teaching writing," each with its own assumptions about the process of writing. "The three theories" included "the classical, the expressionist, and ... the new rhetoric" (p. 86). Within a few years, these categories were replaced by a more widely accepted tripartite distinction that included expressive, cognitive and social views (Berlin, 1988; Bizzell, 1986; Faigley, 1986). In "Competing theories of process: A critique and a proposal," Faigley (1986) wrote:

> Commentators on the process movement (e.g. Berlin, *Writing Instruction*) now assume at least two major perspectives on composing, an *expressivist view* including the work of "authentic voice" proponents such as Williams Coles, Peter Elbow, Ken Macrorie, and Donald Stewart, and a *cognitive view* including the research of those who analyze composing processes such as Linda Flower, Barry Kroll, and Andrea Lunsford. More recently, a third perspective on composing has emerged, one that contends processes of writing are social in character instead of originating within individual writers. Statements on composing from the third perspective, which I call the *social view,* have come from Patricia Bizzell, Kenneth Bruffee, Marilyn Cooper, Shirley Brice Heath, James Reither, and authors of several essays collected in *Writing in Non-academic Settings* edited by Lee Odell and Dixie Goswami. (pp. 527–528)

Cognitive views of process—most often associated with the work of Linda Flower and John Hayes (1977) and Janet Emig (1971)—were based on research in cognitive-developmental psychology, American cognitive psychology, and cognitive science (Faigley, 1986). Proponents of cognitive models of process attempted to understand the actual processes writers went through as they composed, with an eye toward developing ways to intervene in this process, which would allow teachers to assist the student with the actual *act* of composing, instead of commenting only on the products of composition. While cognitive process theories may have seemed (or even still seem) promising, offering instructors a concrete method for intervention and improvement, critiques of these theories quickly followed. Scholars such as David Bartholomae (1985) and Patricia Bizzell (1982) charged cognitivists of ignoring the influence of discursive practices and discourse communities. Others remarked that cognitive theorists were attempting to describe *the* theory or process of writing (e.g. Kent, 1999; Olson, 1999) and, in doing so, were ignoring very real differences in race, class, ethnicity, and gender as well as individual differences.

While cognitivists attempted to describe the cognitive processes associated with writing, expressive process proponents focused their attention on the individual writer. Compositionists such as Donald Murray, Ken Macrorie, and Peter Elbow are often credited for creating a space in which students could find and develop their own original, authentic voices. Stemming in part from a tradition of essayists such as Montaigne, Thoreau, and Emerson, and in part from the Romantic tradition (see Fishman and McCarthy, 1992), expressivists also often focused on personal experience in the composition classroom, and were particularly interested in what we might now call personal writing. Expressivists championed what came to be seen as hallmarks of process pedagogy: individual conferences with the instructor, peer writing groups, revision, freewriting, and portfolio assessment. In order to help students develop their own authentic writerly voices, issues of mechanics and grammar were put on the back burner (which is not to say they were always wholly ignored) while students were encouraged to experiment with language, to write what they knew, and to write to discover.

But expressivists, too, were charged with ignoring the impact of social influences and with dismissing the importance of writing in the academy. By the 1980s, a schism started to form between proponents of personal writing and advocates for academic writing. Indicative of this debate was a conversation between Peter Elbow and David Bartholomae published in *CCC* in 1995. Elbow (1995) put their disagreement in these terms: "I fear that there is a conflict between the role of writer and that of academic" (p. 72). He explained that he sees "specific conflicts in how to design and teach my first year writing course. And since I feel forced to choose—I choose the goal of writer over that of academic" (p. 73). Elbow noted, however, that he imagined himself as both writer and academic, and hoped that his students also imagine themselves in similar ways. The problem, according to him, is that the first-year writing course is the only place in the university where students might be encouraged to see themselves as writers.

During this exchange, Elbow based his view on the definition of a "writer." Elbow explained that, for him, a writer is one who develops an individual point of view. The product may be social, in that it is (sometimes) written for an audience, but the process is often that of an individual mind attempting to best express a unique voice and point of view. Note, however, that the term "writer" for Elbow has often been synonymous with "creative writer"; his job, he said, was to provide an atmosphere in which such a writer can flourish.

Bartholomae (1995) disagreed. He saw his goal as a writing instructor as an attempt to "make the writer aware of the forces that are at play in the production of knowledge" (p. 66). He imagined his project in the classroom, then, as primarily a form of cultural critique and awareness. This is not to say that students in such a class are not writing—of course they are—but Bartholomae argued that students need to be aware of the discursive spaces in which writing takes place, including the academy as a space (a space that they are currently in), and to be aware of the ways in which writing is situated in the academy. In other words, students need to be invited into the world and the writing—the discourse community—of the academy. According to Bartholomae, the focus of a first-year writing course should be on introducing students to the conventions of academic, not creative, writing.

The discussion between Bartholomae and Elbow is indicative of the sort of conversation that still occurs in composition studies. While this particular debate circles around the value of personal writing in the college classroom, what these two scholars are really discussing is the role of the first-year writing course. Is it to prepare students for writing in the academy, writing across the curriculum, writing in the disciplines, or is it to nurture a student's personal identity, personal vision, and sense of self? The terms of the debate may have changed somewhat, but as we will see throughout the remainder of this chapter, the crux of such conversations remains largely the same.

Theorists and practitioners of what Lester Faigley (1986) has characterized as the social view of process have responded productively to many of the challenges leveled against cognitive and expressivist process pedagogies. As Faigley points out, the social view is more difficult to define and categorize as it springs from multiple theoretical sources. Also, the reader will see many similarities between Faigley's social view of writing and "post-process" and rhetorical pedagogies (which we will discuss shortly). Faigley suggests that proponents of the social view of process attempt to place writing in social contexts, believing that "human language (including writing) can be understood only from the perspective of a society rather than a single individual" (p. 535).

This understanding can be rooted in a number of different theoretical backgrounds, however, including "poststructuralist theories of language, the sociology of science, ethnography, and Marxism" (p. 535). Those working from a poststructuralist tradition tend to see writing as situated in larger social contexts (including the academy) and writing itself as always already constructed by prior texts (Bakhtin, 1981). Faigley places David Bartholomae in this faction of social process theories. Faigley explains that in the "more extreme version of this argument, science itself becomes a collection of literary forms" (p. 536). Within this framework, what some may see as "facts," are viewed instead as part of scientific genres and are always already constructed by the practices of the communities of which they are a part. Ethnographers in this context examine the ways in which various communities (including home, work, and school) shape the development of language practices. And finally, those working from critical traditions urge scholars to recognize the implications of language in power, and power in discursive practices.

"Post-process"

Both the expressive and cognitive branches of process pedagogies faced stiff critiques in the 1980s for what was viewed by some as a naïve ignorance of the ways in which social forces shape both writing and writers. Critics decried such theorists' inattention to the social categories of race, class, ethnicity, and gender in the classroom and in the larger social realm (although they also have often failed to consider language differences), and argued that expressivists' focus on unique individual expression not only elided real differences between these social positionalities, but also celebrated a unified sense of self that was being quickly challenged and dismantled by postmodern theory. Furthermore, a focus on personal expression, according to critics, ignored the social and rhetorical contexts in which writing and reading happen.

By the early 1990s, composition specialists seemed to have come to agree on the tripartite classification of process theory and pedagogy into expressive, cognitive and social (Ward, 1994). At about the same time, however, some scholars (e.g. Paré, 1994; Trimbur, 1994) began to redraw the conventional map of the field by introducing a new key term, "post-process." The term post-process quickly became a popular keyword to capture various changes that were taking place in the field of composition; yet, the definition of post-process has long been a point of contention. For instance, the division between process and post-process is a rather tenuous one; Paré (1994), for example, continued to prefer to use the term "social process" in discussing what he referred to in the title as "post-process," implying that post-process was still part of process. When Kent published an edited collection entitled *Post-Process Theory: Beyond the Writing Process Paradigm*, the contributors also seemed to define post-process in various ways, although "all of them agree that change is in the air" (Kent, 1999: 5).

Talking about post-process seems to imply that the field of composition has moved beyond thinking about writing as a process. Yet, instructors in colleges and high schools across the nation continue to teach writing as a process, whether they imagine it as a lock-step sequence of prewriting, writing, and rewriting, or think of it as a more messy, recursive series of events. Most writing instructors, even those who would place themselves within a post-process paradigm, still value multiple drafts and revision as well, and many now view post-process as an extension—rather than a rejection—of process (DeJoy, 2004; McComisky, 2000; Matsuda, 2003). Still, the term "post-process" does mark a more deliberate attempt to focus on the social forces that influence genre, purpose, and audience, as well as writers and the process of writing. Rhetorical pedagogy, critical pedagogy and cultural studies are three approaches that can be placed within such a framework.

Rhetorical pedagogy

Those practicing a rhetorical pedagogy ask students to consider issues of audience, purpose, and form, and often to engage in collaborative writing assignments (see Lauer, 1980). As we have noted, the history of rhetorical education can be traced to fourth- and fifth-century BCE sophists and philosophers such as Gorgias, Plato, and Aristotle as well as first-century CE Roman philosophers such as Cicero and Quintilian. The relationship with many of these ancient rhetoricians is complicated, however. We need to keep in mind that such education was intended for a rather small group of privileged white males and is not always easily transferable to our twenty-first century classrooms. Yet many terms and concepts—such as the rhetorical situation, the rhetorical appeals of *ethos*, *pathos*, and *logos*; terms associated with invention such as *kairos*, *dissoi logoi*, *stasis*, *topoi*; the strong emphasis on audience; various theories of informal argument—have proved useful in the teaching of writing.

Rhetorical education was a staple in early US post-secondary education until the end of the nineteenth century, at which time the focus on public discourse and preparation for civic life was replaced by the culture of taste and belletristic rhetoric, and classical texts were usurped by modern rhetoricians such as Blair, Campbell, and Whately (Crowley, 1998: 51). As we have seen, the focus in such classrooms soon shifted to individual original research, and the new research university replaced the four-year course of rhetorical study with a one-year required course in composition (Kitzhaber, 1953/1990). The sheer numbers of students enrolled in this course, coupled with the influx of attendees from the merchant class, contributed to the emphasis on issues of mechanics and grammar, which, while not inimical to rhetorical education, displaced the broader educational goals of civic discourse inherent in a rhetorical approach.

In the mid-twentieth century, the rise of New Rhetoric stimulated the development of the field of composition as it sought to shift its emphasis from formulaic conception of writing to a more dynamic one. The revival of rhetoric—sometimes referred to as the New Rhetoric—in the 1960s and 1970s attempted to restore this attention to rhetorical invention, audience, theories of informal argument (Toulmin, 1958; Perelman and Olbrechts-Tyteca, 1969), forms, and provide students with the tools necessary to adapt to a variety of rhetorical situations. It shifted the focus away from expressive writing to transactional writing in academic, professional and civic contexts. While the principles of rhetorical pedagogy is important in academic writing, it also adds an emphasis on writing in the public realm by constructing real writing situations for students.

Critical pedagogy and cultural studies

As Berlin (1982) argues, teaching writing as a process is now engrained in all of our pedagogical approaches. But, while process pedagogies of the 1960s and 1970s tended to focus on the individual student or the cognitive processes of the act of writing, cultural studies and critical pedagogies shifted attention toward the realm of the social. Cultural studies and critical pedagogy are sometimes conflated, partially because the two share similar, although not identical, goals. Both approaches attend to the social contexts in which writing happens, both concern themselves with the political in the classroom, and both draw attention to issues of social justice and power within the classroom and in the larger social sphere. It is more, then, a matter of practices and foci that distinguishes one from the other.

Cultural studies pedagogy has its roots in British cultural studies, housed in the Birmingham Centre for Contemporary Cultural Studies, and in the work of Stuart Hall, Richard Hoggart, and Raymond Williams (D. George and Trimbur, 2001: 71–72). Scholars immersed in British cultural studies wanted to shift the focus from high culture and high theory to the everyday lived experiences and artifacts of the common people. In this tradition, cultural studies approaches to composition tend to incorporate popular culture and mass media texts into the classroom in an attempt to dismantle what they see as an elitist barrier between literary texts and more "popular" ones like television, film, and advertising. The emphasis in most cultural studies composition classrooms is on the individual in a social context, and students may be asked to analyze subcultures; read about and examine cultural artifacts like iPods or cell phones, mining such artifacts for their cultural significance; or they may be asked to interrogate such commonly held "myths" as the American dream, the nuclear family, or the multi-cultural melting pot.

Critical pedagogy, while similar in many ways to cultural studies pedagogies, is rooted in the works of scholars Ann George (2001) refers to as the "Big Three" (p. 93): Paulo Freire, Henry Giroux, and Ira Shor. Critical pedagogies make use of many of the same strategies as cultural studies pedagogies, but writing teachers practicing a critical pedagogy are dedicated to an expressed liberatory politics in the classroom. Seeing an important and inextricable connection between language and power, such writing instructors attempt to draw students' attention to unequal power relations in society and try to equip them to resist and remedy this inequality (A. George, 2001: 92). In addition, critical pedagogy often attempts to prepare students for citizenship in a democratic society.

Critical pedagogy and cultural studies pedagogy's focus on politics and socioeconomics characterize what is often referred to as the "social turn" in composition studies. But such a turn has not gone unchallenged. Perhaps the most (in)famous critique is Maxine Hairston's 1992 *CCC* article entitled "Diversity, ideology, and teaching writing." In it, Hairston lambastes compositionists who practice critical or cultural studies pedagogies, arguing that such an approach "puts dogma before diversity, politics before craft, ideology before critical thinking, and the social goals of the teacher before the educational needs of the students" (p. 180). Hairston hopes that "most writing teachers have too much common sense and are too concerned with their students' growth as writers to buy into this [at the time] new philosophy," but worries that, everywhere she looks, she sees evidence to the contrary (p. 180). Hairston's attack provoked a slew of responses, eight of which were published in the "Counterstatement" section of the May 1993 issue of *CCC*, along with a reply by Hairston.

The first of these responses was from John Trimbur, a scholar who Hairston called out by name. Trimbur argues that what Hairston sees as indoctrination (into a particularly leftist political camp), he—and other cultural studies and critical pedagogy scholars—sees as rhetorical education, an attempt to prepare students for participation in a democracy. Trimbur (1993) further argues that all education is political, even classrooms like Hairston's in which students focus primarily on personal experience. While Trimbur's was not the only answer to Hairston's critique, his is paradigmatic of the sorts of responses that her article received. Hairston's critique still rings in many critical and culture pedagogy proponents' ears, evidenced by Ann George's (2001) need to engage the same debate almost a decade later. She responds to Hairston by arguing that there are critical pedago*gies*, not one monolithic approach. She explains, also, that those practicing critical pedagogies need to be wary of excess and of abusing their power (p. 101). Proponents such as Diana George and John Trimbur (2001) hope that an effective practice can help students improve their writing and equip them to resist what such scholars see as problematic and unfair social power structures.

Again, at the center of this debate is the question that haunts all teachers of academic writing: What is this course *for*? What is it supposed to be doing? According to scholars such as Hairston, the focus of the course should be on writing, especially the students' (often personal) writing. Scholars such as Trimbur (1993) argue that while the focus may be on writing, language is always already implicated in the maintenance or dismantling of structures of power. In this framework, a college-level writing course should bring both public discourse and the writing processes of students to the fore (Trimbur, 1993: 249). As we will see, such matters have hardly been resolved in our field.

Where do we go from here?

Thus far we have (very briefly) surveyed the history of composition as a course and as a discipline, and we have discussed some of the major pedagogical approaches to the teaching of composition. So where does that leave us? In other words, where are we now and where do we go from here?

This is not an easy question to answer. One of the more recent attempts to delineate the current shape of composition studies comes from Richard Fulkerson's (2005) *CCC* article, "Composition at the turn of the twenty-first century." He argues that composition studies has "diverged," into three axiological categories: a "social construction view, which values critical cultural analysis; an expressive one; and a multifaceted rhetorical one" (p. 655). He then links these axiological categories with what he sees as "the three major approaches to the teaching of composition" (p. 655). For Fulkerson, these are "critical/cultural studies," "expressivism," and "procedural rhetoric" (p. 655). Fulkerson's third category, the "multifaceted rhetorical" axiology, he further divides into three: "composition as argumentation, genre-based composition, and composition as introduction to an academic discourse community" (p. 671). While he does not engage this approach in the body of his article, Fulkerson also references current-traditional rhetoric, including it as a "perspective on composition" (p. 658).

Fulkerson concludes his article by reducing his original tripartite classification to a binary choice, stating:

> the major divide [in composition] is no longer expressive personal writing versus writing for readers (or whatever oppositional phrase you prefer: "academic discourse," "formal writing," "persuasion"). The major divide is instead between a postmodern, cultural studies, reading-based program, and a broadly conceived rhetoric of genres and discourse forums. (p. 679)

As Fulkerson acknowledges, there is not enough empirical evidence to support his depiction of contemporary composition studies. As such, his does not give us a picture of the *practice* of teaching composition in this country. Because there is very little empirical data that illustrates actual classroom practices, and because it would be difficult to conduct a generalizable nationwide study of classroom practice, Fulkerson relies on conversations currently occurring in leading composition journals. But there is often a divide between scholarly discourse and pedagogical practice. Fulkerson's map, then, while useful, only tells us part of the story. We do not really know what is happening in composition classrooms across the country. Our field would benefit from a more concrete understanding of what is actually happening in writing programs across the country. Until we have such data available, however, articles like Fulkerson's help us imagine the shape of our discipline.

In reading accounts of various pedagogical practices, it is important to remember that such approaches are not mutually exclusive; cultural studies pedagogies and rhetorical pedagogies are not diametrically opposed options from which instructors are forced to choose. Teaching writing is an incredibly complicated act, one that, while informed by composition and rhetorical theory, is not necessarily dictated by it, or at least not dictated by a single approach. Practitioners draw on multiple theories and pedagogies, constructing their own approach out of the appropriate practices present throughout the field. Furthermore, it is important to note that pedagogical approaches are influenced by university policies, individual politics and beliefs, student populations, geography, social constraints, social freedoms, past experiences, and in-the-moment decisions that rarely fall under a single theoretical category.

We believe this is true even for the staunchest of critical pedagogues or the most die-hard expressivists. We remind readers that many first-year programs include personal *and* academic writing; that many include literary *and* popular discourses as well as academic, professional and public discourses; many ask for analysis *and* production of texts. While both doctoral programs and first-year writing programs may certainly emphasize a particular pedagogical approach, we would like to highlight the multiplicity of pedagogical tenets in most teaching acts. In other words, most of the teaching that happens in the classroom includes aspects of current-traditional rhetoric, process approaches, critical pedagogies, cultural studies pedagogies, rhetorical pedagogies, and other approaches that may be developing outside of the purvey of our leading journals.

The disjunction between the disciplinary conversation and classroom practices is also exacerbated by the reality of how composition courses are often staffed. At many colleges and universities, first-year writing courses are staffed predominantly by faculty and graduate students who are trained (or being trained) as literary scholars or creative writers. At many institutions, composition courses are increasingly staffed by part-time or adjunct instructors who are often underpaid without benefits—who often have to teach at multiple institutions just to make ends meet; while their professional qualifications vary, many of them receive little or no institutional recognition for engaging in the disciplinary conversation.

Whatever approach one takes, Patricia Harkin (in Dickson *et al.*, 2006), echoing Berlin, reminds us that "writing teachers should themselves understand their pedagogical and epistemological assumptions and beliefs and should do their best to explain those assumptions and beliefs to students" (p. 756). We agree. We hope that as new instructors approach their teaching and research, they will be encouraged to find their own "best practices" from a number of different theories and approaches, and not feel constrained by binary oppositions in the field. We hope, also, that teachers and scholars, both new and experienced, will continue to read and research in multiple areas, bringing all that they learn into their practices and scholarship, and, by doing so, expand the number of available options. Such work, we believe, pushes productively at the disciplinary edges, and enriches the very important work that we do every day.

Notes

i George Kennedy (1998) notes that evidence of rhetorical terms and concepts can be found in ancient China, Babylonia, and India going as far back as the eighth century BCE.

ii In this chapter, we hope to provide entry points into the complex web of events and ideas that have shaped the development of the composition course in US higher education and various pedagogical practices that take place in that context. For this reason, we will frequently point the readers to various sources that treat each topic in much greater detail.

iii *College English*, which evolved from *English Journal* in 1938, was not a major driving force behind the growth of composition as a discipline during this period because it focused almost exclusively on literature (Goggin, 2000).

References

Bakhtin, M. M. (1981), *The Dialogic Imagination: Four Essays by M. M. Bakhtin* (M. Holquist, ed.; C. Emerson and M. Holquist, trans.) (Austin, TX : University of Texas Press).

Bartholomae, D. (1985), "Inventing the university," in M. Rose (ed.), *When a Writer Can't Write: Studies in Writer's Block and Other Composing-process Problems* (pp. 134–165) (New York: Guilford Press).

Bartholomae, D. (1995), "Response to Elbow," *College Composition and Communication*, 46(1), 84–87.

Berlin, J. A. (1980), "Richard Whately and current-traditional rhetoric," *College English*, 42, 10–17.

Berlin, J. A. (1984), *Writing Instruction in Nineteenth-century American Colleges* (Carbondale, IL: Southern Illinois University Press).

Berlin, J. A. (1982), "Contemporary composition: The major pedagogical theories," *College English*, 44(8), 765–777.

Berlin, J. A. (1987), *Rhetoric and Reality: Writing Instruction in American Colleges, 1990–1985* (Carbondale, IL: Southern Illinois University Press).

Berlin, J. A. (1988), "Rhetoric and ideology in the writing class," *College English*, 50, 477–494.

Berlin, J. A. and Inkster, R. P. (1980), "Current-traditional rhetoric: Paradigm and practice," *Freshman English News*, 8(3), 1–4, 13–14.

Bizzell, P. (1982), "College composition: Initiation into the academic discourse community," *Curriculum Inquiry*, 12, 191–207.

Bizzell, P. (1986), "Composing processes: An overview," in A. Petrosky and D. Bartholomae (eds), *The Teaching of Writing* (pp. 49–70) (Chicago: University of Chicago Press).

Bizzell, P. and Herzberg, B. (eds) (2001), *The Rhetorical Tradition: Readings from Classical Times to the Present* (2nd edn) (Boston: Bedford/St. Martin's Press).

Brereton, J. C. (1995), *The Origins of Composition Studies in the American College, 1875–1925: A Documentary History* (Pittsburgh, PA: University of Pittsburgh Press).

Brown, S. C., Jackson, R. and Enos, T. (2000), "The arrival of rhetoric in the twenty-first century: The 1999 survey of doctoral programs in rhetoric," *Rhetoric Review*, 18(2), 233–242.

Connors, R. J. (1986), "The rhetoric of mechanical correctness," in T. Newkirk (ed.), *Only Connect: Uniting Reading and Writing* (pp. 27–58) (Upper Mountclair, NJ: Boynton/Cook).

Connors, R. J. (1991), "Writing the history of our discipline," in E. Lindemann and G. Tate (eds), *An Introduction to Composition Studies* (pp. 49–71) (New York: Oxford University Press).

Connors, R. J. (1997), *Composition-rhetoric: Backgrounds, Theory, and Pedagogy* (Pittsburgh: University of Pittsburgh Press).

Connors, R. J. (1999), "Composition history and disciplinarity," in M. Rosner, B. Boehm and Debra Journet (eds), *History, Reflection, and Narrative: The Professionalization of Composition, 1963–1983* (pp. 3–21) (Stamford, CT: Ablex).

Crowley, S. (1990), *The Methodical Memory: Invention in Current-traditional Rhetoric* (Carbondale, IL: Southern Illinois University Press).

Crowley, S. (1998), *Composition in the University: Historical and Polemical Essays* (Pittsburgh, PA: University of Pittsburgh Press).

Dejoy, N. (2004), *Process This: Undergraduate Writing in Composition Studies* (Logan, UT: Utah State University Press).

Dickson, A. C., Mejía, J. A., Zorn, J., Harkin, P. and Fulkerson, R. (2006), "Interchanges: Responses to Richard Fulkerson, 'Composition at the Turn of the Twenty-First Century' (June 2005)," *College Composition and Communication*, 57(4), 730–762.

Elbow, P. (1995), "Being a writer vs. being an academic: A conflict in goals," *College Composition and Communication*, 46(1), 72–83.

Emig, J. (1971), *The Composing Processes of Twelfth Graders* (Urbana, IL: National Council of Teachers of English).

Faigley, L. (1986), "Competing theories of process: A critique and proposal," *College English*, 48, 527–542.

Fishman, S. M. and McCarthy, L. P. (1992), "Is expressivism dead? Reconsidering its Romantic roots and its relations to social constructionism," *College English*, 54(6), 647–661.

Flower, L. S. and Hayes, J. R. (1977), "Problem-solving strategies and the writing process," *College English*, 39(4), 449–461.

Fogarty, D. (1959), *Roots for a New Rhetoric* (New York: Teachers College, Columbia University).

Fulkerson, R. (2001), "Of pre- and post-process: Reviews and ruminations," *Composition Studies*, 29(2), 93–119.

Fulkerson, R. (2005), "Composition at the turn of the twenty-first century," *College Composition and Communication*, 56(4), 654–687.

George, A. (2001), "Critical pedagogy: Dreaming of democracy," in G. Tate, A. Rupiper and K. Schick (eds), *A Guide to Composition Pedagogies* (pp. 92–112) (New York: Oxford University Press).

George, D. and Trimbur, J. (1999), "The 'communication battle,' or whatever happened to the 4th C?" *College Composition and Communication*, 50(4), 682–698.

George, D. and Trimbur, J. (2001), "Cultural studies and composition," in G. Tate, A. Rupiper and K. Schick (eds), *A Guide to Composition Pedagogies* (pp. 71–91) (New York: Oxford University Press).

Goggin, M. D. (2000), *Authoring a Discipline: Scholarly Journals and the Post-World War II Emergence of Rhetoric and Composition* (Mahwah, NJ: Lawrence Erlbaum Associates).

Hairston, M. (1982), "The winds of change: Thomas Kuhn and the revolution in the teaching of writing," *College Composition and Communication*, 33, 76–88.

Hairston, M. (1992), "Diversity, ideology, and teaching writing," *College Composition and Communication*, 43(2), 179–193.

Halloran, S. M. (1982), "Rhetoric in the American college curriculum: The demise of public discourse," *Pre/Text*, 3, 245–269.

Harris, J. (1997), *A Teaching Subject: Composition since 1966* (Upper Saddle River, NJ: Prentice Hall).

Kennedy, G. A. (1998). *Comparative Rhetoric: An Historical and Cross-cultural Introduction* (New York: Oxford University Press).

Kent, T. (1999) "Introduction," in T. Kent (ed.), *Post-Process Theory: Beyond the Writing-Process Paradigm* (pp. 1–6) (Carbondale, IL: Southern Illinois University Press).

Kitzhaber, A. R. (1990), *Rhetoric in American Colleges, 1850–1900* (Dallas, TX: Southern Methodist University Press (original unpublished dissertation 1953)).

Lauer, J. M. (1980), "The rhetorical approach: Stages of writing and strategies for writers," in T. R. Donovan and B. W. McClelland (eds), *Eight Approaches to Teaching Composition* (pp. 53–64) (Urbana, IL: National Council of Teachers of English).

Lauer, J. M. (1993), "Rhetoric and composition studies: A multi-modal discipline," in T. Enos and S. C. Brown (eds), *Defining the New Rhetorics* (pp. 44–54) (Newbury Park, CA: Sage Publications).

McComiskey, B. (2000). *Teaching Composition as a Social Process* (Logan, UT: Utah State University Press).

Mao, L. (2007), "Studying the Chinese rhetorical tradition in the present: Re-presenting the native's point of view," *College English*, 69(3), 216–237.

Matsuda, P. K. (2003), "Process and post-process: A discursive history," *Journal of Second Language Writing*, 12(1), 65–83.

Matsuda, P. K. (2006), "The myth of linguistic homogeneity in US college composition," *College English*, 68(6), 637–651.

Matsuda, P. K. and Matsuda, A. (in press), "The erasure of resident ESL writers," in M. Roberge, M. Siegel, and L. Harklau (eds), *Generation 1.5 Ten Years Later: Teaching College Writing to U.S.-educated Learners of ESL* (Mahwah, NJ: Lawrence Erlbaum Associates).

Mills, B. (1953), "Writing as process," *College English*, 15, 19–26.

Murphy, J. J. (ed.) (2001), *A Short History of Writing Instruction: From Ancient Greece to Modern America* (2nd edn) (Mahwah, NJ: Lawrence Erlbaum Associates).

Newkirk, T. (1994), "The politics of intimacy: The defeat of Barrett Wendell at Harvard," in L. Tobin and T. Newkirk (eds), *Taking Stock: The Writing Process Movement in the '90s* (pp. 115–131) (Portsmouth, NH: Boynton/Cook).

North, S. M. (1987), *The Making of Knowledge in Composition: Portrait of an Emerging Field* (Portsmouth, NH: Boynton/Cook Heinemann).

Nystrand, M., Greene, S. and Wiemelt, J. (1993), "Where did composition studies come from? An intellectual history," *Written Communication*, 10, 267–333.

Olson, G. A. (1999), "Toward a post-process composition: Abandoning the rhetoric of assertion," in T. Kent (ed.), *Post-Process Theory: Beyond the Writing-Process Paradigm* (pp. 7–15) (Carbondale, IL: Southern Illinois University Press).

Paré, A. (1994), "Toward a post-process pedagogy; or, what's theory got to do with it?" *English Quarterly,* 26(2), 4–9.

Perelman, C. and Olbrechts-Tyteca, L. (1969), *The New Rhetoric: A Treatise on Argumentation* (Notre Dame, IN: University of Notre Dame Press).

Royster, J. J. and Williams, J. C. (1999), "History in the spaces left: African American presence and narratives of composition studies." *College Composition and Communication,* 50(4), 563–584.

Russell, D. (1991), *Writing in the Academic Disciplines, 1870–1990* (Carbondale, IL: Southern Illinois University Press).

Silva, T. (1990), "Second language composition instruction: Developments, issues and directions in ESL," in B. Kroll (ed.), *Second Language Writing: Research Insights for the Classroom* (pp. 11–23) (New York: Cambridge University Press).

Tirabassi, K. E. (2007), *Revisiting the "Current-traditional Era": Innovations in Writing Instruction at the University of New Hampshire, 1940–1949.* Unpublished doctoral dissertation, University of New Hampshire.

Tobin, L. (2001), "Process pedagogy," in G. Tate, A. Rupiper and K. Schick (eds), *A Guide to Composition Pedagogies* (pp. 1–18) (New York: Oxford University Press).

Toulmin, S. E. (1958), *The Uses of Argument* (Cambridge, UK: Cambridge University Press).

Trimbur, J. (1993), Response to Maxine Hairston, "Diversity, ideology, and teaching writing," *College Composition and Communication,* 44(2), 248–249.

Trimbur, J. (1994), "Taking the social turn: Teaching writing post-process," *College Composition and Communication,* 45, 108–118.

Ward, I. (1994), *Literacy, Ideology, and Dialogue* (Albany: State University of New York Press).

Wright, E. A. and Halloran, S. M. (2001), "From rhetoric to composition: The teaching of writing in America to 1900," in J. J. Murphy (ed.), *A Short History of Writing Instruction: From Ancient Greece to Modern America* (2nd edn, pp. 213–246) (Mahwah, NJ: Lawrence Erlbaum Associates).

Young, R. E. (1978), "Paradigms and problems: Needed research in rhetorical invention," in C. R. Cooper and L. Odell (eds), *Research on Composing: Points of Departure* (pp. 29–48) (Urbana, IL: National Council of Teachers of English).

Young, R. and Goggin, M. D. (1993), Some issues in dating the birth of the new rhetoric in departments of English: A contribution to a developing historiography. In T. Enos and S. C. Brown (eds), *Defining the New Rhetorics* (pp. 22–43) (Newbury Park, CA: Sage).

Academic Writing and the Disciplines

Siân Etherington

Chapter Outline

The focus of this chapter is the teaching of academic writing skills for different subject disciplines. The chapter begins by making the case for discipline-specific writing approaches, outlining some of the arguments in this area and providing some examples of how academic writing can differ across subject areas. The chapter then goes on to discuss some of the practical questions related to teaching this kind of academic writing and provides a collection of useful resources for teachers. Although the chapter aims to provide a general overview of discipline-specific academic writing, the writer's context is that of a UK higher education (HE) institution and thus, the experience drawn on in the course of the chapter is, inevitably, more closely connected to this background.

English for General Academic Purposes/General Composition Classes

Other chapters in this book are concerned with approaches to academic writing which might be used with college students, no matter what their academic subject area or major. Much of the writing tuition which occurs in college settings in the United States (US) and in HE or FE (further education) institutions in the United Kingdom (UK) is of this type.

Within the English for Academic Purposes (EAP) and English as a Second Language (ESL) fields, this approach is generally labelled English for General Academic Purposes (EGAP); for home student writing programmes this could be seen as General Academic Writing, or in the US, as the freshman composition class. For both Learning Assistance and EAP/ESL programmes, this approach is based around a set of skills, text types, and language forms for Academic English which can be presented to any student. The following section briefly considers the arguments in favour of such an approach, before indicating why discipline-specific teaching may be preferable.

Arguments in favour of a generalized approach

Hyland in his 2002 paper on discipline-specific EAP teaching outlines four arguments which support a "one size fits all" approach to academic writing. These can be summarized as follows.

We can teach a common core of academic writing

Perhaps the most persuasive, and certainly the most pervasive, of the arguments used in favour of a general approach to academic writing is the "common core hypothesis" (Bloor and Bloor, 1986). This contends that commonalities across academic writing exist and can be usefully taught to students. Indeed, many researchers have produced taxonomies of generic academic writing skills, tasks and language patterns. For example, Currie (1993) reports on generalizable skills involved in tackling written assignments and Johns (1997) has identified common features of academic prose. These kinds of general features are the basis of many published and successful EAP, ESL, and academic writing textbooks used in writing classrooms across the world. For example, one common focus is on text-type patterns which reoccur throughout academic writing. Overall, supporters of this view feel that the common core approach is efficient and effective.

We are not discipline experts

A second argument centres on the lack of subject knowledge and expertise of academic writing instructors. In a much-cited paper, Spack (1988) maintains that this lack of close involvement in the language of a discipline makes it impossible for English language specialists to make subject knowledge explicit to students. She argues that an attempt to do so may lead to problems of mis-interpretation or wrong emphasis. Leki (1995: 236–237) agrees, suggesting that it is not reasonable to expect "those who do not participate as conversation partners in a discourse … to teach the explicit, let alone implicit, rules of that conversation to others." The recommendation of those who take this view is that academic writing instructors should restrict themselves to teaching broad principles of academic writing and rhetoric. Such features may include academic style, neutrality of tone, use of evidence and argument, reference to other texts and authors, and may also centre on the general text organization patterns mentioned above. Anything else is seen as a step too far for language teachers.

Learners need to get the basics right first

Concern for student needs also feeds the arguments for the EGAP or general academic writing approach. It is argued that learners at lower-levels of English language proficiency and those at the start of student life must first establish proficiency in general aspects of language and writing before they can progress to the more sophisticated realms of discipline-specific language. Supporters of this position feel that it is perhaps allowable for students who are writing theses or research papers to be concerned for the writing of their subject areas, but that for others a grounding in grammar and spelling, general academic structures and style is sufficient. Spending time on the basics makes for more efficient teaching.

It's too expensive

Finally, one of the strong arguments in favour of the general approach to academic writing is that it is cost-effective. An approach which differentiates between discipline areas takes time to accomplish. Teachers may need to work with subject specialists, devote time and energy to the collection and analysis of texts from different discipline areas and create tailored teaching materials based on the results. Hyland suggests that for some institutions this kind of work is seen as an "extravagant indulgence" (2002: 387).

A related question of expense concerns the practicalities of providing discipline-specific classes. Discipline-specific teaching would appear to call for small, specialized classes with dedicated teachers, whose skills may not be easily transferable to other areas. Where a teacher of the language of Engineering may find it difficult to teach Academic Writing for Art History, general principles of academic writing can be taught by one teacher to several different classes. The economic argument for teaching larger general classes rather than small, subject-specific ones is also apparent. Given the financial situation of many HE writing centres, language support or EAP units, these arguments are powerful ones.

The need for discipline-specific academic writing teaching

The ideas discussed above will be familiar to many teachers of academic writing. However, as Hyland (*ibid.*: 387–389) points out, each of these positions can be challenged, making a strong case for the teaching of English for Specific Academic Purposes (ESAP) or discipline-specific academic writing. Again, these arguments can be summarized as follows.

The common core does not exist

The goal of university academic writing programmes is to prepare students for writing "in the real academic world" outside our classes. There the success of student writing is judged by criteria which differ, sometimes considerably, across subject areas.

An example from my own subject-teaching experience illustrates these discrepancies well. In my institution teaching on the Applied Linguistics with Teaching English as a Foreign Language (TEFL) programme is shared between tutors from Applied Linguistics and those from TEFL backgrounds. These tutors were asked to agree on a checklist for postgraduate students to work through before submitting their research projects. Staff from TEFL backgrounds indicated that students needed to make sure that they submitted a references list which matched the citations in their texts. Any source which students had not cited should be excluded from this list. Applied Linguistics staff, however, remarked that they expected a bibliography (a list of sources which students had read and felt had influenced their thinking but had not necessarily been cited in their work). The difference in practice over something as fundamental as references was illuminating: even in subjects as closely related as these two, there can be substantial differences in writing norms, with the consequence that it becomes very difficult to teach a general practice which is applicable to all. Indeed, there is a real danger in teaching general academic writing, if it is assumed by instructors and students that the generalities of practice are absolute and will not differ from subject to subject. An awareness of the differences between disciplines is essential for anyone writing or teaching writing within the HE context. In fact, it could be argued that since all academic writing (outside writing or EAP programmes) must take place in some discipline-specific context, there is no such thing as "general academic writing".

Writing in the disciplines and communities of practice

A "Writing in the Disciplines" approach is closely aligned to ideas concerning "Communities of Practice" (Lave and Wenger, 1991). These theories view the specific context within which student writing has to function as being constructed—and continually being rebuilt and negotiated—by the members of that academic grouping through the practice of reading, writing, criticizing, arguing and working within the discipline. One useful metaphor here is that of academic "tribes" (Becher, 1989); groups who are bound together by shared sets of customs. Outsiders must learn these customs if they are to gain access to the group and acceptance within it. Academic writing is one of the central customs by which an academic community defines itself, and thus its power to exclude or include novice writers is huge.

Another way to view the influence of the subject context on writing is to see each discipline area as having its own rules of engagement, or what Casanave (2003–5) has named "game strategies," which govern academic writing. Without some understanding of the conventions, students cannot hope to succeed in their subject areas. The "rules of the game" of academic writing in the disciplines operate across text types and genres, structure and organization, prose style, and lexicogrammatical language features. We will more fully explore these elements of academic writing and how they may differ across disciplines in the sections below, but here consider text-types as one illustration of this diversity.

Diversity of text-types

For some features of academic writing, the differences between disciplines are clearer than others. For example, if we consider the types of text which students are expected to write, it is easy to see that certain types of texts are more prevalent within some disciplines. For instance, a student who is majoring in Chemistry will be expected to master the laboratory report; a Drama student needs to know how to write a successful critique of a theatre piece; Business students have to write case studies of organizations or business operations.

Indeed, Nesi and Gardner's (2006) recent survey of text types and genres expected in UK university assignments (they interviewed staff in 20 departments across three universities) suggests that the range of texts students are asked to produce is expanding. Professional genres (e.g. reports, client notes) and applied work combining theory and practice are in evidence alongside more traditional, academic genres. Nesi and Gardner's detailed table of possible text-types for discipline areas shows this range (Table 2.1).

The breadth of text-types in Table 2.1 shows that simply learning the standard "essay" format is not sufficient for most students. For each of these genres, a different set of expectations about writing layout, style and language will apply. Writing instructors need to be aware of the range of potential assignment types and have some understanding of what is expected for each.

Differing expectations of text-types and content

However, even where academic writing instructors feel confident that student need *is* focused on the same text types (i.e. "they *all* need to write essays"), the generic approach may be misleading. Academics within different disciplines will have distinct understandings about what constitutes a good "essay" or "discussion paper". We saw above the difference in opinion about the mechanics of a successful dissertation. The different entries for Report, Laboratory Report and Project Report in Nesi and Gardner's table indicate that the text-type "report" can be differentiated widely. Aspects of content can vary too. Historians and Literature specialists, for example, will not share views of what constitutes a good argument or a strong piece of evidence. For the historian, effective argumentation needs to be firmly supported by documentary evidence taken from primary sources. A literary review of a poem or play, in contrast, will make use of the subjective responses of readers or audience.

Indeed, the very basics of academic work are often viewed differently across disciplines. For example, "research" in Law constitutes quite different thinking, actions and investigation from that undertaken in research in Life Sciences, resulting in varied types of writing. Again, as an academic writing teacher it is vital to be aware that differences can operate at such fundamental levels and to be able to explore these issues with subject-specialists.

This brings us to the next argument in favour of discipline-specific academic writing.

Subject expertise is not sufficient

It is important to realize that the discipline-specific conventions of writing are rarely part of conscious knowledge held by subject lecturers. Writing practices

Table 2.1 Text-types in certain disciplines.

Essay	Anthropology, Archaeology, Biology, Computing, Economics, Engineering, English, Food Sciences, Health, History, Hospitality and Tourism, Law, Mathematics, Medicine, Philosophy, Psychology, Publishing, Theatre Studies
Report	Computing, Food Sciences, Hospitality and Tourism, Law, Psychology
Laboratory report	Archaeology, Biology, Physics
Project report	Biology, Economics, Engineering, Mathematics, Sociology
Research project	Biology, Mathematics, Theatre Studies
Dissertation	Anthropology, Archaeology, Biology, Computing, Law, Medicine, Publishing, Sociology, Theatre Studies
Group project	Archaeology, Engineering, Health, Physics, Publishing
Poster	Anthropology, Biology, Engineering, Mathematics, Physics, Psychology
Book review	History, Psychology, Sociology, Theatre Studies
Website evaluation	Medicine, Theatre Studies
Problem sheets	Biosciences, Economics, Food Sciences, Hospitality and Tourism, Mathematics
Case studies	Health, Publishing
Case notes, draft appeal to house of Lords, Advice Notes to a client, Submissions in preparation for a case, Moots, Problem Question (judgment)	Law
Field Study/Ethnography	Sociology
Patient Case Report	Medicine
Letter from publisher to author	Publishing
Reflective writing/journal/blog	Engineering, English, Hospitality and Tourism, Philosophy, Medicine, Theatre Studies
Critical evaluation (of own production or practical task)	Anthropology, English, Computing, Theatre Studies
Marketing proposal/plan	Engineering, Publishing
Narrative fiction	Sociology (several modules)
Press Release, Fact Sheet, Technical Abstract, persuasive writing	Physics (communicating science module)
Letter of advice to friend written from 1830s perspective; Maths in Action project (lay audience)	Mathematics

Source: Nesi and Gardner 2006: Appendix 1

are "taken for granted," implicit knowledge which has been gained through years of reading, writing and working within the area. It is frequently surprising for academic staff to learn that things may be different in other disciplines (and sometimes they react to this information with the feeling that other subjects don't "do things properly").

This lack of conscious knowledge of their subject's conventions of academic writing means that subject specialists do not make the best teachers of academic writing. Since they cannot see the differences easily, they are less likely to highlight or explain these to students. If "everyone knows" what an essay or report is like, there is no need to explain this to students. It takes an outsider to make these features explicit. An academic writing instructor with linguistic and pedagogic knowledge is best able to help both subject specialists and students focus on the pertinent aspects of specific writing and to show students how to start to include these within their own writing. The growth of genre and corpus-based linguistics research has provided EAP and academic writing instructors with a wealth of information which they can use to focus their teaching. However, working with discipline experts in order to discover variations on models and published research is important. Academic writing teachers need to find the best ways of doing this and some suggestions for approaches are offered in the second section of this chapter.

Lower level academic writing does not mean general academic writing

The argument that discipline-specific EAP or academic writing is only for those students who are writing at the highest levels is countered by much of what has been said above. Learners need to know exactly what it is that staff expect from "good writing" if they are going to succeed, no matter what their level. Academic community practices may be most apparent in journal articles or books written by academics because these are the more public genres of the community. However, the implicit assumptions which govern the writing of these also apply to the writing of other genres within the subject. It is never too early for students to start to interrogate the writing practices of their field, as the closer they can come to these, the better the appreciation of their work by the members of the academic community they aspire to join. It may be more appropriate for learners to concentrate on discovery and emulation of good examples of undergraduate essays rather than journal articles, but this nevertheless entails learning about the specific writing practices of their discipline.

It is likely that first generation college students in particular will need more of this sort of support as they very often lack clear understandings of what is expected of their academic performance. These students may not possess good, extensive, reading habits which can help them to pick up the conventions of their subject area or analytical skills which help them to focus on "what the lecturers want." It is important, therefore, that these students are assisted to learn the rules of the game as soon as possible in their educational careers.

Linked to this is another important benefit for all university students in learning about specifically situated writing. Teaching from this perspective provides learners with a fuller understanding of the nature of writing and its place within the university/academic world. As Hyland explains,

> The notion of specificity [thus] provides learners with a way of understanding the diversity they encounter at university. It shows them, in other words, that literacy is relative to the beliefs and practices of social groups and to the purposes of their individual members in accomplishing their goals. (2002: 390)

This approach may, therefore, help learners from all kinds of backgrounds to understand that academic writing is only one of a variety of discourses that they can use. It does not privilege one variety above another, helping learners to retain a sense of value for their own dialect while learning a second. Some of the lack of confidence and personal disturbance sometimes associated with the learning of the "academic voice" may be diminished by promotion of this view. Students can be helped to see that they only need to learn to write for each context as appropriate, not that they must change their language and in doing so perhaps relinquish elements of their identities.

Research-based teaching is vital

Research into the particulars of discipline-specific writing may be seen as expensive and time-consuming. However, given the tacit nature of much of the knowledge about subject specific academic writing held by specialist teachers and writers, it seems that systematic exploration and comparison of subject areas is necessary in order to discover the key differences between discipline writing. Applied Linguistics research within genre studies and corpus linguistics has yielded a great deal of very useful data which is of direct use for teachers in the classroom. For example, the textbooks of Swales and Feak (2000, 2004) are based on years of genre analysis research. Current examples of similar research are published in the journals *English for Specific Purposes* and *Journal of English for Academic English*. Without a basis in this kind of research, there is a danger that teaching simply using instincts about academic writing in an unfamiliar area will be misleading or wrong.

However, despite the wealth of published work, research data does not cover every discipline area. What is a teacher to do where their class's needs lie outside existing published research or where they do not have access to helpful journal articles? There are two possible alternatives: teachers can conduct their own research or they can help students to become researchers of their own disciplines. Usually a combination of these is most effective. By helping students to explore the linguistic features which are common in the academic writing they read, instructors can boost learner independence and also provide some answer to the dilemma of heterogeneous classes. It often is useful to do this exploration in classes with students from other areas, so that contrasts allow the differences to stand out more clearly. In this way, students are helped to see themselves as experts on the practices of their disciplines. The development of focused linguistic analysis skills is extremely valuable for the continuation of learning outside the classroom—something which all students need to do if they are to improve their academic writing.

Strong and weak versions of discipline-specific academic writing

The arguments outlined above make a forceful case for the discipline-specific academic writing approach. However, despite the strength of this position, academic writing instructors may nevertheless face some difficulties in putting these ideas into practice.

A discipline-specific approach may carry more weight in the UK, where students typically major in one discipline area or in closely related subjects. Teachers in the US, however, may find that their students are following major and minor subjects which are far apart in their discipline base. For these students, it is not a clear-cut decision which discipline should be the focus of their academic writing instruction. Teachers in other parts of the world may be faced with similar dilemma as economic pressures mean that it is not always possible to teach students in distinct subject-related groups.

For these reasons, it is perhaps more useful to see discipline-specific teaching as a continuum, with weaker and stronger versions of the approach possible. Where students do not follow one distinct major, it makes sense for teachers to concentrate on more loosely defined boundaries for academic writing; for example, teaching writing for the Life Sciences or the Arts at first and helping students to develop their styles to fit more specific discursive practices as their academic careers progress. In addition to this, an approach which expands students' language awareness and helps them to develop the skills to examine and assimilate the practices of the different disciplines within which they write (developing a range of academic literacies) is advisable. This approach would concentrate on developing students' own textual investigations and experimentation with certain writing styles.

Again for mixed discipline classes a more broad-brush approach, concentrating for example on Social Sciences or Life Sciences, is more appropriate; however, again this needs to be blended with a development of learner analytical skills. Much of the choice of level of detail will be governed by student need. It is, however, of greatest importance that the academic writing instructor has a sense that disciplinary differences exist, an understanding of the range and focus of those differences, and the ability to guide students towards these specifics for their own subjects. The following section considers some of the ways in which an academic writing instructor can work practically to achieve these goals.

Practical advice for teaching academic writing in the disciplines

A writing teacher who wants to work with students within a discipline area faces certain questions about how to proceed. For example, teachers might ask:

- How do I find out what my students need to write?
- How can I best work with faculty members/specialist subject colleagues to help my students?
- Which aspects of writing should I concentrate on?
- How can I help my students to explore their own writing and that within their discipline areas?

The next section examines these questions, providing suggestions and advice about each area. (The account of the creation of online materials in John Morley's chapter is also extremely useful in showing how you might go about developing materials and it should be read in conjunction with this section.)

Needs analysis/target analysis

The importance of needs analysis is one of the tenets of EAP and ESP instruction. Without a strong and clearly motivated sense of what it is their students need to learn, it is impossible for teachers to create a successful syllabus. What then is involved in a needs analysis?

Traditionally, needs analysis involves asking students about their needs, wants and lacks (what does the target situation require of their language?

What do they want to be able to do with language? What is there that they can't do with the language?). However, one of the difficulties for teachers of EAP/Academic Writing is that students very often lack understanding of what it is that they need to do. The hidden nature of many of the rules for writing in an academic context mean that students may know that they have difficulties in writing, but are unable to pin these down to a clear area for improvement. Similarly, and particularly if they are novice writers, they are unlikely to have knowledge about the types of texts they will be expected to write or to have an understanding of the specific nature of these texts within their discipline areas.

This lack of awareness means that academic writing instructors have to use additional sources of information in order to find out about the language and types of writing they need to teach. The subject specialist is the most valuable in this respect: they can provide samples of writing (both successful and unsuccessful in addressing purpose and audience) and explanations about the traditions and norms of the subject area. However, as we outlined earlier, knowledge about the characteristics of discipline specific writing is often tacitly held by subject specialists and therefore part of the needs analysis work of the writing teacher is to draw this knowledge out and make it explicit. The extent to which academic writing instructors collaborate with specialist colleagues can vary, as is discussed next.

Working with subject specialist colleagues

Involvement with faculty members is necessary for academic writing instructors to be confident that the material they are teaching is authentic. The extent of this involvement may vary however, depending on time, circumstances, and often, the personalities involved. Dudley-Evans and St John (1998) have categorized the possible types of liaison into three levels: co-operation, collaboration and team-teaching.

Co-operation involves finding information from departments about the task types students are expected to produce, the content of courses, the expectations of the department and the nature of writing within the discourse community. Specialist staff can also be asked to provide examples of student writing (both good and bad) and journal writing within the discipline which can form the basis of materials. The interview questions used by Nesi and Gardner (2006) in their exploration of student writing in UK HE can act as a useful guide when talking to specialist academics. The Writing in the Disciplines section of the Writing Across the Curriculum website also provides examples of needs analysis interviews with subject specialists (see the Resources section for both).

Collaboration involves a closer working relationship, where academic writing instructor and specialist together create specific activities. These are then used in EAP or Academic Writing classes which run parallel to the subject lectures. For example, for a science class, the two staff members might jointly produce material on how to write a lab report—something which might otherwise not be covered in either a general EAP class (too specific) or Science class (not scientific information). This approach is similar to the US adjunct model proposed by Brinton *et al.* (1989). Here academic content and language/writing skills are taught in two concurrent classes which share both content and assignments. The language teacher may also be consulted on the wording of assignment or exam briefs, so that what is expected of students becomes clearer.

In *team-teaching* academic writing instructors and specialists teach the class between them. Dudley-Evans (2001) gives an example of how this might happen in an class dealing with the organization of written answers to examination essay questions. The session is run by the academic writing instructor, with the subject teacher offering advice and comment on the possible approaches to structuring an answer. Subject specialists also help students to clarify their answers in terms of content knowledge. Each participant benefits from the presence of the others. Subject specialists are helped to see the difficulties which students have with exam questions and to clarify the ways in which they would like the question answered. The language teacher is able to discuss an authentic question while relying on the guidance of the subject specialist as to the requirements of the discipline. Students, of course, gain expert guidance on both content and language. The team-teaching approach also helps students to see the ways in which they can interrogate the language presented to them within the academic content, acting as a model for their own investigation of the linguistic aspects of their subject.

The choice of which of these three approaches to adopt will depend greatly on the amount of input which subject specialists are able and willing to provide. The ways in which the two staff members work together also needs some careful consideration. Indeed, Dudley-Evans (2001: 228) cautions that collaboration or team-teaching approaches are more likely to be successful if

1 The amount of time expected from subject specialist is limited (around 1–2 sessions per week over a 10–11 week term).
2 There are clearly defined roles for the subject and language instructors. This is particularly important in team-teaching situations.
3 Both parties have respect for each other's professionalism and judgement.

Related to this last point is a concern about the working relationship which may develop between language teachers and subject specialists. This may be more of an issue for the UK HE context where there is a frequent lack of parity in status and pay between these two groups. Language instructors here are often employed on academic-related rather than full academic contracts and may be viewed as service-staff rather than academic colleagues. Given this kind of setting, collaboration may result in a "servant" like stance among language specialists in relation to subject staff. However, writing instructors are able to assert their position by taking a more Critical stand in their teaching (e.g. Benesch, 1996). This approach purposefully sets out to help students to challenge some of the assumptions and traditions of their subject area. Thus, Academic Writing or EAP support becomes about more than simply explaining or translating a discipline area for students under the guidance of a content specialist. (For more reading on working with subject specialists, see the Useful Resources section.)

Working with samples of writing

The other important source of information about discipline-specific writing is texts themselves.

Again there are several questions which teachers may have about the use of authentic texts to inform teaching.

Collecting texts

The first of these questions is, what kind of texts to use? For many classes, it is appropriate for students to work with samples of student writing at their level and within similar text-types to the ones they are expected to produce. For others, usually postgraduate or research students, it can be valuable to investigate the features of published research. For these students it is also essential to consider theses and dissertations, since writing of this kind is these students' main goal. An important guide is to consider the type of writing that students themselves will have to produce.

The collection of samples of writing can be done through specialist staff (as outlined above) or students themselves. You may be able to persuade your unit or faculty to fund the purchase of scripts from students, facilitating the creation of a fairly large collection (corpus) of texts for analysis. Snowballing sampling techniques also work well: asking those who help you to contact other teachers or students who may also be interested in submitting texts. Texts should be in electronic form in order to aid with exploration and exploitation for materials.

It is often suggested that textbooks or popular writing related to a subject area can be used as input for classes in discipline areas. For example, many teachers may use newspaper or magazine articles relating to Business matters in Business English/EAP for Business classes. The difficulty with the use of this kind of material, however, is that it is usually of a different genre/text type to that which students are expected to produce themselves and thus it is unlikely to provide a useful model of whole text writing. Some aspects, usually at the level of specialist vocabulary, may be useful, but teachers should guard against the promotion of "journalese" and the inappropriate use of technical terms which may occur. The gap between journalistic treatment of a topic and that which is required within a subject discipline is often large, particularly at graduate levels. It is also sometimes the case that the emphasis on vocabulary of a subject area which this sort of material encourages provides too narrow a field for exploration of discipline-specific writing. This brings us to the next point.

Working with texts

Once a teacher has collected a sufficiently large group of texts, the next stage is an analysis of the writing within these. The question to ask here is "Which features of writing are likely to be the most valuable foci for teaching?"

Most of those working on this sort of textual analysis consider that investigation of the features of texts is best done at three levels:

- the wider context in which the text operates (how it is viewed within the community of practice);
- the organization and structure of the text (related to the genre);
- the lexico-grammatical choices made within the text (the register).

These three elements all combine to differentiate the text as a piece of writing within its discipline area. (e.g. Gardner and Holmes 2006 use all three aspects as the basis for their analysis of British student writing across different disciplines).

Consideration of the *wider context of use and meaning* involves discussion with subject staff about the nature of the texts and how they are viewed by readers and writers within the discipline area. Investigations of the types of texts most often written (or demanded of students) within a particular subject is helpful. Questions about the value of certain types of text are also important. This provides the writing instructor with a better understanding of why certain texts are written. Finding out about the text types and subject specialists' understandings of what is meant by certain labels for texts is an important part of this stage of analysis. The section above on working with subject staff gave more details on this aspect of exploration.

Organization and structure of the text

In Part 1, we discussed the differences between subject areas in the types of texts they require and expectations of what is included in those texts. Text types which are shared across subject areas (e.g. dissertation or research report) may differ in structure and organization. For example, the majority of scientific research reports follow the pattern shown in Table 2.2.

For other disciplines, however, there are likely to be additions to or deviations from this format. In practice-based social science research, sections on the context of the research and implications for practice of findings are expected. Academic writing instructors can survey texts in a particular subject area in order to discover typical stages.

Structure of writing can also be usefully analyzed through the "moves" or patterns of rhetoric which a text uses to fulfill its main purposes. This way of considering the development of the meanings within a text was established by Swales (1990), primarily through his analysis of research articles. Swales and Feak identify a "move" as a "defined and bounded communicative act that is designed to achieve one main communicative objective" (2000:35). It can be as short as a clause or as long as several paragraphs. Any text will have several moves which act to develop the logic or functions of a text in particular directions.

Table 2.2 Research report organization.

Title

Authors

Abstract

Introduction

Methods

Results

Discussion

Acknowledgements

References

Appendices

Table 2.3 CARS model of research article introductions (Swales and Feak, 2004: 244).

Move 1: establishing a research territory

1a) by showing that the general research area is important, central, interesting, problematic or relevant in some way (optional)

1b) by introducing and reviewing items of previous research in the area (obligatory)

Move 2: establishing a niche

2a) by indicating a gap in the previous research, or by extending previous knowledge in some way (obligatory)

Move 3: occupying the niche

3a) by outlining purposes or stating the nature of the present research (obligatory)

3b) by listing research questions or hypotheses

3c) by announcing principal findings

3d) by stating the value of the present research

3e) by indicating the structure of the research paper

A very useful example of moves analysis at work is in Swales' CARS model of research article introductions, which shows how different moves are combined to **C**reate **A** **R**esearch **S**pace for the research which follows. These moves are as shown in Table 2.3.

The model does not claim that this pattern works for all research paper introductions, however. Swales acknowledges that this model is a generalized one and that there are differences between academic disciplines in the moves and sub-moves which are more commonly employed. He indicates, for example, that moves 3b–e are more probable in some fields than others. In support of this, work by Kanoksilapatham (2005) has found a clear difference between moves in Biochemistry and Computing Science introductions. In his sample, all Biochemistry articles include Move 1b (establish value of research by reviewing previous research), whereas Computing Science introductions tended to omit this move. Kanoksilapatham suggests that this difference may be due to the lack of rich research history within the Computing Science discipline, leaving less for writers to draw on, and the influence of the commercial world on the discipline, meaning that previous work becomes less important.

Genre analysts have also considered other sections of the dissertation: Hopkins and Dudley Evans' work on moves within Discussion of Results sections mapped the stages shown in Table 2.4.

Again, not all of these moves are present in each Discussion section and there are likely to be differences in use across disciplines. It is important to view findings of this kind as descriptions of what is frequently done by writers and which can provide guidance, rather than prescriptions for student writing.

Table 2.4 Organization of Discussion of Results section.

Discussion
1 Background Information
2 Statement of results
3 (Un)expected result
4 Reference to previous research (comparison)
5 Explanation of Unsatisfactory Result
6 Exemplification
7 Deduction and Hypothesis (since modified to Claim)
8 Reference to Previous Research (in support of a claim)
9 Recommendation
10 Justification

Source: Hopkins and Dudley-Evans, 1988: 118

An investigation of the typical moves used within the key sections of research journals or dissertations/theses within particular subjects can provide a teaching framework for Academic Writing instructors and/or areas for exploration for students.

One example of the use of moves analysis to produce a framework for writing is the Academic Phrasebank of the University of Manchester (see Useful Resources section for URL). The author of this resource analyzed a collection of student writing against the Swales and Hopkins and Dudley-Evans' models, noting the language used to fulfill each move. Other categories of functions arose through reading of the texts. The resulting list of phrases is a very valuable resource for writers, but does not take account of disciplinary variations. However, teachers can conduct a similar exercise with a corpus of texts from one subject area to establish more specific sets of moves and connected phrases. Indeed, the construction of a discipline-specific Phrasebank is something that teachers and students could work on together.

Lexicogrammatical patterns

There are many different patterns of lexis and grammar across discipline writing which have been explored by researchers and can form the basis of teaching materials for Academic Writing instructors. However, some aspects are more easily accessible for students than others. For example, a consideration of the use of "I" or "we" in texts is something which students can grasp without too much linguistic explanation. In contrast, work on "epistemic modality to express certainty and uncertainty" (Rizomiloti, 2006) may be beyond the linguistic and analytic abilities of most students. This is something to bear in mind when choosing areas for materials development.

Some reasonable starting points might be:

- Vocabulary choice.
- Collocations (words which frequently occur together or form "set phrases" within the discipline).
- The use of personal pronouns.
- Use of other "informal" features (e.g. And/But in initial positions, contractions).

Lexicogrammatical choices within texts are often explored using corpus linguistics and concordance-based research methods. Researchers in this area of linguistics use text analysis software to interrogate patterns of language use within collections of texts. These copora vary from the general to more specific; for example, the British National Corpus is a 100 million word collection of texts which is designed to represent a wide cross-section of current British English. A more focused example is the British Academic Writing English corpus (BAWE), currently under construction. (Findings from exploration of this corpus are expected to inform the future teaching of discipline specific EAP and Academic Writing.) Other researchers have used mini-corpora based around specific disciplines in order to find out about specific features of writing in these fields (e.g. Mudraya, 2006, compiled an Engineering corpus; Rizomilioti, 2006, worked with corpora in the fields of Biology, Literary Criticism and Archaeology). Details of corpora, text analysis software and free concordancing packages available to teachers are given in the Resources section. The sections below provide some examples of the kind of teaching material which can be produced using this approach.

Lexical items

One way to focus on vocabulary choices within texts is to provide students with concordance data and ask them to investigate the features of particular words. This data is produced by concordancing software and is a collection of all the lines from the corpus of texts which contain the key word, showing its immediate context. E.g. one section from the concordance output for the word "solution" from a set of Chemistry texts looks like Table 2.5 (Mudraya, 2006: 246).

The meanings and collocations of the word "solution" can be explored in the following ways.

Activity 1. Study the concordance data and find the instances of the word solution used (1) in the general sense (e.g. solution of a problem) and (2) in the technical (chemical) sense.

Table 2.5 Example of concordance output for "solution".

1 What if the gas were not ideal. A **solution** can still be found

2 the calculations required to obtain a **solution** An average constant velocity

3 k-wall properties do not complicate the **solution** a great deal and give a better

4 is dried and a water-based caustic soda **solution** is added. Following a timed mix

5 the equation of state. A trial and error **solution** is the simplest way to proceed.

6 the last trial so this is an adequate **solution**. Notice how quickly the new solution …

(55 more lines follow)

Activity 2a. From the concordance data, supply the adjectives that collocate with the word solution used (1) in the general sense and (2) in the technical (chemical) sense. Underline the adjectives that can be used with both senses of solution.

Activity 2b. From the concordance data, supply the verbs that collocate with the word solution used (1) in the general sense and (2) in the technical (chemical) sense. Underline the verbs that can be used with both senses of solution.

Answer key 2a

General	**Chemical**
adequate, analytical, (not) possible, particular, optimum, similar, following, explicit, known, sensitive, insensitive, straightforward, ideal, alternative	aqueous, acid, dilute, concentrated, strong, weak, ideal, saturated, following, similar, liquid, particular, partially miscible

Answer key 2b

General	**Chemical**
find, obtain, complicate, is/are, attempt, add, yield, exist, take, lead to, give rise to, have, lengthen, print, contain, calculate, simplify	add, be/is, has, pump, form, immerse in, enter, flow out of, absorb, plate out of, take, exist, contain

This kind of exercise is useful in that it draws students' attention to the meaning of a piece of "subtechnical" vocabulary and it is this vocabulary which usually proves difficult for students to use accurately. Technical or specialist vocabulary is more easily learned since this tends to be explained by subject staff or textbooks. Subtechnical vocabulary can be confusing however, since such words have a common meaning in general use, but a second more specific use inside the discipline area (here "solution" generally means "solution to a problem", but in a technical sense means something different). These different meanings are often taken for granted by subject specialists and not explained.

Grammatical choices

Corpus work can inform grammatical choices too. Table 2.6 is an example of a piece of teaching material produced for a seminar for a group of medical professionals, based on a corpus of articles from medical journals (Feak 2006).

These examples give some indication of what instructors can do with this sort of information, using published research findings or through their own research. However, teachers do not have to be experts in concordancing or text analysis software in order to explore such patterns in discipline writing. It is possible to use the same principles and investigate "by hand", collecting examples of language used in particular ways within the disciplines.

The Internet can also be exploited: Google can provide a rough indication of the frequency of particular words, phrases or collocations within a subject area. Type into the Google search box the phrase you are investigating in inverted commas followed by the name of the discipline and search. The number of resulting hits will give you guide to the frequency of use, at least in web-based documents and writing. Students can use this technique to compare the usage of slightly different phrases in their field. For example,

Phrases searched for	Google hits
"this paper investigates" Medicine	187,000
"this paper wants to suggest answers to ..." Medicine	53

Results are only a rough guide, since teachers cannot control the materials on the Web to ensure a principled sample of texts as their search field.

Table 2.6 Teaching material based on a corpus of medical journals.

Medical research papers typically contain non-verbal data of various kinds – tables and figures. There are four main options for referring the reader to this kind of non-verbal data:

a. Survival rates were high (see Table 4)/Survival rates were high (Table 4).

b. As shown in Table 4, survival rates were high.

c. The survival rates are shown in Table 4.

d. Table 4 shows the high survival rates.

In a study of a small corpus of 50 medical research papers (from thoracic surgery), 125 instances of the four options above were found. In your experience, which is likely to be the most common? The least?

Nevertheless, this is sort of information can be useful for students who are trying to decide which phrases to use in their writing.

Personal pronouns

An absence of personal pronouns is often viewed as one of the hallmarks of general academic writing. However, research shows that their use varies across disciplines. Science and Engineering writing tends to be more impersonal, but writing in the Humanities and Social Sciences often uses a great deal of first-person personal pronouns in particular sections. For example, a writer describing their involvement as a participant researcher in a piece of qualitative research may use "I" quite freely. Those writing about practice-based research are likely to use "I" or "we" in describing the context of the study. The humanistic disciplines tend to use more personal pronouns in order to achieve certain interpersonal goals (Hyland, 2001).

Instructors can explore this aspect of writing with their students through the study together of journal articles or a collection of dissertations. A frequency count of the use of personal pronouns and the sections in which they occur can lead to some interesting comparisons across disciplines. The research abstract is an interesting, and manageable, text for investigation of this feature. Swales and Feak (2004: 284) indicate that abstracts they investigated in Physics, Chemistry and Astrophysics journals were more likely to take a personal stance, using phrases such as "we discuss", "we compute" and "we conclude". They suggest that the use of "we" may function to shorten the abstract, giving it pace.

Students as explorers of their own disciplines

The final section considers more closely ways in which teachers can help students to explore the customs and rules of their subject area for themselves. For many teachers the development of this skill in their students is key: not only does it provide students with linguistic analysis abilities to apply outside class, thus aiding extra-curriculum learning, this approach also makes the teaching of mixed-subject groups manageable.

Several writers have described this sort of approach within their classes. Currie (1999) encouraged undergraduate students to keep "journalogs" to report on particular practices within their parallel content classes. In considering academic writing practices, students were required to interview a subject class teacher about their own writing and the writing they asked of students. Students submitted a report on their findings and also took part in a class discussion around the differences and similarities between disciplines. This approach helped students to appreciate the importance of writing in the academy and the role of writing in the creation and dissemination of knowledge within the community. Some students were surprised to find that writing was important in areas where they had thought it would not matter so much (e.g. Maths, Chemistry, Physics). This approach promotes the role of students as ethnographers of their subject areas: providing them with skills and opportunities to learn more about their own "educational culture" or "academic tribe".

Other approaches can be based around textual analysis. For example, Hirvela (1997) required her students to build a portfolio of analyzed texts from their subject area. Lee and Swales (2006) gives an account of a class which helped NNS doctoral students to compile and analyze corpora in their subject areas. The two examples below show how this sort of analysis could be initiated.

Comparing Phrasebank With Writing In Your Discipline Area

1 Go to the University of Manchester Phrasebank site http://phrasebank.man.ac.uk/ and find the section on Introductions (Writing Introductions).

2 Identify phrases that you could use for
- Establishing the importance of a topic
- Establishing the importance of a topic (time frame given)

What is (generally) the difference in grammatical structures used in these two types of phrase?

3 Read the introductory sections from the two journal articles you have chosen.
- Can you identify the phrases which establish the importance of the topic?
- What tense do they use? Why?
- Are the phrases similar or different to those listed in Phrasebank?
- Is there any word or phrase which is particular to your academic subject?

	Phrase(s) used to establish importance of topic	Tense used/ why?	Same or different to Phrasebank?	Particular for my subject because …
Journal article 1				
Journal article 2				

4 Now do the same exercise for phrases which "Highlight the knowledge gap in a field of study".

	Phrase(s) used to highlight knowledge gap in field	Tense used/ why?	Same or different to Phrasebank?	Particular for my subject because …
Journal article 1				
Journal article 2				

5 Repeat this exercise with phrases for other functions in academic writing.

Comparing the Use of "informal" Features Across Disciplines:

(adapted from Hyland, 2006: 162)

The figures below come from Chang and Swales' study of writing in three discipline areas (1999)

Feature	Statistics uses	Linguistics uses	Philosophy uses	Total uses
I/my/me	29	307	684	1020
Begin a sentence with an inappropriate conjunction (e.g. And/But)	57	229	446	732
Final preposition	3	20	21	44
Contraction	0	21	71	92
Question	9	62	153	224

- Which discipline area has the most informal writing style?
- Which is the most formal?
- Which discipline area is being described?

A: "It appears that the _____ ... exhibit a more interactive writing style. They achieve their intended rhetorical purposes through the manipulations of overt personal pronouns and sentence rhythm (e.g. initial conjunctions and contractions). _____ has to be more rhetorical in a way because it's dealing with issues which there isn't an established way of settling ... if you want to give demonstrations in _____, you would have to be doing something more like therapy to get people over confusions."

B: "As for _____, its status as a field not comfortably categorised as either humanities, sciences or social sciences seems to be well reflected in its textual presentations."

C: "researchers in _____ seem to believe ... that scientific studies are factual and hence best designed to be faceless and agentless. ... to be prudent scientists, the _____ avoid using features which reveal personal involvement or emotion".

Select one of these informal features and conduct a small research study of its use in 4–5 journal articles from your research area.
- How do your findings compare with those for the subject areas above?
- Can you explain the similarities or differences?

Both of these exercises help students to begin a structured investigation of the linguistic patterns of their own discipline area. Once students are helped to see that language is used differently within subjects and the reasons why this may happen, they are very enthusiastic to consider these differences more closely for themselves.

Conclusion

This chapter has discussed the need for discipline-specific Academic Writing tuition, indicating that mastering writing within a subject area is a key to academic success for students. It has also argued that it is language instructors who need to work to make these elements clear for student writers. The chapter has suggested some ways in which teachers can proceed to work with subject specialists and in the analysis of discipline-focused texts, but has also stressed the language teachers' role in students' development as explorers of their own discipline practices.

The following useful resources provide further sources of information and guidance relating to the areas discussed above.

Some useful resources for teaching academic writing in the disciplines

There are many resources available which provide further information and guidance on teaching academic writing in the disciplines and it is impossible to list all of these. Therefore, the references below are a selection only. Links from some of these will lead you to other useful information.

Web-based resources:

What is Writing in the Disciplines?
http://wac.colostate.edu/intro/pop2e.cfm
Part of the Writing Across the Curriculum Clearinghouse website.

This is an excellent set of resource with several sections devoted to Writing in the Disciplines, including print resources and ideas for useful activities to use in class. For example,

- Asking students to keep a "jargon journal" of specialist terminology from their subject area.
- Analyzing an expert's revisions (examining a series of drafts from an academic writer with the class—and the writer if possible—in order to learn more about their processes of writing and choices in writing).

There are also links to transcripts of interviews with teachers of academic subjects showing their expectations of student writing both in terms of text types and content. These can act as useful models for your own interviews with members of faculty about the writing they expect students to do.

Link to e-lists to join.

Writing Across the Curriculum George Mason University Guides in the disciplines http://wac.gmu.edu/guides/GMU%20guides.html

This page provides links to online guides for the following curriculum areas:

Biology
History 100
Information Technology and Engineering
School of Management
New Century College
The College of Nursing and Health Science
Psychology
Public and International Affairs
Religious Studies

The guides include information on particular aspects of writing for each discipline area, including ideas from interviews with subject tutors (some of these, however, may confirm the notion that subject tutors are not sufficiently aware many of the features of their own writing to be able to make this clear to student writers).

OWL at Purdue University—Resources for Documenting Sources http://owl.english.purdue.edu/handouts/research/ r_docsources.html

Links to style sheets and explanatory websites for referencing in different discipline areas.

University of Toronto: advise on Writing in the Disciplines http://utoronto.ca/writing/advise.html#types

Provides advice on specific types of writing, including Writing about Poetry, Writing about Art History, Writing about Physics and how to write a Lab Report.
http://utoronto.ca/writing/books3.html#socsci
University of Toronto site with a bibliography of books describing how to write in various discipline areas (Humanities, Social Science, Science, Health Sciences).

Cornell University, J.S. Knight Institute for Writing in the Disciplines
http://arts.cornell.edu/Knight_institute/index.htm

The institute supports writing seminars and writing intensive courses in a broad spectrum of academic disciplines and at all levels of undergraduate education; it also engages in a variety of outreach activities. The website includes information on research project focusing on Writing in the Majors. From 1997 to 2005 the institute hosted a Writing in the Disciplines consortium.

Model writing assignments for a Biology Course
http://indiana.edu/~cwp/assgn/biomods/index.shtml

Campus Writing Program at Indiana University, Bloomington provides an overview of a project working with Biology Faculty to produce writing assignments. Links to list of possible assignment types and advice on writing in Biology discipline.

Academic PhraseBank, The University of Manchester
http://phrasebank.manchester.ac.uk/

The Academic Phrasebank is a general resource for academic writers. It aims to provide examples of some of the phraseological "nuts and bolts" of writing organized under rhetorical and functional headings. It was designed primarily with international students, whose first language is not English, in mind. However, native speakers will also find the materials very useful.

Miller T (ed.) Functional Approaches to Written Text
http://exchanges.state.gov/education/engteaching/
pubs/BR/5111TOC_nof.htm

Web publication of this book hosted by US Department of State, Bureau of Educational and Cultural Affairs. A useful section on genre approaches, including

Applied Genre Analysis and ESP

VK Bhatia http://exchanges.state.gov/EDUCATION/ENGTEACHING/PUBS/BR/functionalsec4_10.htm

Paper which describes a genre-based teaching approach for professional writing in Business and Law.

Corpus Linguistics and Concordancing: Tools and further information

Corpus linguistics provides one approach to investigation of differences between discourse in discipline areas at the level of lexis and grammar.

Text Corpora and Corpus Linguistics
http://athel.com/corpus.html

Includes an Introduction to using corpora, existing corpora which you can use (although these tend to be non-academic texts or spoken language), corpus software, web concordancing and online corpus linguistics courses. Also links to a host of other useful sites.

WordSmith Tools
http://lexically.net/wordsmith/

Mike Scott's pages on his WordSmith tool for linguistic analysis of texts. You can download demonstration versions for free. There are also useful links to other sites with information on corpus linguistics and use of concordance packages.

VLC Web Concordancer at Polytechnic University of Hong Kong
http://vlc.polyu.edu.hk/concordance/

A simple to use concordancer with a range of corpora to choose from, including several of student writing and academic texts from business, applied linguistics and computer studies.

Tim Johns Data-Driven Learning Page
http://eisu2.bham.ac.uk/johnstf/timconc.htm

An excellent collection of materials, handouts, exercises and links connected with data-driven learning using corpora and concordancing approaches.

British Academic Written English Corpus
http://coventry.ac.uk/researchnet/d/505

This corpus is a collaboration between the Universities of Warwick, Reading and Oxford Brookes. It is part of the project "An investigation of genres of assessed writing in British Higher Education". The aim is to provide a database for use by researchers who are investigating the nature of academic writing, and also by tutors who are designing teaching and assessment materials for their students. The project is funded by the UK Economic and Social Research Council and due to end in December 2007 when the full corpus will be made available.

One of the questions the project is seeking to answer is "What are the similarities and differences between genres produced in different disciplines, and for different degree programmes?".

The website provides links to research papers and conference presentations on the project including Gardner and Holmes' 2006 paper comparing student writing in History and Engineering.

Books

Coffin C, Curry MJ, Goodman S, Hewings A, Lillis TM, J Swann 2003 *Teaching Academic Writing: A Toolkit for Higher Education* London and New York: Routledge

Chapter 3 covers Writing for Different Disciplines. It contains very useful classroom activities which focus students on differences between subject areas in text types, data representation, discipline-specific terminology, and examples of case study and essay writing.

Swales JM and Feak CB 2004 *Academic Writing for Graduate Students* (Second Edition) Ann Arbor: The University of Michigan Press

Swales JM and Feak CB 2000 *English in Today's Research World: A Writing Guide* Ann Arbor: The University of Michigan Press

Both of these books focus on general Academic Writing (and in the introductions Swales and Feak explain why they prefer this approach), however, they also include specific tasks which are designed to start students thinking about disciplinary differences in writing. For example, Unit 5 of AWGS (2004) reports Hyland's 1999 study of frequently used reporting verbs across disciplines and asks students to investigate the use of reporting verbs in journals in their own subjects. *English in Today's Research World* includes more of these kinds of activities and allows teachers to move from the general to discipline–specific within a mixed group.

Other writing in disciplines guides

Weissberg R and Buker S 1990 *Writing up research: Experimental research report writing for students of English* Englewood Cliffs, NJ: Prentice Hall.

Journals with research on disciplinary-based writing

English for Specific Purposes (Elsevier)

This journal has published a large number of discourse and genre analysis research papers on Academic writing/EAP. It is a very useful source of data for classroom use. It also provides some examples of programmes which focus on ESAP/AW in disciplines.

E.g. Lee and Swales 2006 "A corpus-based EAP course for NNS doctoral students; Moving from available specialised corpora to self-compiled corpora" pp. 56f. This paper gives an account of a class which encouraged students to compile and analyze their own corpora in their subject areas.

Journal of English for Academic Purposes (Pergamon/Elsevier)

This is a newer journal than ESP but has also published great deal of work on EAP, discourse and genre analysis and corpus linguistics. It has published several comparisons of linguistic features across discipline areas in addition to papers which describe approaches to teaching Academic Writing in the Disciplines.

Further reading on collaboration with subject specialists

Johns and Dudley-Evans (1980): the earliest account of teacher collaboration in EAP describing the team-teaching experience with small classes of PG students.

Johns and Dudley-Evans (1980), "An experiment in team-teaching of overseas postgraduate students of transportation and plant biology," *in Team Teaching in ESP 6-23 ELT Documents 106* (London: The British Council).

Flowerdew, J. (1993), "Content-based language instruction in a tertiary setting," *English for Specific Purposes*, 12, 121-138. Account of work with foundation year university students in Oman in team-taught, parallel science and science-support classes.

Northcott, J. and Brown, G. (2006), "Legal translator training: Partnership between teachers of English for legal purposes and legal specialists," *English for Specific Purposes*, 25(3), 358-375. This paper deals with a very specific situation of legal translation and indicates some of the difficulties which can occur if a non-legally trained teacher tries to "go it alone".

Interviewing subject specialists about writing in their disciplines
Interview questions used by Nesi and Gardner (2006).

- What role does assignment-writing play in your department?
- Can you tell us what different types of written assignment you set your students?
  - Could you tell us more about ZZ?
  - Are there other types of assignment task that you haven't mentioned?
  - Do you set assignments of type [pre-existing genre] as well?
  - Do you use other formats, e.g. non-written assignments, such as videos?
- What are the main ways in which the various types of assignment you set differ?
  - How could we tell a YY from an XX?
  - e.g. an experimental report from a case-study?
  - e.g. a critical review from an essay?
- What sort of differences do you expect to find between the written work of first and second year students on the one hand and final-year undergraduates and masters-level students on the other hand?
- What do you value most in student written work?
- What are the sorts of things that you most dislike finding in student's written work?
- In your opinion, how much does presentation matter?
- How do the various assignment tasks that you set enable you to judge whether a student has shown evidence of the qualities you value?
- Do you find that overseas students have particular problems with written assignments, compared to native English speakers?
  - Do you have any particular ways and means of helping them overcome these problems?
- Who should we talk to about collecting assignments?
- Is there a good time to collect assignments on module MM999?
  - Opportunity to explain that we're hoping to get 5 or 6 good-quality assignments from 2 or 3 modules at each level (years 1-3 and masters).
- Are there any modules in your dept which you think we should definitely include in our sample?
  - if so, which are they? and why?

References

Becher, T. (1989), *Academic Tribes and Territories: Intellectual Enquiry and the Culture of Disciplines* (Buckingham: The Society for Research into Higher Education and Open University Press).

Benesch, S. (1996), "Needs analysis and curriculum development in EAP: an example of a critical approach," *TESOL Quarterly*, 30/4, 723–738.

Bloor, M. and Bloor, T. (1986), Languages for specific purposes: practice and theory. *CLCS Occasional Papers 19*. Dublin: Trinity College, Centre for Language and Communication Studies.

Brinton, D. M., Snow, M. A., and Wesche, M. B. (1989), *Content-based Second Language Instruction* (New York: Newbury House).

Casanave, C. P. (2002), *Writing Games* (Mahwah, NJ: Lawrence Erlbaum Associates).

Chang, Y. and Swales, J. (1999), "Informal elements in English academic writing: threats or opportunities for advanced non-native speakers?" In Candlin, C. and Hyland, K. (eds), *Writing: Texts, Processes and Practices* (London: Longman).

Currie, P. (1993), "Entering a disciplinary community: conceptual activities required to write for one introductory university course," *Journal of Second Language Writing*, 2, 101–117.

Currie, P. (1999), "Transferable skills: promoting student research," *English for Specific Purposes*, 18/4, 329–345.

Dudley-Evans, T. (2001), Team-teaching in EAP: changes and adaptations in the Birmingham approach. In J. Flowerdew and M. Peacock (eds), *Research Perspectives on English for Academic Purposes* (Cambridge: Cambridge University Press).

Dudley-Evans, T. and St John, M. J. (1998), *Developments in English for Specific Purposes: A Multidisciplinary Approach* (Cambridge: Cambridge University Press).

Feak, C. B. (2006), "Further reflections on collaborative practice in EAP materials production," paper given at AAAL and ACLA/CAAL Montreal, Quebec.

Gardner, S. and Holmes, J. (2006), "Multiple perspectives on specialist English for EAP tutors," paper given at the BALEAP PIM: 18 November 2006. Durham University Language Centre, From *Astrophysics Papers to Student Business Case Reports: Teaching Specialist English in the University Context.*

Hirvela, A. (1997), "Disciplinary portfolios and EAP writing instruction," *English for Specific Purposes*, 16/2, 83–100.

Hopkins, A. and Dudley-Evans, T. (1988), "A genre-based investigation of the discussion section in articles and dissertations," *English for Specific Purposes*, 7, 113–122.

Hyland, K. (2001), "Bringing in the reader: addressee features in academic articles," *Written Communication*, 18/4, 549–574.

Hyland, K. (2002), "Specificity revisited: how far should we go now?" *English for Specific Purposes*, 21, 385–395.

Hyland, K. (2006), *English for Academic Purposes: An Advanced Resource Book* (Abingdon: Routledge).

Johns, A. M. (1995), "Teaching classroom and authentic genres: initiating students into academic cultures and discourses", in Belcher, D. and Braine, G. (eds), *Academic Writing in a Second Language: Essays on Research and Pedagogy*, pp. 277–291.

Johns, A. M. (1997), *Text, Role and Context: Developing Academic Literacies* (Cambridge: Cambridge University Press).

Kanoksilapatham, B. (2005), "Rhetorical structure of biochemistry research," *English for Specific Purposes,* 24, 269–292.

Lave, J. and Wenger, E. (1991), *Situated Learning: Legitimate Peripheral Participation* (Cambridge: Cambridge University Press).

Lee, D. and Swales, J. M. (2006), "A corpus-based EAP course for NNS doctoral students: moving from specialized corpora to self-compiled corpora," *English for Specific Purposes,* 25/1, 56–75.

Leki, I. (1995), "Good writing: I know it when I see it," in Belcher, D. and Braine, G. (eds), *Academic Writing in a Second Language: Essays on Research and Pedagogy* (pp. 23–46) (Norwood, NJ: Ablex).

Mudraya, O. (2006), "Engineering English: A lexical frequency instructional model," *English for Specific Purposes,* 25/2, 235–256.

Nesi, H. and Gardner, S. (2006), "Variation in disciplinary culture: university tutors' views on assessed writing tasks," in Keily, R., Clibbon, G., Rea-Dickins, P. and Woodfield, H. (eds), *Language, Culture and Identity in Applied Linguistics* (British Studies in Applied Linguistics, Vol. 21) (London: Equinox Publishing).

Prior, P. A. (1998), *Writing/Disciplinarity: A Sociohistoric Account of Literate Activity in the Academy* (Mahwah, NJ: Lawrence Erlbaum Associates).

Rizomilioti, V. (2006), "Exploring Epistemic Modality in Academic Discourse using corpora," in Arnó, E., Soler, A. and Rueda, C. (eds), *Information Technology in Languages for Specific Purposes* (New York: Springer Science and Business Media).

Spack, R. (1988), "Initiating ESL students into the academic discourse community: how far should we go?" *TESOL Quarterly,* 31, 765–774.

Swales, J. M. (1990), *Genre Analysis: English in Academic and Research Settings* (Cambridge: Cambridge University Press).

Swales, J. M. and Feak, C. B. (2000), *English in Today's Research World* (Ann Arbor: University of Michigan Press).

Swales, J. M. and Feak, C. B. (2004), *Academic Writing for Graduate Students* (second edition) (Ann Arbor: The University of Michigan Press).

Teaching Writing Teachers to Teach Writing

3

Akua Duku Anokye

I began my teaching of writing career in the early 1970s. A recent graduate with an MA degree in Speech and Hearing Science and Urban Linguistics, I had little thought of teaching first-year writing. After a one-year stint at Bowie State College where I worked in the Speech Department and with Upward Bound, I was looking for a job that would be more rewarding. One afternoon while shopping in northern Virginia, I passed a community college campus that seemed inviting. Who would have thought that stopping to inquire about a part-time teaching position (in any department) would lead to my lifelong career as a first-year composition specialist? I had stopped at the personnel office to make my inquiry and they ushered me up to the second floor where they introduced me to the Chair of English. OK, that was a good start. In the brief interview the chair asked me whether I thought I could teach English composition. Of course, that wasn't the name of the course. It was called Verbal Studies, distinguishing written from spoken discourse. Hey, I had been enchanted by words and stories all my life, and I was an excellent reader. Why not? She gave me several books to look over and I was to get back to her the next day. Before I arrived home, she had called and left a message that she wanted to offer me two courses to begin with and I should come to orientation the following week.

Sitting in that room the evening of the orientation, I was shocked when the Chair came to the door and motioned for me to come outside. Right then and there, she offered me a full-time teaching position because they had just received a last-minute resignation. Like a deer caught in the headlights, I accepted and returned to the orientation, little of which I remember except it was a three-hour meeting that spoke little of pedagogy, philosophy, or any of the things I would be desperate to learn in the following years.

As I prepare for my thirty-fourth year of teaching writing and my tenth year of directing a first-year composition program, I am still imagining and reflecting on what a meaningful orientation for teachers of academic writing might be. I have had some excellent role models over the years like Linda Stanley at Queensborough Community College during the 1980s and early 1990s and during the later 1990s, Joan Mullin, who is now at UT-Austin. I have worked with MA and PhD students teaching for the first time as TAs in the English Language and Literature Department at University Toledo; at the same time, I was working with seasoned adjuncts with varying degrees, mostly in English. Few of these teachers, student or adjunct, had degrees in what we now call rhetoric and composition. Ten years later at Arizona State University's West campus where I am now working, I have no TAs, but a wonderful collection of faculty associates with MAs, mostly having taught first-year composition as TAs in their former schools and one with more than 15 books to his credit, a former high school teacher with 30 years' experience and a PhD in English, another with a PhD in English, and finally a PhD in speech communication mass media. I also have a full-time cohort of faculty with PhDs specializing in sociolinguistics, composition and pedagogy, and English and another with an MA in literature and writing studies. I've come a long ways. My faculty is now as widely diverse as the student body, coming from as far as Taiwan, Brazil, New York, Nebraska and the Southwest.

In preparation for orientation and workshops for faculty teaching academic writing, over the years, I have read everyone from Paulo Freire to P. J. Corbett, Geneva Smitherman to Mina Shaugnessy, Brian Street to Victor Villanueva, Wendy Bishop to Elaine Richardson. Sondra Perl, Keith Gilyard, David Bartholomae, Arthur Applebee, Cheryl Glenn, Linda Flower, Mike Rose, Steve North, Maxine Hairston, Lester Faigley, Jackie Jones-Royster, Min-zhan Lu, Bill Stewart, Walt Wolfram, George Hillocks, Lee Odell, Andrea Lunsford, Deborah Tannen and of course Zora Neale Hurston have been my bedside companions. Regardless of the multiple realities they explored and the range of experiences they displayed, there is one constant that I believe should be first communicated to all teachers—the concern for student lives and the experiences they bring to the classroom. To set the tone for a classroom experience that values students I like to begin orientation with a program philosophy such as this:

> The teaching and study of composition is a complicated undertaking that not only benefits the university but prepares students for lifelong learning opportunities. It is a multifaceted process, both individual and social, that takes place over time with continued practice and informed guidance. The teacher of composition must be a

student of the many ways meaning is constructed by writers and their readers, and how meaning is conveyed and received via codes that are explicit as well as implicit in the language used.

Our basic writing theory rests on a notion that writing is an active, interactive, recursive process with writers discovering meaning as they think, write, interact with their own emerging texts, listen to responses from others, and revise. The students then are participants in active learning and meaning construction. We teachers must have a strong sense of respect for students, a high level of interaction with those students, and a commitment to reflect on what we observe, searching for patterns, questions, and assumptions while generating and playing with new possibilities. We examine and re-examine our assumptions about ourselves, our students, what and how we teach, and we assess our program. Our aim is to engage in a dialectic that challenges our students to look deeper into their assumptions about the world as we challenge our own assumptions. Keeping a teaching journal facilitates this type of interaction.

We believe that effective teaching utilizes both oral and written discourse activities coupled with constant feedback. Writing promotes, and is nurtured by, dialogue and conversations with meaningful others about a preliminary idea, draft, and final text. Thus, writing can be facilitated through classroom interaction, discussion, and oral monologue. Constant juxtaposition and interaction of spoken and written discourse provides students with a systematic process for developing the critical writing skills necessary to be successful in their academic and professional lives. Sequencing assignments that progress from oral to written, from group discussion to soloing, to informal writing to formal writing keep the discursive and recursive nature of composition in mind.

We also examine the interaction between theory and practice. There are many approaches to theory and practice. We welcome all constructive voices and seek to create positive tension necessary for theoretical and practical development. We seek opportunities for competing theories to "talk" to one another and use that dialogue to reflect on and assess our teaching practices, our program. Each of us brings a unique configuration of experiences to the learning table. Rather than one dominating another, we hope to encourage our students and our colleagues to enrich one another with their ideas, their questions, their experiences, and their points of view.

In the final analysis we respect our colleagues and invite them to participate in the teaching of writing in all disciplines and to assist in the review of our student work and the program initiatives via an annual portfolio assessment. (Anokye, 2005–2006)

With this philosophical statement I attempt to establish a community of thinkers, teachers, and colleagues. During the orientation, we begin with an overview of this philosophy and discuss how our own personal teaching styles, experiences, education and writing prepare us to be successful teachers of academic writing at the university. I believe that the best teaching practices involve modeling of the methods and strategies, so I like to engage the faculty in reflection on assumptions we make about ourselves and how those assumptions affect us as teachers. We work in groups interrogating ourselves and our colleagues on such issues as: Who do I think I am?; What makes me suitable for teaching composition?; What gives me my authority?; What can I offer my students?; How do I think my students see/think about me when they first meet me?; and How right are they? These are very personal questions that are intended to strip away much of the veneer we've built up over the years. Not only do we examine assumptions we make about ourselves, our identities, our language, but we also examine assumptions we make about what we teach, the theories upon which we base our methods, our approaches, our practices. Following this exercise, we have created a cognitive map to help us track our progress as we talk about our students. These reflections become the basis for each faculty to write a statement of philosophy about the teaching and learning of writing that will later include brief examples of how they plan to implement their philosophy in their courses.

A good writing program anywhere must account for the students being taught. Following intense self-examination, we engage in a dialogue about our student profile. Our goal, as the program philosophy intimates, is to establish a student-centered classroom. To accomplish that goal we look at our student profile. Is our campus a residential or commuter campus? Do the students have jobs? What are their average ages? What kind of ethnic, racial, economic population do we serve? Is our school urban, suburban, or rural? Do our students have families they are raising or live with? Are they self-supported or on financial aid? What is their career focus? As we carry out this analysis we also ask ourselves: What is the history of our campus? What are our expectations for students? What is our university or college mission? How will we assess our students and ourselves? What are the civic, social, labor demands in the area? Are our students properly placed in the courses we offer and how can we determine that? We often devote a half day to this practice by which time we can begin to tackle the actual pedagogy of academic writing.

We use the "Writing Outcomes Statement for First-Year Composition" adopted by the Council of Writing Program Administrators (WPA) in April 2000. A version of the WPA statement was published in WPA, *Writing Program Administration*, 23(1/2) (Fall/Winter 1999), at pages 59–66. This statement articulates what composition teachers nationwide have learned from practice, research, and theory. In the introduction to the outcomes it asserts "learning to write is a complex process, both individual and social, that takes place over time with continued practice and informed guidance. Therefore, it is important that teachers, administrators, and a concerned public do not imagine that these outcomes can be taught in reduced or simple ways. Helping students demonstrate these outcomes requires expert understanding of how students actually learn to write" (*ibid.*, Introduction). I like opening with this statement because it reiterates, supports and illuminates the teaching philosophy that we have already explored. It provides a context for which we think about teaching academic writing, what we hope to achieve, and provides some guidance for assessing student and program success.

The outcomes include statements about intellectual, rhetorical knowledge, critical thinking, reading, writing, processes, and knowledge of conventions all which cover the wide range of skills we would like for students to attain as citizens of their academic, social and civic communities.

I used to begin the second day of workshop/orientation sessions with a discussion of critical thinking one of the major categories from the WPA outcomes. I'd share Bloom's Taxonomy and demonstrate how thinking about higher order thinking skills assist the teachers in leading students to understand the moves they need to make to be good readers, thinkers and consequently writers. Bloom's Taxonomy, of course, works something like a pyramid with higher order thinking skills built on the more fundamental ones ranging from knowledge, to comprehension, to application, to analysis, synthesis and evaluation. This discussion is always enlightening because not all teachers have read Bloom, nor taken an education course, or thought about the importance of this hierarchy and its application.

I introduce faculty to the concept of cue words as a means for helping them see the hierarchy that exists among some words and the level of thinking they elicit. Cue words clue students into the type of information that they should be looking for or the kind of thinking that they should be doing. For example, students may need to "identify" or "define" certain concepts before they can "analyze" or "compare/contrast" them. This embedding of tasks within tasks needs to be kept in mind both as teachers work for clarity in phrasing their assignments and as they explain their expectations to students.

Cue Words	Definition
agree/disagree	to consent or differ in opinion
analyze	to examine the parts of
compare/contrast	to give similarities or differences
define	to state the meaning of a word; to give the distinguishing characteristics of
describe	to give details based on sensory observations
explain	to give reasons for; to make comprehensible; to account for
illustrate	to give examples

list/identify	to give a series of
name/state	to point out
paraphrase/restate	to tell in one's own words

In the process of discussing critical thinking with my new TAs, however, I discovered that I had made a tactical error in assuming that teachers would understand or know the connection between the critical thinking skills we were aiming for and rhetorical criticism. I can recall once having gone through an entire four-day workshop and two sessions of the Teaching Composition Seminar only to realize that my new teachers, ones who had just come to us fresh from English degrees from around the country, had not thought about or discussed rhetoric. I had given my TAs the task of coming up with assignments that would help their students use strategies that had rhetorical effects. I could not understand why they struggled with the assignment until one was bold enough to say to me, "Dr. Anokye, what do you mean by rhetorical effect?" In those days many of them had not experienced talking about rhetorical criticism as an analytical method used to examine a discourse in context, paying attention to its situation, purpose, and audience, and observing how the writer or speaker controls the context with language. Rhetorical criticism is a highly empowering tool which can be applied to the world of language and communication that surrounds us. Historically, rhetoric has been the study of persuasion. What makes a discourse persuasive? One of the most challenging breakthroughs a student needs to experience is discovering how writers not only say things, but also do things. The study of rhetorical criticism helps us understand what is being done to us when we listen and read (Horning and Sudol, 1997). Today when I talk about critical thinking I talk about rhetorical criticism in tandem. But also today more students taking English degrees are exposed to rhetoric and composition in their undergraduate degrees. I now end our workshop on this topic with a writing assignment, "How is critical thinking related to rhetorical criticism?"

Satisfied that academic writing workshop participants are well disposed to rhetoric and composition bedrock practices, I turn our discussion to teaching the writing process. That process is where the struggle begins for many composition instructors. How does an instructor, especially a first-year teaching assistant, teach beginning writers the writing process? There are many ways to get from a blank piece of paper to an effective text. During our discussion of the writing process we come to agree that:

• Many students come into a writing course with a specific set of assumptions about how to write a paper. They have been taught to design rigid outlines, or to follow a five-paragraph essay format. Students need to understand that there are guidelines to follow when attempting to write a paper, but they can tailor those guidelines to their own process. They can be guided with draft writing, small group feedback, and teacher evaluation, but in the end, they need to use these in ways that help them, not convolute their writing even further. When students learn to think of writing as a process, they will become aware of the components that will increase their repertoire of strategies and activities. By giving students many different examples of the process, it enables them to design their own system.

- Writing is unlike any other academic skill in the sense that it is not something that necessarily gets easier with time. Whereas a beginning writer may complete only one draft in an attempt to get the distasteful project over as quickly as possible, an experienced writer may spend a great deal of time agonizing over drafts and revision. The important thing to note about this phenomenon is that beginning writers need to realize that writing is a difficult process for everyone, and not to get discouraged. One thing that comes to mind in an effort to prove this to students is to write with them sometimes, and especially for them to share work with each other.

- Although many of these strategies are introduced to composition instructors, this is often easier said than done. Students come to conferences with nothing on paper, explaining that they work better in one big draft, despite requirements that they have a draft for conferencing. They fight against the process, because it usually consists of a much longer period of stress over the paper. Each instructor may need to evaluate his or her class separately in order to encourage the step-by-step process.

- One way to encourage student feedback and therefore more than one draft on a paper may be email. Writing over email is a much more low stress situation than being confronted with living, breathing peers. Students can post parts of their process for students to look over, and this also would make it easier for students to edit others' work right on a computer screen. In order to avoid too much borrowing of ideas, this kind of feedback could even be on post-graded papers, for people to get ideas for the next assignment.

- With the course delivery systems that are used by many universities today, even more creative opportunities are available through discussion boards and drop boxes for students to brainstorm, write, and workshop online. Teachers have to think outside the box and bring their own experiences with the writing process and new experiences of technology to enhance student learning.

Creating effective writing assignments plays a large role in how students respond to their writing experiences. During the workshop we practice creating writing assignments for a variety of purposes. We review important steps in creating those assignments. Not wanting to leave it to chance, we make sure the assignment has a purpose related to our course objectives and outcomes. So we ask ourselves questions like: Will it help students learn? Will it demonstrate proficiency? Is it more than required busy work? We also want to be certain that we explain the purpose of the assignment to the students. They should know why they are doing a particular exercise; how it fits in with the instruction that day, and of what use will it be. Students should know from the beginning of the assignment the assessment procedures. They should know given the assignment objective what criteria will be used to assess it. We should let them know that the assignment is based on the recursive nature of writing and what drafting expectations are in place. I also like to let students know how my assessment complements the objectives of the course, who will be the primary evaluator; whether students will have opportunities to evaluate their own assignments; will the grade be based on whether they learn or how much they demonstrate that they learn; and how their performance on one assignment might affect their performance on a final exam/project.

Not only do the answers to questions such as these help students as they work through the writing assignments, but thinking carefully about how the writing assignments are related to our overall purposes creates a sense of coherence for the teachers. We work together using a handout and each of us takes a topic of interest and creates a brief writing assignment using that handout. The steps include:

Step 1: Identify the task
Review your course syllabus to determine a point at which a brief writing assignment would help students learn content for an early unit in your course.

Step 2: Review "cue words"
All teachers do not agree on the exact definitions of these various words. Most students do not even think to ask what is meant by these words; they just assume that they know. It is essential that teachers share their definitions of cue words with students.

Step 3: Clarify the task
Use the cue words that elicit the precise information you want, and write out a single statement or question that is brief and clear and that identifies the exact information required.

Step 4: Make the task concrete and challenging
You might try defining a persona for the writer, or insisting upon a particular audience for the work, or merely creating an imaginative wrinkle in the terms of the project.

Step 5: Define the terms in your assignment
Define those words in your assignment so that there is no confusion about them.

Step 6: Add to the statement of task any special instructions about form and content
You might want to specify a required length or define a structure students can use handily.

Step 7: Put all these steps together in a clear, precise, concise statement of task.

In sum, this exercise shows teachers that they should specify the content, suggest or identify some prewriting stimuli, give the assignment some rhetorical context—that is, give the students an audience and purpose to write for, and finally negotiate the meaning of the assignment with their students. Time spent on such an exercise gives teachers an opportunity to be creative and thoughtful about what they are asking for their students to do and how they use language to communicate the ideas.

Further, I am very fond of sequencing writing assignments. I usually give participants time to think about how the assignments they have been considering might contribute to an overall semester project in which the students can engage looking at some meaningful issues, topics, concerns, problems, proposals relevant to them and their community. Using a model such as this leads easily into a general sequencing of activities that conveys the importance of various activities that comprise the writing process. This step-by-step work also gives the teachers and students many opportunities for feedback before the final project. David A. Jolliffe's *Inquiry and Genre: Writing to Learn in College* supports this notion of sequenced writing.

Convenient steps for using the sequencing model include a careful introduction of the overall writing assignment. During our workshop we discuss methods for explaining to students the components of the writing project, using examples, and possibly even activities that will require the students to participate in constructing ideas surrounding the project. The project most importantly must be specific in subject, aim, genre, and audience. In the class, students can engage in discovery activities that both respond to the assignment and brainstorm issues they'd like to explore further. Eventually students will propose topics, work through rough drafts, peer review and workshops, conference with their instructors, and expect periodical assessment as they work through meaningful reading, discovery, research, reflection, and solution processes. Each essay/writing assignment along the way has embedded tasks that illuminate the writing process, critical thinking as well as academic and personal achievement. The orientation workshops allow teachers time to think carefully and collaborate with their colleagues about all components of the process, proposal, drafts, and assessments.

Workshops throughout the year are devoted to conducting peer review workshops, conferencing, class discussions, the revision process, and a host of other important pedagogical concerns of teaching academic writing. Over the summer, teachers are asked to read a variety of theoretical and pedagogical experts and discuss them in discussion boards or other mechanisms set up for that very purpose. However, the subject of evaluation cannot be left until later in the semester. Having completed the second day of a four-day workshop the third day is devoted to the important issues of evaluating and responding to writing.

Commenting on and evaluating is one of the most important and most challenging parts of an instructor's job. Comments on papers, email, and student/teacher conferences are chances for one-on-one instruction. Paper comments are also the major form of feedback a teacher can give when the student is outside of the classroom. The challenging part of this process is finding a style of grading that benefits the students and is also efficient for the instructor. In the workshop we discuss our ideas about what good writing is, what it looks like, what it entails.

My hope is that we conclude that good writing is a successful combination of content, organization, and expression used in a rhetorical context. Good writing should have an audience in mind and should effectively address that audience. Good writing also requires a certain amount of accuracy and even eloquence. Good writing is often not achieved in one draft, and students use peer review, teacher comments, feedback, and self-evaluation to achieve good writing. These criteria inform our discussion. Without intent to be prescriptive, we share with one another some of the following helpful procedures for evaluating essays:

- Read through all of the papers briefly, without comments. This can give an overall view of how the class responded to the assignment.
- Go through each paper, making marginal comments that pertain to student success at keeping to his or her topic, and writing to a certain audience.
- Finally, go back over each paper more carefully, looking at marginal comments, and thinking back to the student's previous assignments. This is when an instructor may make a final evaluative comment. Although it is important to focus on both the weak and strong points in the student's paper, we try to remember to reward what has been done well, and keep our comments supportive.
- It should take about 20 minutes per paper to go through this entire process.

Other helpful ideas include:

- After finishing comments, group papers according to above average, average, and weak.
- Using final comments, evaluate what this means for a grade.
- Remember that C is satisfactory, not failing. Giving students inflated grades may ease initial class tension, but it could also serve to lower a student's standard for good work.
- Early papers should count less than final papers, so that improvement is taken into consideration.
- It is unnecessary to grade everything a student writes; however, in order to reinforce the writing process, drafts, in-class writing, and journals should be credited in some fashion perhaps with a holistic score.

- A percentage of the final grade, maybe 10 percent, can be allotted for class participation. You want to take into consideration the different learning styles of the students; therefore, those who excel in oral participation, for example, should receive credit for this contribution.
- Don't use red ink.
- Identify fundamental problems so that the student does not become so overwhelmed, he or she does not know where to begin to improve.
- Do not rewrite your student's paper—you are not a copy-editor.
- Do not impose your own writing style on your students.
- Use legible handwriting for comments, and make them understandable comments, not symbols. A student will not learn anything if he or she cannot understand the comments. Today many teachers are using technology like that available to them with the Commenting feature of word processors.
- Do not insult your students. Comments should not use the language of personal criticism.
- Both praise and criticism need reasons. A simple good grade may please a student, but a reason for the good grade may teach something.
- Reinforce excellence. Praise good writing.
- Use conferences to expand on a comment that could not be articulated in 20 minutes on a student's paper.

I also encourage teachers to teach students how to self-evaluate using a rubric that clearly identifies purpose, and criteria for each writing assignment. Equipped with a general rubric adapted from the Educational Testing Services SAT-II rubric, in the workshop, teachers practice adapting the six-point rubric to each individual assignment and discuss how they can best communicate expectations to their students. In my own classroom, I introduce this rubric to students early on. It seems fair for them to have experience with applying such a rubric prior to their own writing exercises. I give them samples of essays that represent points along the scale; I highlight characteristics of each essay explaining why I would assign a particular score to each paper. As they become more adept at identifying characteristics and justifying scores, I gradually have them transfer those skills to assignments they have completed themselves. Part of each workshop on their essays involves students applying the rubric, identifying characteristics that have been selected for that assignment and explaining to one another why one score is more appropriate than another. Even though this exercise is somewhat removed from the concept of holistic scoring, many of the same skills are used. The important concept is that we begin to transfer the skills of analysis and evaluation to students. They use these skills to revise and strengthen their writing.

Faculty often use this holistic evaluation method for short assignments, in-class essays, journals, etc. Not only does it save instructors time, but it gives students feedback about their writing while encouraging them to formulate specific questions during one-on-one conferences and track their own progress as well.

I'd be remiss if I didn't take time during my orientation workshops to discuss academic writing teachers' goals to foster social responsibility. I have long followed the belief espoused by Brian Street "that writing is socially implicated in power relations and embedded in specific cultural meanings and practices" (Street, 1995). For me it means exploring and interrogating issues of diversity, racism, ethnicity, gender, and learning disabilities to name only a few. It also means that we are teacher/researchers and understand the power of language to destroy self-esteem, motivation, and self-respect. We have to let our students know that we are ourselves lifelong learners and participants in a society that we don't always agree with but that we never shirk from. In a recent email conversation with Vivian I. Davis, past Chair of the Conference on College Composition and Communication, she was helping me think through some important issues that were facing the National Council of Teachers of English (NCTE). She said, "I keep hoping we have come beyond the notion of trying to celebrate differences. I wish now we could be focused on inclusion. That would mean we would be doing some very different kinds of things than we have done before. I think we need to be seriously challenging the elitist community that values only certain types of researches, certain accepted teaching models and strategies, and that rewards and awards only the kinds of work in our discipline that hews to the status quo." My belief is that is where we should also be in the classroom. I invite teachers to explore these issues from the stance of inclusion. Not that we are sending out our students to learn about "those people" and "their problems," but that we are aware that the problems and issues belong to us. It is imperative that we communicate these ideas to our students. That we convey our desire to learn more. That we share in their exploration. That we are civically engaged.

Our foray into such a discussion during the workshop gives teachers another moment on which to reflect about their own teaching and personal philosophies and how they affect our students. Huey P. Newton was often misquoted, but the thought is certainly relevant, "If you are not part of the solution, you are part of the problem."

In the end, I ask all faculty in my first-year writing program to keep a journal. To have a running conversation with themselves about what is going on in their classes; what they observe in groups, with individual students as their writing develops; what activities they have tried; what student responses were to activities, movies, art, readings, assignments, etc. At the end of the semester, they submit this journal along with support materials (lessons, activities, etc.) that demonstrate their own development as composition teachers. Like their students, I ask them to write a reflective letter introducing their portfolio and discussing their discoveries about themselves as teachers, linking their activities and assignments with the development of student understanding and utilization of the writing process. Finally, I ask them to include self-directed advice for their future teaching endeavors. I find this practice, though time-consuming, brings more clarity to teachers about how they engage in teaching and also serves as a strong assessment for how the first-year program may be revised.

I'd never suggest that a four-day orientation workshop before classes begin can answer all of the questions a new or even returning teacher of academic writing might face. Computer technology and the writing classroom is another wide-open topic in today's academic writing classroom. We can hardly keep up with the technology. With BlackBoard, WebCT, ITune University, podcasts, hybrid, and online teaching, there are almost too many choices. Even how we present our syllabi are drastically affected by the medium in which they are presented. If you are in a program like mine where nearly all writing is done in a computer classroom environment, the portfolio as a major mode of semester-end assessment is nearly inescapable. Let's not even talk about the impact of textbook merchants who clamor for your attention to get their books into your classes. There are enticing web pages, CDs, and enough support materials to leave us breathless. I have not talked about the community outreach projects, and pilot programs, and learning communities, they will all have to be saved for another day. I keep communication open with the teachers in our program and direct them to statements like the NCTE's "Beliefs about the Teaching of Writing" or the Conference on College Composition and Communication's February 2004 Position Statement on "Teaching, Learning, and Assessing Writing in Digital Environments" or the April 1974 "Students' Rights to Their Own Language" that was reaffirmed in November 2003, and given an annotated bibliography in August 2006. This is only to name a few. Suffice it to say, teaching writing teachers to teach writing is a full-time commitment, not for the faint of heart.

References

Anokye, A. D. (2005–2006), "Teaching Composition—FYC Handbook for ASU's West Campus" (third edn), 62 pages.

Bloom, B. S. (1984), *Taxonomy of Educational Objectives* (Boston, MA: Allyn & Bacon).

Horning, A. and Sudol, R. A. (eds) (1997), *Understanding Literacy: Personality Preference In Rhetorical And Psycholinguistic Contexts* (Cresskill, NJ : Hampton Press).

Jolliffe, D. A. (1998), *Inquiry and Genre: Writing to Learn in College.* (Boston: Allyn and Bacon).

Street, B. (1995), *Social Literacies* (Harlow, UK: Longman Publishing Group).

 "Students' Right to Their Own Language CCCC Guideline." *Conference on College Composition and Communication*, April 1974, reaffirmed November 2003, annotated bibliography added August 2006.

Assignments and Activities in Teaching Academic Writing

Christine M. Tardy and Jennifer Courtney

4

Chapter Outline

After identifying a pedagogical approach appropriate to the local classroom and institutional context, teachers face the sometimes daunting task of developing assignments and activities. Writing assignment can vary widely, depending on classroom culture, goals, and needs. This chapter focuses on describing assignments and activities that may be used to teach academic writing within the context of a first-year composition classroom, focusing particularly on research-based academic writing; however, many of these assignments and activities can be modified and adapted to suit other teaching situations.

The term "academic writing" is used to describe a wide range of writing, from personal writing in educational contexts to very specialized disciplinary writing; we focus here on research writing because it often poses the greatest challenge to new university students. This chapter begins with a discussion of key concepts for understanding the writing in disciplinary contexts. Starting with a discussion of academic writing can also benefit students, as disciplinary writing is often a new way for students to think about writing. After outlining foundational concepts, the chapter describes various activities and assignments that can be used in a progressive sequence or even as isolated stages where needed.

Key concepts for understanding academic writing in different disciplinary contexts

A "*discourse community*," according to James Porter, is "a group of individuals bound by a common interest who communicate through approved channels and whose discourse is regulated" (pp. 38–39). The academic community is composed of numerous discrete and overlapping discourse communities: the faculty senate, for example, members of the civil engineering department, and eighteenth-century literary scholars. Together, the communities share many of the same ideas about, for example, the university mission or shared governance. Separately, each community has distinct values and expectations governing communication in field-specific publications and other professional venues.

For students enrolled in composition courses, the idea of discourse communities can be both confusing and enlightening. First-year students are just getting accustomed to being a part of the academic community, with its rituals (like convocation) and conventions for behavior (such as emailing a professor). They are also new members of their disciplinary discourse communities. Learning the content, as well as the genres and communication conventions, is one key to becoming a full-fledged, confident member of any academic discipline. For students who receive different messages about writing from different teachers,understanding the disciplinary basis can provide students with a tool for writing successfully for different audiences.

In many cases, academic writing as it is taught in English departments often privileges humanities genres. While there are goals for writing that most practitioners of most disciplines can agree on (e.g. writing should be sophisticated, analytical, controlled), the expectations for writing in the disciplines vary widely in areas like content, research methods, citation styles. For engineering students, the ability to write a collaborative team report is often fundamental to success in the discipline. The citation systems used within engineering differ from humanities citation styles, and the use of the passive voice is preferred in nearly all instances. These patterns are simple but diverge from the conventions most students learn in their general writing courses.

Given the range of the disciplinary expectations, what should an instructor do? We suggest that rather than teach only humanities genres, instructors consider how information literacy and rhetorical and genre analysis can form the conceptual underpinnings and pedagogical focus for academic writing courses. With this background, students can approach writing tasks within their majors with sensitivity to audience and with the understanding that writing is contextual and discipline-specific. Further, we see this approach to academic writing as in line with a prominent rhetoric/composition statement on first-year writing outcomes, the WPA Outcomes Statement for First-Year Composition (http://ilstu.edu/~ddhesse/wpa/positions/outcomes.htm), which highlights the importance of collaboration and disciplinary conventions.

Activities:

1 Ask students to create a list of the discourse communities they are a part of. For two or three of these, ask students to identify some key features of that community: Is there a specialized language used for workplace procedures? Does a club or organization have terms for activities or specific interests that would not be readily understood by non-members? How does one pick up the language and traditions of that community?

2 Ask students to reflect on the differences in the writing they did in high school and in college. What are college expectations? How do expectations differ in different courses? Encourage students to move beyond the notion that good writing is determined by individual teachers and is instead part of a larger disciplinary view of academic communication.

Improving students' *information literacy* is a cornerstone for academic writing pedagogy. Defined very generally, information literacy is the ability to find information using a variety of tools and the ability to evaluate that information in terms of credibility, relevance, and usability. For students in first-year writing, information literacy can encompass a working knowledge of their library's catalog, electronic databases, the World Wide Web, and specialized Internet search tools like Google Scholar. As we will discuss below, information literacy also includes the ability to recognize a need for information, to develop research questions, and to become adept at formulating search terms and choosing information-gathering strategies.

Particularly relevant to an academic writing course is academic integrity (for further information, refer to Chapter 10). Whether by citing according to the appropriate disciplinary conventions or by representing the work or ideas of another truthfully, using information ethically is a fundamental outcome in many first-year writing sequences. While many students enter the university with technological savvy, we distinguish technical skill with computers or specific software from true information literacy and see explicit instruction in locating, evaluating, and incorporating sources as a crucial part of academic writing pedagogy.

Activities:

1 Assign students to locate the university honor code or statement on academic integrity. As a class, discuss what it means, and how expectations for integrity might be even more specific in particular fields or with individual instructors. Encourage students to clarify expectations with instructors for each writing assignment if there is any ambiguity about citation conventions or research expectations.

2 Design a mini-lesson on paraphrasing, summarizing and quoting. Present students with a passage of academic prose, and examples of a summary, a paraphrase, and an instance of plagiarism. Ask students to identify which is plagiarized and why. It can be useful to show several examples of inappropriately attributed work, from sentences or phrases used verbatim to passages mimicking the structure and organization of the original. For homework, ask students to practice summarizing, paraphrasing, and quoting, using either an assigned passage or one they select.

3 If your university subscribes to turnitin.com, ask students to write a brief reflection on or to discuss in small groups the effect they feel the service has on them as students. Do they find it insulting? A hassle? A deterrent? What are pros and cons of using the service?

4 Present information about online paper mills and paper writing services. Ask students to spend some time browsing the free websites and assessing the quality of the papers. As a class or as individual reflections, invite students to speculate about the effect these services have on the frequency of cheating. Are there any cases when using a service would be OK? What should penalties for students using the services be? Why?

Stages of academic research writing and related assignment and activities

Research writing is a messy process. One difficult task that teachers of academic research face is clarifying the process for students without over-simplifying it. Although research is not linear, it does generally occur in stages—stages which may, of course, recur and overlap. Breaking the process into stages can help students develop the many skills involved in research. Through a staged approach, teachers scaffold tasks for students, gradually building on the skills they are developing in the course. We describe some of the major stages of research below.

Gathering sources

Discussions of research in writing textbooks often come at the end of the book, and present research as a step-by-step process by which students acquire information about their chosen topics. We see source gathering as a much more complex process, wherein students interact with and respond to information. Through the process students come to know about their research area and about the often hazy boundaries that separate a manageable focused area of study from an unwieldy generalized "topic." For example, a student interested in writing about childhood autism might find thousands of sources discussing autism from a variety of angles: cognitive, causal, behavioral, social, or therapeutic. The audiences for sources might also vary widely, from parents to educators to medical researchers to counselors to journalists. Presented with such a range, students might be inclined to patch the different sources together into a document that provides "an overview" of autism. While a task of this sort may be a valuable learning opportunity in terms of content, it falls short of helping students to develop a disciplinary orientation or a rhetorical focus. To steer students into more focused research, we suggest discussing the idea of disciplinary discourse communities, and showing lots of examples, early on in the semester.

Activity:

Ask students about their majors and about other majors on campus, and provide course catalogs, academic journals, and trade publications about a variety of disciplines on campus. The campus library can often lend out a variety of journals to faculty for short periods. It can be particularly revealing to show examples of how different disciplines study the same, or a closely related, topic, such as cloning, standardized testing, or media violence. Becoming familiar with the range of approaches disciplines take to inquiry can also open up research areas for students who may be accustomed to thinking of research as report-writing or argument writing on binary or controversial topics. Seeing and handling examples of disciplinary writing can also be helpful for undeclared students because they have a chance to examine texts in many different areas, which can be more informative than simply talking with other students or relying on impressions.

Once students have been introduced to the notion of disciplines, teachers can develop heuristics that enable them to articulate the parameters of their knowledge and their goals for the project. These heuristics can be revisited throughout the course of the project as new ideas develop or directions change. An early heuristic might ask questions such as:

- What is my area of interest?
- What do I know about it so far?
- What else do I need to know?
- What disciplines might be interested in my topic?
- What do I want to accomplish in writing about this topic?

After developing a focus and tentative goals, library instruction can become more detailed as students work on finding information directly relevant to their projects. We suggest having students keep a research log in which they record search terms, brief summaries of sources, and notations on the credibility and potential usefulness of sources. This log can serve as both an analytic tool as well as an organizational aid, particularly useful for long-term projects.

Before students begin researching in earnest, help them to distinguish between types of sources and resources by incorporating lessons in information literacy. For many students, any computer resource might be considered "online"; we find it helpful to explain the differences between web sources, database sources, and reference sources used at the computer, like CDs. Some key source types and research concepts include:

- General Internet searching
- Google Scholar searches
- Library catalog searches
- Database searches
- Academic journals
- Database archiving (how databases archive and make academic journal articles searchable)
- The differences between periodical sources and books
- The differences between periodical types
- The concept of academic peer review.

Depending on the institutional subscriptions at your university, beginning library instruction with general academic databases and moving into more specific ones builds students' repertoires of information-gathering strategies and enables them to begin seeing the databases in terms of specific usefulness. When possible, we prefer working with librarians who are able to tailor sessions to a class project or to best reflect the current class focus.

Activities:

1 If possible, work with a librarian to design a customized library tutorial for students. We suggest requesting that students receive a general introduction to one or two key databases and then work independently on a specific task. Instructors and librarians can work one-on-one with students as needed.

2 In the library or in a computer lab with full library access, ask students to find one or two specific articles using databases. Students should be comfortable searching for and retrieving sources. Suggest that students practice emailing sources to themselves or using the "book bag" or other account features offered by the library for tracking sources.

3 Students should review one of the many Web-based sources, often available through university library websites, on determining the credibility of sources. In class, review key ideas to prepare students for the *rhetorical analysis*.

Conducting a rhetorical analysis

To analyze the sources in-depth, we suggest using a technique called *rhetorical analysis*. Broadly defined, rhetorical analysis is a way to understand a source (whether an academic journal, a chat room, or a trade publication) in terms of its purpose, scope, audience, biases, and conventions. Jack Selzer explains rhetorical analysis by distinguishing the textual and contextual aspects of the activity. Roughly, textual analysis looks at organization, data methods, evidence representation, argument type, and mechanical conventions, while contextual analysis looks to the author's disciplinary context, prior publications and cultural influences. For instructors looking for a detailed discussion of this analytical tool, we suggest this reading. Instructors may also find James Porter's heuristic for rhetorical analysis to be of use for upper-level writers and easily adapted to a first-year writing classroom.

Students can use rhetorical analysis to analyze journals, Web sources, and other research venues. It is not intended for analyzing individual articles, though understanding how an individual article is situated within, say, a specific journal can be important for understanding purpose, scope, and genre expectations. Students can conduct rhetorical analyses individually, in small groups, and with varying levels of formality.

Activities and assignments:

1 To introduce the concept of rhetorical analysis and its usefulness in understanding discourse communities, we might ask small groups of students to review the following sources: the satirical Onion.com "reporting" on a science topic, an issue of the journal

Activities and assignments: (Continued)

Science Educator, the journal *Science*, and an issue of kid-friendly *Ranger Rick*. Students might be asked to sketch a demographic or disciplinary portrait of the targeted audience, focusing on the likely levels of background knowledge, education, and interests. They might look at how advertisements reveal information about the consumer habits or material aspirations of the audience. Further, while examining publications, students might also consider who is excluded from the forum and why. Examining readers who are part of the community serves to emphasize the idea that by and large published pieces are not meant for "anyone," a concept that students accustomed to the idea of inclusivity may be resistant to. Students might be asked to point to specific features of the text that clue them into audience-based rhetorical choices. For example, an article in a science education journal discussing how children use dioramas might be contrasted with a how-to article in *Ranger Rick* geared to boys interested in building science models. Once students have a general idea of audience and purpose, they can begin to move on research sources closely linked to their own interests.

2 As an early assignment, students can locate an academic and a non-academic source on a topic of their choice—childhood, business, or media—and then conduct rhetorical analyses on both, followed by a brief reflective component explaining the differences or overlaps between the texts.

Analyzing disciplinary discourses

Through rhetorical analysis activities, students build an awareness of the many ways in which context and discourse community influence writing. Students may already hold an awareness of the ways in which broadly defined contexts and communities—such as "public" or "academic"—carry visible influences on texts, but first-year students are less likely to be familiar with the weight that academic discipline exerts on writing. While academic disciplines share many common practices and values, they also differ in significant ways; for example, "rigorous" research in literary studies draws on different approaches and methods than "rigorous" research in biology. These distinct approaches to constructing and sharing knowledge are visible when we contrast the written communication of literature scholars and biologists. For the undergraduate student, these distinctions, however, are usually quite mysterious. As writing scholar David Bartholomae famously pointed out:

> Every time a student sits down to write for us, he has to invent the university for the occasion—invent the university, that is, or a branch of it, like history or anthropology or economics or English. The student has to learn to speak our language, to speak as we do, to try on the peculiar ways of knowing, selecting, evaluating,

reporting, concluding, and arguing that define the discourse of our community. Or perhaps I should say the various *discourses* of our community, since it is in the nature of a liberal arts that a student, after the first year or two, must learn to try on a variety of voice and interpretive schemes—to write, for example, as a literary critic one day and as an experimental psychologist the next; to work within fields where the rules governing the presentation of examples or the development of an argument are both distinct and, even to a professional, mysterious. (1986: 134)

For students entering the university, the very notion of "discipline" may lack meaning, and so the idea öf writing differently for different disciplines may well be hard to grasp initially. One way to introduce the idea of academic disciplines is by describing them as cultural communities. Like other cultural groups, academic disciplines hold a shared set of practices and beliefs—in this case, those practices and beliefs concern research and knowledge construction. Also like other cultural groups, academic disciplines are not homogenous or monolithic; while they share a common focus and set of activities, they also allow for a range of variation. In other words, while members of an academic discipline may disagree, they share generally agreed upon *ways* to do so.

Activities:

1 Ask students to create maps of "typical practices" for teaching and assessment in various disciplines in which they have taken classes. Brainstorm a few examples first as a whole class, and then ask the students to continue lists in small groups. For example, a map for a science class may include lab work, lab reports, lecture, discussion, textbooks, exams, and exercises; a map for a literature class might include novels, poems, lecture, discussion, student presentations, and essay papers. As a class, discuss possible reasons for the differences in classroom practices, connecting these to differences in what constitutes "truth" and how knowledge is constructed in different academic fields of study.

2 As a potential follow-up to Activity #1, students can generate lists of common words used in the various disciplines discussed and then discuss the ways in which such words might illustrate disciplinary values. For example, what are some differences between a "report" and "essay," or an "experiment" and "study"? Pay particular attention to words which may be found across disciplines but used in slightly different ways, such as the term "discourse," which carries slightly different meanings in philosophy, literature, and linguistics.

After students have begun to understand academic disciplines as cultural groups, they can more easily understand how disciplinary ways of thinking, acting, and communicating are somewhat unique. Disciplinary discourses may be distinguishable by "different appeals to background knowledge, different means of establishing truth, and different ways of engaging with readers" (Hyland, 2004: 3). As such, disciplinary writing varies in multiple ways. Linguists who have researched disciplinary texts have shown how writing across disciplines may differ, for example, in ways of structuring an argument, stating knowledge claims, use of first person pronouns, and citation patterns.

Activities:

1 Create a randomly ordered list of ten titles taken from journal articles in three different disciplines, such as philosophy, marketing, and engineering. First, ask students to sort the titles by discipline. Compare their answers and discuss the clues they used to complete the task. Students are likely to focus on the content, or object of inquiry, at this stage. Next, ask students to analyze the linguistic differences among the three different groups of titles. For example, they may look at title length, use of additional punctuation (such as colons), jargon, cultural references, or level of generality or specificity. Discuss the ways in which the titles may reflect certain cultural values of the disciplines.

2 As a class, examine sample journal articles from three different disciplines. Ask students to note patterns in the articles' linguistic features, including: overall length, length of introduction, number and style of references, format (headings, sub-headings, section divisions, footnotes), typical sentence and paragraph length, use of first person pronouns (*I*, *we*), terms for positive and negative evaluation (e.g. *rigorous*, *elegant*, or *lightweight*), and use and type of visuals. Compare and contrast the three disciplines' uses of these linguistic features, discussing how the patterns may be linked to disciplinary cultural values.

Writing assignment:

To investigate patterns within one disciplinary community, students collect a range of texts within a discipline that is of interest to them. Ideally, students should collect texts that will be of value for their research project. Drawing on their sample texts, students can analyze typical linguistic and rhetorical features (see Appendix A for a sample guide). Next, students can interview a faculty member in the discipline to check their analysis against an "insider's" view. Through the interview, the student can also collect additional insight into the discipline's preferences and expectations for particular ways of building and presenting arguments, both for experts and for students. Finally, students write up their findings in a paper or share them with the class in a presentation.

Conducting field research

Most academic disciplines conduct field research. Generally, field research consists of interviews, surveys, experiments, and field observations; the purpose of field research is to collect data for analysis. As students conduct rhetorical analyses, they will develop a sense of the typical research in their field. Encourage students to notice the methods and how data is handled in journal articles, as understanding and using disciplinary research methods is crucial to full participation in a discourse community. While entire courses can be dedicated to field research methods, we will discuss the purposes, as well as advantages and disadvantages of field research for beginning students.

Interviews

For beginning students, interviewing a disciplinary expert about their topic can be enormously enriching. Students can use interviews to understand disciplinary writing conventions as well as to put a face to often daunting-sounding or overwhelming content. Most universities have experts in nearly every field. For students beginning their research projects, talking to an expert about possible directions can quickly focus a project or clarify a field concept. Students might also ask professors for their take on a current field discussion or for perspective on what a particular issue might mean for further research. For example, a first-year communications student might ask a media scholar to comment on a presidential campaign or to provide context for the many arguments about the effect of media on violence.

Before students begin to conduct field research, it is prudent for instructors to check with their institution's research office for Internal Review Board (IRB) procedures. If classroom research is acceptable, consider making field research a part of the course after sharing the following points with students.

These are the advantages of interviews:

- Allow for specific questions for known experts
- Enable clarificatory questions and spontaneous discussion
- Establish contact between expert and student researcher allowing for future contact.

There are some disadvantages of interviews, however:

- Can be controlled by interviewee
- Can be difficult for shy individuals
- Provide only one perspective on given issue.

The etiquette and procedures to be followed are:

- Contact the expert and ask for time for the interview; be specific and flexible about times and dates.
- Create a list of questions well ahead of the interview time.
- Ask permission to record the interview; in the event permission is not granted and as a matter of good practice, take detailed notes of the interview.
- Follow up with a brief summary of the interview, including any quotes or key points that may be inserted into a research essay.
- Be sure to send an email or written thank you.

Surveys

Surveys are used widely on most campuses, a fact which can be a double-edged sword; on the one hand, students are familiar and comfortable with the instrument. On the other hand, many feel as though they are being "surveyed to death" and may be unwilling to participate in peers' surveys or to subject other students to yet another survey. When students investigate campus issues, public health concerns, or current events knowledge, surveys can provide information that may well serve as a "thermometer" of local opinion. We encourage students to use interviews when local, very timely, information is preferable, and to use the results sparingly and in conjunction with other published research (also known as "triangulation").

These are the advantages of surveys:

- Can yield a large amount of information relatively quickly
- Can reach a targeted population easily
- Can be useful for gauging general opinions and trends.

There are also some disadvantages of surveys:

- Often have a low-response rate
- Must be well designed to yield valid data
- Can be difficult to analyze.

The etiquette and procedures to be followed are:

- Be very explicit about the survey's purpose and how results will be used.
- Select appropriate population for the survey.
- Specify whether participant anonymity will be protected.
- Design surveys that do not "lead" participants to respond in a way that benefits the hypothesis.
- Acknowledge when survey results are surprising, contradictory, or inconclusive.
- Thank participants; check with the institution on policies for providing food or small incentives to participants.

In addition to providing students with basic background on field research, we suggest that instructors consult one of the many sources on basic field research methods and providing the information to students. We also recommend that instructors meet with students interested in conducting field research to review their purposes, questions, and design. Students should turn in all data along with the final paper or project.

Finally, many writing courses are organized around the field research method known as ethnography. There are several excellent books on this topic if local research, and/or service learning, are of interest.

Writing with sources

One shared feature of academic writing, regardless of discipline, is that it relies on both implicit and explicit reference to other sources. Writing that is purely personal may be labeled "anecdotal"—nearly always a negative adjective in academic contexts. Even writing that is of more personal nature (a generic variation that has become increasingly common in many humanities and social science disciplines) situates the writer's individual perspective within a frame of prior disciplinary work.

The practice of drawing upon additional texts is a complex one, which immediately raises for most teachers the question of how to tackle issues of plagiarism. As Chapter 10 of this volume addresses this issue in full detail, we will focus instead on more general issues of working with sources. As students begin to work with sources, they will quickly be faced with a wide range of source types, including popular magazine articles, newspaper articles, online information sites, homepages, Wikipedia, print books, book reviews, and journal articles. As they organize their resources, students should keep track of the kinds of sources they have, and they should develop their ability to evaluate these sources' relative usefulness and appropriateness for the project.

Building on previous activities related to disciplinary discourses, students can benefit from exploring how sources are used in academic writing in general but also how sources are used and represented within particular disciplines. It may be useful to begin such a discussion by introducing students to key terms used to describe academic uses of sources. Looking at a textbook, scholarly book, or article, students can identify *references* to complete works that appear at the end of a text (or in footnotes) and *citations*, which appear within the text. They may contrast the use and form of reference citations in academic texts with those found in trade magazines such as *The Economist* or newspapers like *The New York Times*.

Helping students to see more specifically how works are incorporated into academic texts can provide them with tools to apply to their own writing. Research of academic writing has shown that disciplines vary in their preferences for *integral citations*, in which the author's name appears in the citing sentence, versus *non-integral citations*, in which the author's name appears only in parentheses. For example:

> Hyland (2004) illustrates how citation patterns vary by discipline. [*integral citation*]

> Research shows that citation patterns vary by discipline (Hyland, 2004). [*non-integral citation*]

Additionally, some academic disciplines include *quotations* (short excerpts from another text, appearing in quotation marks) or *block quotes* (longer excerpts from another text, indented from the writer's text). Use of quotations, block quotes, or even an absence of explicit quotations of any sort is dependent to a large extent on disciplinary preference, with scientific writing showing a much lower use of quoted source texts than writing in the social sciences or humanities. Citation patterns are therefore complicated, varying by discourse community as well as genre.

Activities:

1 Students examine a range of texts (e.g. journal article from multiple academic disciplines, or multiple genres written on a single topic) for citation patterns. Discuss as a class the typical citation patterns found within different disciplines and/or different genres and the possible uses of those patterns. As a follow-up homework assignment, students can examine a paper that they have written for a university course, identifying their own citation pattern and comparing it with findings from class.

2 Students create a list of common verbs and phrases used to refer to outside sources and to introduce quotations (e.g. *according to, argues that, describes*). Using this list, students re-write a passage of research writing which is written in a repetitive and redundant style.

While source texts can provide useful examples of academic writing, their primary role is to build a writer's content knowledge within a particular area of inquiry. Students who are relatively new to university writing may find the task of reading and distilling information from so many sources to be somewhat overwhelming. Writing instructors can therefore provide students with strategies for tackling these tasks, such as tips for identifying a reading's main purpose or thesis, taking and keeping track of reading notes, and annotating texts in the margins.

Writing assignment:

Students create an annotated bibliography of their sources, beginning with a full reference, followed by a summary of each source. Annotated bibliographies may also include key words, the genre of the resource, or even a critical analysis of the source's credibility or relevance to the writer's research. An assignment like this helps students to gather their sources early on, to practice summary skills, and to begin to work with academic documentation styles, such as MLA, APA, or Chicago.

Developing research questions

Many students are accustomed to thinking about research as supporting an argument rather than investigating the complexities of an issue. Rather than simply selecting a topic of research—a pursuit that is likely to lead to very broad and un-focused investigations—students can be encouraged to develop research questions within a particular topic area. Such development can begin with classroom discussions of possible topics. Beginning with a broad topic like *global warming*, instructors may facilitate brainstorming of possible questions that may prompt further research within this area. For example:

- What are the causes of global warming?
- What are the effects of global warming?
- What, if anything, can be done to stop global warming?
- What are the politics of global warming?

Students might consider how such questions relate to disciplinary inquiry. For example, which disciplines are likely to explore each question? Where there is overlap, how might the approaches differ by discipline? Students may then work with one or two questions to identify possible resources for research. Where might they turn to investigate, for example, the politics of global warming? What kinds of information are likely to be provided by different resources?

In the process of developing research questions, it may be useful for students to identify poor research questions and revise these into more focused questions. Students can consider why a question like "*Is bilingual education effective?*" may be problematic for a short-term research project. Questions may be raised to narrow the research focus: What kind of bilingual education? In what contexts? At what grade levels? Toward what goals? How is "effective" defined and measured? Students may gradually refine questions like this to become more manageable for short-term research. Students might also be encouraged to begin broadly, but to refine their questions as they gather resources and learn more about the topic. In academic research, questions arise out of knowledge of prior research and of an on-going scholarly conversation. Writing students rarely have the time to fully research a topic area before forming research questions, but they can be encouraged to gradually refine their questions as they become more familiar with their areas of investigation.

Assignment:

Students keep a research blog, taking notes from the readings on their topics in an online forum, which may be anonymous if the student prefers (though it must be shared with the instructor). After each entry, students can add tags or threads to identify the sub-topics of the readings. Over time, students can view all of the entries related to one tag to help gain a sense of the resources they have accumulated within each thread. This process of labeling their reading notes can gradually serve to help them develop and refine research questions.

Synthesizing information

As students gather resources and refine their research questions, they move toward the often difficult step of synthesizing information. Synthesis is a higher-order skill which requires students to recognize themes among diverse genres, arguments, and contexts. Students can be aided in this process through the use of graphic displays of information which help to highlight the relationships among texts. Tables, grids, webs, and continua are some of the visual forms which can be used to map information in meaningful ways. Using visuals in this way may not appeal to all learners, so instructors should consider providing options and also modeling the use of such aids. For example, the

Table 4.1 Source comparison grid.

	Text #1	Text #2	Text #3
Is the author for or against English only?			
What kind of law (if any) does the author call for?			
What is the author's stance on bilingualism or use of home languages?			
What is the author's stance on bilingual education?			

whole class can read several texts and then work as a group to create a grid which illustrates each text's ideas for means of comparison. For example, after reading a set of texts on the English Only movement, students may create and complete a grid like that shown in Table 4.1.

Grids can be defined based on the shared set of issues that the articles deal with, so that the very act of creating the grid requires students to identify common themes. Once the grid is filled in, students can see where authors agree and disagree, where gaps exist, and where the arguments may even be inappropriate to compare. In some cases, students may find it more helpful to map authors along a continuum. For example, one end of the continuum may represent full support for English Only legislation, while the other end may represent support for a fully multilingual society. Students can map the texts they've read along the continuum, noting how their views relate to one another. Again, the mere act of deciding what the ends of the continuum represent is an important step in understanding the dynamics of the issue being researched and the ways in which the resources address the issue.

After students have analyzed relationships among their sources, they will face the more difficult task of describing these relationships in written form. Grids or webs can provide students with ideas for organizing their writing. For instance, they may organize the ideas by grid rows, addressing various elements of the issue and discussing the range of voices within each element. Analyzing prior student papers, if available, or published research which synthesizes sources can be tremendously helpful for students at this stage. Students can look for organizational patterns, outlining or mapping these patterns to make them more visible. They can also highlight useful phrases and expressions used for various rhetorical functions. For instance, students may identify phrases which are often used to refer to resources, such as *According to … * or *X argues that …* Important for synthesis, students may also identify phrases used to express generalizations (e.g. *Others have pointed out that … * or *Advocates for X note that …*) versus phrases used to express ideas or content from single texts (e.g. *One study shows that … * or *In her book, {title}, X takes an opposing stand.*). Students can begin incorporating such phrases into their own writing, also considering the various nuances of different phrases in terms of formality, style, and even ideology.

Activities:

1 Students interview at least four peers outside of class about a topic of interest, perhaps related to a debate of current importance or a hot-button issue on campus. Students should bring their interview notes to class where they annotate the notes to identify themes among the various interviewees. Students then integrate these views into a short summary of the issue. They may choose to organize their writing in any way *except* by author. In other words, they cannot write one view after the other, but instead must synthesize the interviews to show common and contrasting themes. Alternatively, students may be asked to write two separate summary paragraphs. The first should be organized by interviewee (i.e. describing each interviewee's view separately) and the second by common themes, integrating the interview answers.

2 As a variation on the above, students write one paragraph which uses integral citation and a second paragraph which uses only non-integral citations.

3 Small groups of students are given a set of index cards, each of which includes a quote, paraphrase, or summary from a different source on the same topic. Students sort the cards into piles that make sense to them. Compare the piles as a class, then vote on the most effective logic for sorting the information. Finally, students compose a paragraph based on the synthesis patterns that were voted on. Paragraphs can be compared and discussed.

Conclusion

The tasks and assignments described here are intended to help students develop some of the skills involved in academic writing. We imagine them as a springboard for teachers, who will alter them to suit their own teaching contexts and their students' needs. While we have focused here specifically on activities and assignments for teaching academic discourse and research writing—as opposed to expressive or personal writing—the principles that we have drawn upon are not tied to research writing.

Demystifying writing and the writing process, scaffolding tasks, and helping students make their own discoveries are principles that instructors can draw upon in developing other pedagogical strategies for teaching a broad range of writing skills.

References

Bartholomae, D. (1986), "Inventing the university," in Mike Rose (ed.), *When a Writer Can't Write*, pp. 134–165 (New York: Guilford Press).

Hyland, K. (2004), *Disciplinary Discourses: Social Interactions in Academic Writing* (Ann Arbor: University of Michigan Press).

Selzer, J. (2004), "Rhetorical analysis: Understanding how texts persuade readers," in Bazerman, C. and Prior, P. (eds), *What Writing Does and How It Does It*, pp. 279–308 (Mahwah, NJ: Lawrence Erlbaum Press).

Porter, J. (1986), "Intertextuality and the discourse community," *Rhetoric Review*, 5, 34–47.

Appendix A: A guide to analyzing linguistic and rhetorical features of disciplinary writing

Collect several examples of published research writing within one discipline that you are interested in. Based on those samples, answer the following questions.

1 Do the titles contain a common pattern? How long is a typical title? Does it include any punctuation, such as a colon, semi-colon, or dash?

2 Do the articles use any headings or sub-headings? If so, are they general (e.g. Introduction, Method, Conclusion) or text-specific?

3 What is the average length of the sentences? What is the average length of the paragraphs?

4 What phrases are used to describe the objective or purpose of the paper?

5 Does the author use first person pronouns (*I/my/me* or *We/our/us*) at all? If so, when and how often?

6 Do the texts tend to use more integral or non-integral citations?

7 How many block quotes are used, if any? What phrases are used to introduce them?

8 When referring to other work, does the author use any evaluative language, such as adjectives, adverbs, or verbs with evaluative connotations? List these and indicate whether they are positive or negative.

9 Do the texts tend to rely on logical appeal, emotional appeal, and/or ethical appeals? Which seems to be most important? Explain.

10 Are there any other features of these texts that you think may be unique to this kind of writing and/or this discourse community? Explain.

Feedback: Issues and Options

5

Dana R. Ferris

Chapter Outline

Introduction

Feedback on student writing is a critical issue for the writing instructor. It easily consumes more time and energy than any other aspect of writing instruction. Feedback also allows the teacher to invest in and communicate with each individual student, thus allowing for a unique and important instructional opportunity. At the same time, feedback can be challenging, frustrating, and even fear-producing. Consider the following thoughts shared by an experienced writing teacher:

> Few things cause me more anxiety than waking up to a full set of essays, knowing I must read and respond. This is not just because responding is the most time-consuming activity in writing pedagogy. The seemingly infinite number of unknown factors in responding makes it an extremely complex exercise as well ... As I read a set of papers, I wonder: *Will my students benefit from my comments? Will they even understand them? Is there a better way to approach this task?* For about thirty minutes, I labor over a paper, reading, underlining,

writing numbers, typing comments, biting my fingernails. By the twentieth or twenty-fifth iteration, I have inevitably begun to question the wisdom of my career choice. (Segade, 2004)

It is safe to say that most if not all writing instructors feel this way about responding to student papers at least some of the time. To such self-doubting introspection is added the gloomy assessment of some composition experts. For example, Elbow (1999) said that "writing comments is a dubious and difficult enterprise" (p. 201), and response has been called an "exercise in futility" (Marzano and Arthur, 1977, cited in Knoblauch and Brannon, 1981, p. 1).

The problems and challenges surrounding feedback may come from several different sources. The first is teacher time and energy. Various studies on responding have noted that it can take 15–30 minutes at minimum to respond in writing to one student paper or to conduct a one-to-one conference. If those times are multiplied by an entire class of students or several classes, it is not hard to see why one author referred to writing teachers as "composition slaves" (Hairston, 1986). A second but related concern is teacher competence and confidence. Teachers may not know what to look for in student papers or how to communicate suggestions in ways that are clear and helpful to students. They often fear demoralizing, confusing, or frustrating students with feedback that is too negative, unclear, not specific enough, or which "takes over" the student paper.

Other concerns about feedback revolve around the students. First, students may not comprehend the intent or substance of teacher (or peer) feedback and not understand what the problem is; even if they do understand the issue, they may not always know how to resolve the problem (Ferris, 1995; Straub, 1997). Also, students may not be adequately or appropriately engaged in utilizing feedback, once they have received it, to improve their writing but rather may view "revision" or "editing" as simply a matter of surface clean-up once their teacher or peer "proofreader" has provided an extra set of eyes. Such a perspective reflects a misunderstanding of the nature of revision and the potential value of feedback from a peer or expert reader.

Notwithstanding these frustrations and concerns, writing teachers continue to respond to student writing and to require and facilitate other types of response, such as peer feedback, tutor feedback, and guided self-feedback. We do so because we have been trained to provide feedback, because students expect and desire it, and because at some level, we believe that thoughtful, well-constructed feedback actually *can* help students to improve their texts and to grow as writers. As Segade (2004) concludes her thoughts about responding, she notes: "Given the amount of effort and time that goes into responding, it is imperative that we find response practices that make sense and learn how to change those that don't."

In this chapter I will explore "response practices that make sense." I will examine teachers' *approach* to feedback, specific *response* techniques and suggestions, and *follow-up* with students after they have received feedback.[i] I will conclude with options for self-evaluation of our own feedback so that we can also "learn how to change [response practices] that don't [make sense]." In addition, I will explore in passing response issues particular to multilingual writers and to language-specific feedback or error correction.

Approach to feedback

philosophy
we all have one

By "approach" I am referring to an instructor's philosophy of response or set of guiding principles or assumptions that operate when we sit down with a set of student papers or meet one-on-one with students for a conference. The first observation about a teacher's feedback approach is that we all have one, whether we are conscious of it or not. If we have not received training on response and/or reflected on the hows and whys of responding, we most likely will respond in ways similar to those used by our own teachers—or, if we have had bad experiences, in ways opposite to them. The components of an approach to response can be described through several "reporter" questions (why, when, what, who, and how) which can also be cast as decisions the teacher must make (see also Fig. 5.1).

Approach: Why?

Perhaps the most overlooked aspect of an approach to response is to articulate why feedback is being provided to student writers. There are at least four

1	*Why* (or for what purposes) is feedback being given?
2	*When* should it be provided?
3	*On what issues* should feedback be focused?
4	*Who* should provide the feedback?
5	*How* should feedback be given?

Fig. 5.1 Articulating an approach to response: Some questions
Source: Outline adapted from Ferris (2006).

reasons

distinct purposes for teacher feedback, depending upon the context and timing of the response. The most common is to *explain or justify a grade on a completed paper*. In non-composition class settings, this type of feedback is usually the only response students will receive, and in fact, most instructors outside of composition would not even be aware that there is any other potential purpose for feedback. Another similar and sometimes simultaneous purpose for feedback on a completed paper is to *assist students with future writing assignments in the course*—in other words, though it may be "too late" for that particular paper, the teacher can provide feedback to help students know what to do differently the next time. Feedback to accomplish the first purpose (grade justification) will likely be fairly brief and general. For example, the teacher might explain that the paper received a "C" because it had some weaknesses in organization, did not cite enough sources, or was poorly proofread. If the teacher is also trying to assist the student for the future, these general comments might include an example or two for illustration. For instance, to "weak organization" could be added the observation that specific body paragraphs were not well focused and could have benefited from a controlling idea (topic) sentence around which the content of the paragraph was structured. However, because the paper is "finished," it is unlikely that the teacher will provide detailed marginal comments or in-text corrections, as this would be a poor use of the teacher's time and potentially frustrating to the student. ("You've marked up my paper, but there is nothing I can do about it now.")

In contrast to the "final product" responses described above, teachers' purposes for providing feedback are likely to be quite different in a process-oriented writing class organized around multiple-drafting and revision. When a teacher provides feedback on a preliminary draft(s) of a paper, it is primarily *to aid students on a current paper before it is finalized*. Such feedback may be quite extensive and detailed and may cover big-picture issues of content (ideas, arguments, support) and organization (of the entire paper or specific portions) as well as micro-level issues of style, accuracy, word choice, and format. Finally, a teacher's purpose in responding may (and should) be *to assist students in improving their writing skills*. In other words, feedback is not merely a "fix-it" list for a particular paper but rather individualized and contextualized instruction about ways in which the student writer has been successful and ways in which s/he could still improve or grow. Such feedback may also be directly linked to in-class instruction the students have experienced. To illustrate, perhaps the teacher has been working with the class on ways to connect ideas logically and elegantly across sentences and paragraphs using

process

transitional phrases and other cohesive devices. On the next set of papers, the teacher might look specifically at how well the students have incorporated the instruction and provide praise where students have been successful and suggestions where improvements could be made.

The point of discussing these various purposes for feedback is not to argue for the value of one over another but rather to observe that any instructor who responds to student writing, whether in the disciplines or in a composition class, may have any one (or all) of these objectives operating as they provide written or oral feedback. In fact, the same instructor might respond in all four ways at different points of the course and the writing process, for instance providing detailed feedback on a preliminary draft and briefer responses on final or more developed versions of the paper. Further, the primary purpose for response at that point in time can and should direct the nature of the response (including volume and substance).

Approach: When?

A related question is at which point(s) in the writing process the student should receive feedback from others. There are several assumptions or sub-points to this question. First, will students be allowed or expected to produce multiple drafts of versions of their papers? In most writing courses these days, multiple drafting, feedback, and revision are the norm, but they are not always, and even in a process-oriented writing class, there may be particular pieces of writing that will not be revised, such as in-class writing, journal entries, or homework assignments. As already noted, when a piece of writing is in its final iteration, the goals of feedback may be quite different than when it is still being developed. Second, if students do produce multiple drafts of papers, will they receive feedback on all drafts, or will they be expected to do their own self-evaluation and revision work at some points? Some instructors prefer to vary modes and sources of feedback throughout the writing process or course, for instance having peer response sessions after first drafts, one-to-one conferences on second drafts, extensive written comments on third drafts, and brief written comments on final drafts or portfolio essays. Finally, will students have the opportunity or be required to revise their work after receiving feedback, or is the feedback mainly advisory for future assignments? Research suggests that students are more likely to reread their papers and carefully consider teacher commentary after preliminary drafts than after final, graded drafts (Ferris, 1995).

of course

Approach: What?

One of the most difficult and sometimes controversial questions about feedback is on what aspects of the student text instructors (and peers) should focus in providing feedback. Grading rubrics available in the composition literature suggest that teachers have a variety of options with regard to this question. For example, in some courses, the teacher may be looking for mastery of course content; in a composition course, this might include accurate analysis of textual sources assigned and/or cited in the student paper. In other cases, the teacher may focus attention (especially in the early stages of the drafting process) on whether or not the student has completed the assigned task or written the paper to the specifications of the assignment. Instructors may also focus on rhetorical issues such as overall organization, paragraph structure, transitions, thesis or topic statements, and so forth. Another possible area for feedback is language issues (spelling, grammar, punctuation, word choice). Finally, some instructors may also give feedback about apparent student engagement in the writing process, such as evidence of careful planning, thoughtful revision, and conscientious editing.

Clearly there are many different issues on which a teacher may focus in providing feedback or structuring peer review sessions. Some teachers prefer to focus on different aspects at various stages of the drafting process, such as content in early drafts and language issues on penultimate drafts. Others respond to individual students and texts at the point of their greatest need, rather than rigidly adhering to a "content first, grammar later" formula. From the "approach" standpoint, what does seem clear is that teachers should not attempt to respond to all of these issues simultaneously every time they read student papers, as this is a prescription for teacher burnout and student overload. Rather, the teacher should prioritize the most important issues in feedback, and these priorities will depend both upon the instructor's philosophy and the needs of the particular students involved. As an example, a teacher may feel strongly about not overemphasizing language issues in feedback but may also have multilingual students who need extra help with grammar and vocabulary issues because their language is not as developed as that of their native-speaking counterparts. Teachers in such situations need to balance their own preferences with the unique characteristics of the students under their care.

Approach: Who?

Writing instructors may have conflicted feelings about their role as respondents to student writing. Experts for several decades have warned teachers about the dangers of "appropriation," meaning that the teacher "takes over" the student paper or subverts the writer's intentions through their feedback (Brannon and Knoblauch, 1982; Sommers, 1982; Zamel, 1985). Others have responded that in efforts to avoid appropriation, teachers have in effect abandoned their students by failing to provide them with direction or guidance through feedback (Reid, 1994).

It can be hard to define what constitutes "appropriation" and what types of teacher commentary cross the line between "guidance" or "intervention" and "appropriation." US Supreme Court Justice Potter Stewart once famously said about pornography: "Maybe I can't define it, but I know it when I see it." Perhaps the same is true of teacher appropriation of student texts. Generally speaking, though, if the teacher is trying to add specific content to a student's text, to direct the student to change a stated opinion, or crossing out words, phrases, or entire sentences (possibly rewriting them, sometimes just eliminating them), there is a good chance that s/he has crossed the line into appropriation. A clear example of this comes from the paper of a student named "Antonio" who was asked to write an essay about the effects of being a member of a minority group (Ferris, 2003). Antonio started his paper by stating clearly that being a minority had affected him negatively. However, as his paper progressed, he discovered that there were also many positive aspects to being part of two cultures (he was an immigrant student from Mexico) and that overall, the experience had made him a stronger person. However, the teacher was troubled by Antonio's straying from his initial thesis and suggested that he should talk about "negative effects" and that he should change "stronger" to "weaker"—in effect, asking him to deny what he really thought rather than simply rewriting his thesis to accurately reflect what followed in his paper. His revised (and less effective) paper, in which he obediently did what the teacher told him to do, provides a chilling reminder of the influence teacher commentary can have on students—and that such influence is not always positive.

Teacher appropriation is alive and well and a serious problem for teachers and students. Student survey research clearly shows that students resent teachers attempting to take over their papers and tell them what to say and how to think (Straub, 1997). However, students also want teacher feedback to help them improve their writing and to succeed in their endeavors and will feel anxious and resentful if they do not receive it. While teachers should take care to avoid the appropriative behaviors described above, they should also be realistic that given the power differential between teacher and student, *any* feedback they provide is likely to influence student papers, simply because it comes from the teacher, and students care about pleasing the teacher and getting good grades (Elbow, 1999; Sperling and Freedman, 1987). This power disparity is inevitable, so teachers should focus on being helpful rather than controlling and collegial rather than authoritarian in the tone and substance of their commentary.

One "who" question that probably should be asked more often in forming an approach to response concerns the various potential *source(s)* of feedback. Feedback can come from the teacher, from peers, from outside helpers such as tutors, from self-evaluation, and from other external sources such as handbooks or websites. Some teachers may believe that they should be the sole respondent to student writing because (a) they are the teacher/expert and it is their job; (b) they are dubious about peer feedback; (c) they are wary of self-feedback because it sounds like abandonment; and (d) they are unsure about sending students for outside help for fear that someone else will be writing or at least editing their students' work. Others may be enthusiastic proponents of peer feedback because they believe it reduces their own workload or because they assume students would find it less threatening to receive criticism from a peer than from a teacher (actually, in most cases the opposite is true).[ii] Still others may take a minimalist approach to response, preferring to provide students with a list of guided self-evaluation questions and perhaps some resources to consult and let students provide themselves with feedback.[iii]

Despite the attempts of some researchers to set these various sources of feedback in competition with each other (see, e.g. Jacobs *et al.*, 1998; Zhang, 1995, 1999), the truth is that teacher/expert, peer, and self feedback are all different from one another and each has benefits for students as well as possible disadvantages. Thus, a better approach for teachers is a judicious mixture of different feedback sources throughout the writing process and course. One principle to consider as a writing course progresses is *increasing student autonomy*, meaning that the teacher may start off providing a good deal of feedback but, after modeling both what to look for and how to respond appropriately, gradually turning the task over to peer and self evaluators.

Besides asking "who" the respondent(s) should be, another important aspect of the "who" question concerns the student audience. For instance, in many US postsecondary settings, "mainstream" composition classes may include monolingual native speakers of Standard English, native speakers of a nonstandard English variety, and multilingual students, including Generation 1.5 students (Harklau *et al.*, 1999) who may have lived in the US most or all of their lives but who nonetheless have non-native features in their writing. As these distinctions relate to response, teachers need to bear in mind that these groups of students start out with different knowledge bases, both as to how much accurate, idiomatic, academic Standard English they have acquired and can demonstrate successfully in their writing and as to how much formal English instruction they may have received. A Generation 1.5 student, for instance, may not have enough acquired knowledge of English to be able to self-correct a word choice or sentence structure error if it is simply underlined or circled, but s/he may also not recognize terminology such as "subject–verb agreement" (or its shorthand) if a teacher writes it on a paper. (This may also be true of many monolingual English student writers.) It is thus important for teachers to find out about their students' backgrounds (e.g. language and education background; to what rhetorical and grammatical terminology they have already been exposed) and to be informed by the students' knowledge base(s) when constructing feedback.

Approach: How?

In the next section I will look in some detail at the mechanics of providing feedback and offer some suggestions. More generally, however, the teacher has several "how" questions to consider. First, what will the "mode of delivery" be? Many teachers provide handwritten or typed comments to students, either written directly onto the student text, inserted using a computer "Comments" function (such as in Microsoft Word), or appended as a separate form. Others prefer to meet individually with students in face-to-face oral conferences so that discussion of the student paper can be "two-way" and so that clarification and explanation is facilitated. Computers provide teachers and students with virtual commenting and/or conferencing options which can be either asynchronous (i.e. exchanges of email with papers and comments attached) or synchronous (real-time instant messages or live chats).

There are advantages and disadvantages to all modes of delivery. While some experts view conferencing as the best (or even only acceptable) way to provide feedback, others have observed that teacher–student conferencing dynamics can be awkward and uncomfortable, especially for the student, and that some students may have trouble remembering what was discussed when they work on their papers later (Arndt, 1993; Elbow, 1973; Garrison, 1974; Goldstein and Conrad, 1990; Newkirk, 1995; Patthey-Chavez and Ferris, 1997). Others have observed that teachers' written commentary can pose a variety of problems for students, ranging from difficulty with the instructor's handwriting, lack of understanding of codes or symbols used, or inability to comprehend or apply criticisms or suggestions made. "Virtual" feedback is only useful to the degree that both teacher and student have the technology available and are adequately conversant in using it—and even under optimal conditions, it seems too impersonal for the tastes of some.

Another general "how" issue for teachers to consider is whether or not they will use a standard feedback form or rubric to provide feedback (Ferris, 2001, 2003; Ferris and Hedgcock, 2005; White, 1999). Most secondary and postsecondary English writing programs in the US have some sort of departmental or standard course rubric available or required for teachers to use. Secondary English teachers, often grappling with 150 or more student papers per week, tend to rely on rubrics (circling or checking relevant issues on the list) as a means to manage time and workload by not writing the same comments over and over. Even college instructors with fewer students may find rubrics helpful as a starting point for identifying and prioritizing feedback points in individual papers and to reinforce for students the standards and expectations for successful writing in the course. However, other experts caution that rubric-based feedback can be too generic, vague, and impersonal.

A final philosophical question as to the "hows" of giving feedback concerns whether the teacher will provide comprehensive or selective feedback (i.e. responding to every issue of concern versus choosing a few of the most important on which to focus commentary). Proponents of comprehensive feedback would argue that teachers have limited opportunity to communicate with students through personalized feedback, so when it is provided, it should be thorough. Further, teachers worry that it is unfair to students to neglect commenting on a particular issue, giving them a false sense of security that could be shattered later if they receive a low grade. Advocates of selective feedback counter that it is overwhelming to teachers and demoralizing to students when commentary is provided on numerous issues, and that a few well-constructed comments on the most important issues will have a greater short- and long-term effect than many comments on problems both big and small. Teachers' practices may vary depending upon how many students they have, what the students' needs and preferences are, and the stage in the writing process and course at which feedback is given.

Approach: Summary

As noted at the outset, response to student writing is important and time-consuming. The ways in which teachers view the goals and act of responding will influence both the process they use to provide feedback and its effects on students. Thus, it is critical that new teachers learn to think through the various issues behind responding and for experienced teachers to review their own philosophies and assumptions behind their current practices. Finally, once teachers have articulated a philosophy of or approach to response, it is also valuable to communicate that approach in some form to their students. For instance, if the teacher plans to provide selective rather than comprehensive feedback, or if the teacher intends to vary both the sources and modes of feedback delivery, it is helpful for students to know this so that misunderstandings do not occur. If the teacher has a clear, confident, and consistent rationale for the provision of feedback and shares it with the students, they are more likely to be cooperative and supportive of the teacher's approach and of the feedback process itself.

The mechanics of response

Once a teacher has thought through the big-picture reasons behind feedback and the issues surrounding it, the real work begins: Sitting down with a set of student papers and providing responses. With the previous discussion in mind, this next section offers several practical suggestions for responding to student papers (see Fig. 5.2 for a summary). Several assumptions are made in this section: (a) I am discussing primarily teacher feedback as opposed to peer or self feedback. Though many of the suggestions can be adapted for peer feedback sessions of self-evaluation guidelines, readers are also directed to sources

1 Use a course rubric or checklist and the specifications of the writing task to identify feedback points for a particular paper.
2 Read through the entire paper without making any comments.
3 Select 2–4 "feedback points" (areas for suggestion or improvement) that seem most critical to the paper at that point in its development.
4 Write a summary note or cover memo outlining the strengths and weaknesses of the paper as you see them.
5 As necessary and desired, make a few comments in the text itself to amplify or illustrate the points made in the cover memo.
6 Review your comments to make sure they are encouraging, text-specific, clear, and helpful. Monitor especially for jargon and ineffective questioning techniques.

Fig. 5.2 The responding process: Some suggestions
Source: Suggestions adapted from Ferris (2003, 2006) and Ferris and Hedgcock (2005).

which discuss alternate sources of feedback in more detail (see Note ii); (b) I am discussing written feedback as opposed to one-on-one conferencing, though again the suggestions can be adapted to oral feedback and to "virtual" feedback; and (c) I am assuming a selective rather than comprehensive approach to commentary in most instances.

Knowing what to look for

One of the most common concerns expressed by pre-service teachers learning about response to student writing is that they will not be able to identify the problems in a student paper—or conversely, that they will see so many issues that they do not know where to begin. Even experienced teachers will admit that their responding practices can be haphazard and lack consistency or clear prioritization.

Fortunately, there are several straightforward ways to "narrow the universe" of the issues in student papers. As previously noted, many teachers utilize a course grading rubric or a checklist based upon that rubric in providing feedback. Such tools are perhaps even more helpful at the preliminary stage of identifying issues for response, as they remind teachers of the expectations they and their students are required to meet by the end of the writing course. However, I am not suggesting that teachers use rubrics as a substitute for more substantive and personalized feedback but rather as a starting point for responding. Fig. 5.3 suggests a procedure for utilizing a rubric in giving feedback to student writers. Appendix 5.1 shows a student paper with a completed rubric based upon that text.

Another objective means of identifying priority issues for feedback is to look at the specifications for the particular assignment. For instance, a personal narrative assignment might call for good storytelling and analysis of the

---

- Use course/departmental grading criteria to create or adapt your checklist OR design your own for each assignment. (See sample in Appendix 5.1.)
- Read through a student paper and complete the checklist with a √, √–, or X. Use the "Xs" and "√–s" to identify and prioritize feedback points.
- Then compose an end note and (if desired) marginal comments.
- If desired, highlight or otherwise mark errors or other language-related issues.

Fig. 5.3 Suggested procedures for using a rubric or checklist in giving feedback

significance of the story. In contrast, excessive detail can actually weaken a persuasive essay. A text based upon one or more outside sources will require different feedback than a paper based entirely on the writer's experience or observations. Further, in the preliminary stages of the writing process, the teacher may wish to alert the student writer if s/he has strayed too far from the task specifications. Learning to follow directions and to write according to a prompt is an important academic skill. Finally, as previously mentioned, if the teacher has been focusing on particular writing issues in class, it may be appropriate to provide feedback to students about whether they have effectively implemented the instruction they have received.

Looking at the entire paper _– can pose problems_

Nearly all veteran writing teachers have had the embarrassing experience of writing a comment on a student paper and then finding that the question or problem was resolved on a subsequent page. One way to avoid such time-wasting mistakes is to read the entire paper first before responding to it either orally or in writing. Perhaps more importantly, if the teacher intends to prioritize issues in the paper and respond selectively, it is obviously impossible to do so until the whole paper has been read. While some teachers feel that it is too time-consuming to read through a paper and then go back and make comments, it can actually be more inefficient to make comments during a first reading.

Identifying feedback points

Again assuming selective rather than comprehensive feedback, the point of reading the paper first and using focusing tools such as a rubric and assignment specifications is to identify several high-priority issues on which to comment. In addition to comments about what the student has done well, the _selecting feedback points_ teacher should identify several areas, or "feedback points," in which improvement is possible or necessary. I am unaware of any empirical research that has established an optimal number of feedback points on a given paper, but from my own experience, about 2–4 is preferable, giving the student several substantial issues to work on without being overwhelming. Returning to the "what" issue discussed previously under "approach," feedback points can cover any areas of the text the teacher deems appropriate, from ideas to organization to language issues.

As an illustration, consider the paper written by "Tong" in Appendix 5.1. From reading the paper and looking at the checklist, two major issues become apparent. First, in his introduction, Tong suggested that lying could be either a good or bad thing depending upon the intentions of the person telling the lie. However, all of the arguments in the body of the paper and the conclusion were one-sided, discussing only the positive reasons for lying (or circumstances under which lying might be appropriate). Tong needs either to rewrite his thesis/introduction or to add information to his paper to reflect both sides of the issue. Second, Tong's third body paragraph is unclear and needs to be amplified with some kind of example or explanation about what he means by "protecting yourself" through lying. While these are not the only problems with the paper (there are grammar and word choice issues, and the example in the first body paragraph is not very convincing), they are arguably the most important for this early stage of the writing process.

Constructing a summary note

In responding to student writing, teachers have the choice of responding to specific issues in the margins of the paper or responding more generally to the entire paper in an end note or cover memo returned to the student—or some combination of marginal and terminal feedback. While there is utility to both types of feedback, a summary note may be more valuable for several reasons. First, as its name suggests, it provides a cogent *summary* of what the strengths and weaknesses of the entire paper rather than a disconnected stream-of-consciousness conversation in the margins. Second, because the summary note is separate from the body of the paper, the teacher can use complete sentences and make more substantive (and legible) comments than may be possible in the margins. Students in survey research have complained about short, cryptic, illegible teacher commentary (Ferris, 1995; Straub, 1997).

Building on the completed checklist in Appendix 5.1 and the two feedback points discussed above for Tong's paper, a summary end note to Tong could look like the one in Fig. 5.4.

While there are different ways to construct a summary memo of this type, this particular example approaches it like a letter, beginning with the student's name and signed by the teacher. It provides specific encouragement at the outset about what Tong has done well before launching into the two feedback points. The memo explains what the concerns are and then suggests in general ways how Tong might go about solving the problems—but giving Tong options as to how exactly he will approach those suggestions. While the comments are clear and substantive, they are also not excessively long or wordy. The memo ends with a final (rather generic) word of encouragement. It could either be appended to the back or the front of the student paper when it is returned to him.

Dear Tong,

   This is a very nice first draft. I especially appreciated your thoughtful response to the essay question: That lies can be either good or bad depending upon the person's intentions. You also did a nice job of identifying arguments to support your opinion and providing good examples in the first two body paragraphs.
   I have a couple of suggestions for you to consider as you revise:

1   In your introduction, you argue that people may lie with good or bad intentions. But in the body of your essay, all of your points and examples are about lying with good intentions. You might consider either changing your introduction or adding a paragraph or two that talk about lying with bad intentions.
2   I think your third body paragraph—about lying to protect yourself— needs some more thought and additional detail. What would be an example of an appropriate lie to protect oneself? How is this different from a child who lies to his/her parents or teacher to escape punishment (also "protecting" oneself)?

Great job so far. I'll look forward to reading your second draft!

Best wishes,

Teacher

Fig. 5.4 Summary end note for "Tong's" paper

Adding marginal commentary

While it is my view that summary notes are the most valuable type of feedback, additional marginal comments that further amplify or illustrate the points made in the summary note can also be valuable if the teacher has time to provide them. What is perhaps different about the process outlined in Fig. 5.2 is that the summary note is constructed *first* and is based upon a reading of the entire paper and thoughtful selection of key feedback points. In contrast, many teachers read through the paper, write comments in the margins as they go along, and then write a brief note at the end of the paper which is either fairly general ("Good job" or "Needs work") or which basically reiterates what has already been said in the margins. In my nearly 24 years of teaching writing, I have provided feedback both ways, and I find the two approaches about equivalent in terms of time required—but that the "summary note first" approach leads to better quality feedback that I am more satisfied with and which is more beneficial to students. That said, marginal notes can provide specific illustrations of points raised in the summary note, and the immediacy of their placement in the text makes the comment clear to them. Appendix 5.2 provides an example of marginal comments for Tong's paper. They amplify what is said in the summary note (Fig. 5.4) and add a couple of other minor issues for Tong to think about as well as complimenting him in spots. However, it is important to note that the marginal commentary is not lengthy, excessive, or hard to read or understand. I have seen student papers so heavily marked by teachers that by the time the marginal comments and end note are completed, the teacher has actually written more than the student did in the original paper!

Further, in-text commentary may, at the teacher's discretion, also include some feedback on error or language issues. For instance, Tong, who is in a multilingual writing course, makes a number of errors in grammar and morphology. The teacher may wish to highlight or underline the errors to call them to his attention as he revises. The sample feedback shown in Fig. 5.4 and Appendix 5.2 does not address grammar issues because in my judgment, there are more important problems for Tong to think about at this point. However, if a student makes serious errors that interfere with the comprehensibility of the message or frequent errors that are patterned, this may be one of the feedback points that the teacher deems worth mentioning in a summary note ("As you revise, be sure to check whether your verbs should be in the present or past tense") and/or marking in the text so that the student has some specific feedback about the issue(s). A teacher's approach to language-focused feedback or "error treatment" (Ferris, 2002, 2003; Ferris and Hedgcock, 2005) may vary according to the needs of the individual student and the stage of the writing process.

Reviewing commentary for clarity and effectiveness

It is safe to say that feedback students do not understand and cannot apply will not help them and is a waste of the teacher's time. Unfortunately, constructing clear and effective commentary is easier said than done. There are several specific issues to consider in providing feedback to student writers.

Words of encouragement. Most students (in fact, most people) appreciate some feedback about what they have done well. While they understand that it is the teacher's job to instruct them and give constructive criticism, it is human nature to be a bit demoralized if the response to something one has produced is entirely critical or negative. In a study of student views on teacher feedback (Ferris, 1995), I was struck by how clearly and specifically students remembered notes of encouragement they had received, often quoting them word-for-word. To be frank, it may be hard sometimes for teachers to think of anything about the student paper to praise, which is again why a checklist or rubric like the one in Appendix 5.1 may be helpful. At opposite extremes, sometimes a teacher may be so afraid of hurting a student's feelings that they write nothing but effusively positive comments—but abandon their important role in providing expert feedback and mentoring to the student writer. All things considered, a judicious combination of praise and constructive criticism is probably what serves most students best. Comments of encouragement should be specific so that students know what they have done well (i.e. "Good job" is not especially helpful if that is the sum total of the praise). Note that the summary note to Tong in Fig. 5.4 specifically noted his response to the prompt and his setting of a thoughtful task in the introduction.

As a final note on the role of praise and criticism, teachers can sometimes actually be abusive to students through their commentary. In my own teacher-preparation courses for future writing instructors, I always ask the pre-service teachers in my classes to reflect upon feedback they have received from instructors about their own writing. I am stunned and even appalled at some of the stories they tell. For instance, one teacher talked about how her high school English teacher ripped up her paper in front of the class saying, "*That's* what I think about your paper!" Another student said that his college composition teacher told him that "Not everyone is cut out for college." (The student is now completing a master's degree and is teaching his own writing class.) Teachers should avoid any comments that are mean, sarcastic, or which disparage the student's effort, character, or intelligence.

Clarity. Comments which are too vague and abstract might confuse and frustrate students. Teachers should avoid comments like "Vague" or "Awkward," as they fail to specify either what the problem is or how the student might address it. They also should avoid cryptic remarks like "Really?" or "Why?" or "No!" Most beginning composition students will not be able to read their teacher's minds and know what to make of that type of feedback.

Another barrier to clarity is the use of rhetorical or linguistic jargon. Teachers cannot always assume that students will enter their classes knowing what "thesis" or "transition" or "agreement" or "coherence" mean. Unless they have previously assessed their students' knowledge and/or taught those terms themselves, they should be avoided in providing commentary. This is

> *Student Original:*
> But it was unbelievable that when I visited New York City.
>
> *Teacher Comment:*
> INC SEN (in margin)
>
> *Student Revision:*
> It was unbelievable that when I visited New York City.

Fig. 5.5 Example of ineffective jargon use with a multilingual student writer
Source of example: Zamel (1985).

especially true when some or all of the students are multilingual writers (see Fig. 5.5). A classic example of this (shared with me by a colleague) is when a teacher told an ESL student that his essay needed "an introduction." In the next draft, the student obediently began, "How do you do? My name is Le. I am 19 years old. I have black hair and a girlfriend …" "Le" knew the most basic form of the term "introduction" but not its application to the composition classroom.

Finally, teachers should be careful when using questions as part of their feedback. Many writing teachers have been explicitly trained to ask questions rather than using imperatives when giving feedback as a means of being nondirective and allowing the student to retain ownership of his/her paper. However, some questions are more effective than others. Some are straightforward requests for more information unknown to the teacher ("What happened next?"). However, others are not questions at all but rather indirect requests ("Can you give an example here?"), while others are higher-order rhetorical questions designed to push the student's thinking or argumentation (e.g. "Isn't it true that …" "Don't you think …"). Research on the effects of teacher commentary on student revision suggests that students can deal with requests for information fairly well but may not know what to do with more abstract questions, which require not only additional thinking but substantial reworking of the paper to accommodate the new thoughts (Conrad and Goldstein, 1999; Ferris, 1997, 2001). Further, students educated in other languages or cultures may misunderstand the "indirect request" question and think "Yes, I could give an example, but I prefer not to," or wonder whether the teacher's indirectness shows a lack of competence or confidence. To address these issues, teachers should consider whether in some instances a straightforward statement ("Please provide an example here") would be preferable to a question. As to more challenging "thought questions," the teacher could provide some specific guidance about what the student could do to incorporate

> **TEACHER COMMENT:** *Is this really a crossroads friendship if you're not in contact?*
>
> **WHAT SHE MEANT:**
> You may be misunderstanding Viorst's definition of a "crossroads friendship." Take a look at the article again and decide if you need a different example or a different category for your example.

Fig. 5.6 Ineffective teacher question
Source of example: Ferris (2007: 172).

> *Student Text Excerpt:* My best high school friend was a great influence on me. Even though she is now at San Diego State and I'm at Sac State, I'm still following her good example.
>
> *Teacher Comment: What is her major?*

Fig. 5.7 Irrelevant or counterproductive teacher question
Source of example: Ferris (2007: 172).

the new information (e.g. "Consider rewriting your introduction," or "Add a sentence/paragraph in which you discuss your thoughts about this issue"). See Fig. 5.6 for an example of an unsuccessful teacher question and a possible restatement.

Another problem that arises with questions is when teachers, in an effort to appear as engaged, interested readers, ask questions that are irrelevant to the overall goals of the student paper. In the example in Fig. 5.7, if the student actually responded to the question, it would weaken the paper. In reviewing their own questioning strategies, teachers might ask themselves the following question: "If the student writer actually answered this question in the paper, would it make the paper better or worse?" The student may not understand the difference between "conversational" questions from the teacher and questions which are intended to be acted upon in a revised draft.

Response: Summary

The above discussion should demonstrate that response to student writing is a complex endeavor, more of an art than a science, and one that requires some thought and some practice. That said, if teachers follow the process suggested in this section (Fig. 5.2), they will at least have a starting point from which to refine their responding skills. While there definitely are a number of pitfalls to avoid, teachers can learn to respond effectively in ways that encourage, challenge, and support their students.

Follow-up: What students do after receiving feedback

One of the most frustrating aspects of response to student writing is the sense that students do not understand or care about feedback they have received and thus do not attend to it or utilize it to improve their current or future writing. Considering the substantial time and effort most writing teachers devote to feedback, such concerns, if true, are certainly discouraging and demoralizing. Thus, it is important for teachers to consider what students do after receiving feedback from peers or the instructor. Far too often, teachers will simply hand back a set of papers at the end of class, say "The revision is due a week from today," and leave it at that, hoping that the students will read comments carefully, take them seriously, and utilize them successfully in their future writing. When this does not happen, teachers start to question the efficacy of feedback, regardless of its source, in the writing process. However, there are several simple and practical methods to ensure that students can benefit from the feedback they receive.

The first important step is to allow students time to ask questions about the comments they have received, whether they are written or emailed or delivered orally in a teacher–student conference or peer review session. In the case of written commentary returned in class, the teacher could give students a few minutes to reread their papers and the teacher's feedback and ask any questions that might arise. Students should be given explicit permission and encouragement to ask such questions so that they do not worry about appearing disrespectful or argumentative toward the teacher. This is especially important for students previously educated in other cultures with more rigidly hierarchical teacher–student relationships. The truth is that any form of two-way human communication can and does misfire sometimes, and teacher or peer feedback is no exception. Even the most well-constructed feedback can be misinterpreted. A possible follow-up exercise would be to have the student writers, after rereading their own papers and examining and asking questions about feedback, write a brief paragraph about what they have learned from rereading and from the suggestions they have received and what changes they might make as a result.

Once students have completed a revision of a paper after getting feedback on a previous draft, they can be asked to submit with the revision a cover memo that explains how they addressed the comments and suggestions given by teachers and/or peers, what changes they made, and what suggestions they chose not to act upon and why. This exercise accomplishes several things. First, it validates the importance of the feedback students have received. They cannot simply ignore the commentary, as they are required to analyze and explain how they have responded to it. Second, it requires them to think analytically on both micro- and macro-levels about their own writing and revision processes. Third, because one option for writers is to explain why they did *not* follow a suggestion they received, it reinforces their control and ownership over their paper, helping to balance the appropriation/power/intervention issues discussed earlier.

Finally, after students have completed revisions on a particular paper, they can submit all drafts, feedback, responses to feedback, and revision cover memos. The teacher can consider all of this material as evidence of effort and engagement in the writing process and factor it into the grading scheme for a paper, a portfolio, or the final course grade. Having to submit evidence of careful thought and effort during the writing process again affirms the importance of feedback and subsequent revision.

As a postscript to this follow-up stage, it is important for teachers to understand that feedback alone may not be adequate for students to revise successfully and develop as writers. Many students need actual instruction on revision, starting with the understanding that good writing goes through multiple iterations and can undergo substantial change along the way. Some student writers arrive at secondary and postsecondary instruction believing that "revision" is just a matter of proofreading, spell-checking, and surface clean-up. Revision is a complex process, and while feedback can assist in this process, students themselves need to understand and take responsibility for the development of their papers. In short, before turning students loose on assigned revisions with teacher or peer comments in hand, they need to understand the whys and hows of revision.

Evaluating the effectiveness of feedback

As a final note, whether one is a new teacher or a veteran, there is benefit in occasionally monitoring the effectiveness of one's own feedback practices.

1 Do my comments reflect my own philosophy of response? Do they reflect my own sense of (a) the major needs of this student/text; and (b) my understanding of the course grading criteria and the specific task?
2 What is the balance between marginal and end comments?
3 What is the balance between positive and critical comments?
4 To what degree are my comments personal and text-specific?
5 Are my comments clear and specific? If I have used any questions, are they helpful? Will the answers to the questions, if provided, potentially improve the paper?
6 Have I struck the proper balance between being clear and helpful yet allowing the student to retain ownership of his/her paper?

Fig. 5.8 Self-evaluation questions for teacher feedback
Source: Adapted from Ferris (2003); Ferris and Hedgcock (2005).

Feedback is, after all, costly in terms of time and effort, and it has great potential, if well done, to facilitate students' writing development. In short, it is too important to the overall success of a writing teacher to take its success or effectiveness lightly or for granted (see Fig. 5.8.)

There are several practical ways in which teachers can monitor and evaluate their own feedback (and/or peer review sessions they assign). One is to analyze one's own commentary objectively and quantitatively, looking at issues such as comment length, purpose (question, praise, suggestion, etc.) and style (question, imperative, statement). Analysis models designed for research purposes can be adapted for teacher self-evaluation; one example is provided in Appendix 5.3. By analyzing and charting one's own commentary, a teacher can get a sense of his/her patterns and practices and make adjustments as needed. Second, the teacher can reflect on commentary in a more qualitative manner by thinking through the questions provided in Fig. 5.7 for one or more student papers. Third, the teacher can trace the effects of feedback on revision by numbering each suggestion and assessing its impact on a four-point scale: (1) Not revised; (2) Negative effects; (3) Mixed effects; (4) Positive effects (Appendix 5.3; adapted from Ferris, 1997). The teacher can then look more closely at which types of comments seemed more or less successful in facilitating revisions and why (see Ferris, 2001, for a sample analysis; see also Conrad and Goldstein, 1999). Finally, the teacher can ask the students to

1   Do you read your teacher's comments and corrections?
2   What does your teacher comment the most about (content, writing, grammar, etc.)?
3   Do you use your teacher's suggestions when you write your next paper?
4   Do you usually understand your teacher's comments and corrections?
5   Does your teacher give you positive or encouraging comments?
6   What do you do if you do not understand your teacher's comments?
7   Do you feel that your teacher's comments have helped you to succeed in this course and improve your writing? Why or why not?
8   In what ways do you wish your teacher would change or improve his/her comments?

Fig. 5.9 Student reactions to feedback: Questions to ask
Source: Ferris (2006).

respond to questions about feedback they have received (see Fig. 5.9 for some sample questions; see also Ferris, 1995, for a sample questionnaire used in several studies).

Conclusion

For good or ill, feedback has potential to affect student writing—and thus, there are pitfalls to consider. Excessive or overly controlling feedback can frustrate, disempower, and demotivate student writers who may feel they have lost ownership of their texts. Abusive or ineffective feedback can demoralize students, mislead them, and actually impede their progress as writers. On the other hand, thoughtful, constructive, respectful feedback can be very motivating and encouraging to writers and thus can have great power and be of tremendous benefit to students. In fact, it may be the single most significant gift teachers can provide, as it demonstrates personal interest and investment in the progress of each individual student. Because of feedback's potential benefits *and* its dangers, it is critically important for new teachers to learn the skills and art of commenting and for experienced teachers to regularly evaluate the impact and effectiveness of their feedback. To reiterate the point made at the beginning of this chapter: "Given the amount of effort and time that goes into responding, *it is imperative that we find response practices that make sense and learn how to change those that don't*" (Segade, 2004, emphasis added).

Notes

i   The outline for this chapter is adapted from Ferris and Hedgcock (2005, Ch. 5).

ii Space does not permit a detailed treatment of the topic of peer feedback. Readers interested in reviewing some of the arguments for and against its use and suggestions for utilizing it successfully are encouraged to look at some recent work on this issue (e.g. Ferris, 2003; Ferris and Hedgcock, 2005; Liu and Hansen, 2002).

iii While cynics might observe that "self-feedback" sounds like a rather transparent effort on the part of teachers to reduce their workload, it is only fair to say that for some teachers, this view is indeed principled: They believe that (a) Students will learn more about writing by being required to analyze and revise their own work; and (b) Any form of feedback from others takes ownership away from the writer and can be disempowering and demotivating (for further discussion, see Brannon and Knoblauch, 1982; Elbow, 1999; Ferris, 2003; Sommers, 1982; Sperling and Freedman, 1987).

References

Arndt, V. (1993), "Response to writing: Using feedback to inform the writing process," in M. N. Brock and L. Walters (eds), *Teaching Composition Around the Pacific Rim: Politics & Pedagogy* (pp. 90–116) (Clevedon, Avon, UK: Multilingual Matters).

Brannon, L. and Knoblauch, C.H. (1982), "On students' rights to their own texts: A model of teacher response," *College Composition and Communication*, 33, 157–166.

Conrad, S. M. and Goldstein, L. M. (1999), "ESL student revision after teacher-written comments: Text, contexts, and individuals," *Journal of Second Language Writing*, 8, 147–180.

Elbow, P. (1973), *Writing Without Teachers* (Oxford: Oxford University Press).

Elbow, P. (1999), "Options for responding to student writing," in Straub, R. (ed.), *A Sourcebook for Responding to Student Writing* (pp. 197–202) (Creskill, NJ:Hampton Press).

Ferris, D. R. (1995), "Student reactions to teacher response in multiple-draft composition classrooms," *TESOL Quarterly*, 29, 33–53.

Ferris, D. R. (1997), "The influence of teacher commentary on student revision," *TESOL Quarterly*, 31, 315–339.

Ferris, D. R. (2001), "Teaching writing for academic purposes," in J. Flowerdew and M. Peacock (eds), *Research Perspectives on English for Academic Purposes* (pp. 298–314) (Cambridge: Cambridge University Press).

Ferris, D. R. (2002), *Treatment of Error in Second Language Student Writing* (Ann Arbor: University of Michigan Press).

Ferris, D. R. (2003), *Response to Student Writing: Implications for Second Language Students* (Mahwah, NJ: Lawrence Erlbaum Associates).

Ferris, D. R. (2006), "Responding to student writing: Approach, response, follow-up, & evaluation," keynote address presented at the Third Annual UC Berkeley Symposium on Multilingual Writers, Berkeley, CA, 14 October.

Ferris, D. R. (2007), "Preparing teachers to respond to student writing," *Journal of Second Language Writing*, 16, 165–193.

Ferris, D. R. and Hedgcock, J. S. (2005), *Teaching ESL Composition: Purpose, Process, & Practice* (Mahwah, NJ: Lawrence Erlbaum Associates).

Garrison, R. (1974), "One-to-one tutorial instruction in freshman composition," *New Directions for Community Colleges*, 2, 55–84.

Goldstein, L. and Conrad, S. (1990), "Student input and the negotiation of meaning in ESL writing conferences," *TESOL Quarterly*, 24, 443–460.

Harklau, L., Losey, K. M. and Siegal, M. (1999), *Generation 1.5 Meets College Composition* (Mahwah, NJ: Lawrence Erlbaum Associates).

Hairston, M. (1986), "On not being a composition slave," in C. W. Bridges (ed.), *Training the New Teacher of College Composition* (pp. 117–124) (Urbana, IL: NCTE).

Knoblauch, C. H. and Brannon, L. (1981), "Teacher commentary on student writing: The state of the art," *Freshman English News*, 10 (Fall, 1981), 1–4.

Jacobs, G. M., Curtis, A., Braine, G. and Huang, S. (1998), "Feedback on student writing: Taking the middle path," *Journal of Second Language Writing*, 7, 307–318.

Liu, J. and Hansen, J. (2002), *Peer Response in Second Language Writing Classrooms* (Ann Arbor: University of Michigan Press).

Marzano, R. J. and Arthur, S. (1977), "Teacher comments on student essays: It doesn't matter what you say," ERIC Document Reproduction Service No. ED 147 864.

Newkirk, T. (1995), "The writing conference as performance," *Research in the Teaching of English*, 29, 193–215.

Patthey-Chavez, G. G. and Ferris, D. R. (1997), "Writing conferences and the weaving of multi-voiced texts in college composition", *Research in the Teaching of English*, 31, 51–90.

Reid, J. (1994), "Responding to ESL students' texts: The myths of appropriation," *TESOL Quarterly*, 28, 273–292.

Segade, G. (2004), "Book review: *Response to Student Writing* by Dana R. Ferris," http://writingproject. org/cs/nwpp/lpt/nwpr/1990 (retrieved 10 June 2006).

Sommers, N. (1982), "Responding to student writing," *College Composition and Communication*, 33, 148–156.

Sperling, M. and Freedman, S.W. (1987), "A good girl writes like a good girl: Written responses to student writing," *Written Communication*, 4, 343–369.

Straub, R. (1997), "Students' reactions to teacher comments: An exploratory study," *Research in the Teaching of English*, 31, 91–119.

White, E.M. (1999), "Using scoring guides to assess writing," in R. Straub (ed.), *A Sourcebook for Responding to Student Writing* (pp. 203 –212) (Creskill, NJ: Hampton Press).

Zamel, V. (1985), "Responding to student writing," *TESOL Quarterly*, 19, 79–102.

Zhang, S. (1995), "Reexamining the affective advantage of peer feedback in the ESL writing class," *Journal of Second Language Writing*, 4, 209–222.

Zhang, S. (1999), "Thoughts on some recent evidence concerning the affective advantageof peer feedback," *Journal of Second Language Writing*, 8, 321–326.

Appendix 5.1 Sample student paper with completed checklist

Background: "Tong" was a junior enrolled in a class called "Writing for Proficiency," an upper-division course for multilingual writers who had failed the university writing proficiency examination. The approximate proficiency of students in this course is one semester below the college level. "Tong" and his classmates wrote this essay in 50 minutes in class during the first week of the semester after reading a short newspaper article on the topic of "lies." They were asked to respond to the question: Is lying always wrong? Why or why not?

Everyone have been a liar once in their life. People who lie intentionally to harm others are bad people and their lies are harmful too. However, there are lies that are done with good intention. So, there are times that lies are appropriate. A lie is either a good or bad one base upon the liar's intention. Only one person can really tell whether a lie is intended to harm or do good.

Many people lie with good intention. There were times where kids were upsett that they didn't get to finish their candy. Parents are not evil. Many parents would lie that they would like to have some candy too in order to reduce the amount of candy their kid is consuming. The kid may realize that the parents may just set the candy aside and accuse them of lying, but the parent's intention was good. If the kid would continue on to finished the candy it would be bad for the kid's teeth and health. When parents lie its usually not that they are intentionally trying to harm, but to provide the kid with good teeth and health in the future.

Some people lie when judging others. In the article "Lies Are So Common Place, They Almost Seem Like The Truth," by Terry Lee Goodrich, the author points out that most guest at a dinner would never said a prepare meal was terrible. Instead, most would lie and complement the meal. Many people do so to protect the other person's feelings. The intention was not to offend a friends feelings after all the hard work he had done to get dinner ready. Sometimes it is better to lie and not hurt your friends.

Lying can sometimes be necessary. An example is when you feel threaten by the situation that is given then lying may be the only options. There are times where you need to protect yourself and the only way to do so is by lying. No matter how bad the situation maybe majority of the people lie with good intention. If they were to told the truth they would of face serious problem. Protecting yourself is always good intentions.

Lying is such a negative word. However, if use correctly with good intentions lying can be appropriate. Wanting the best for your child is a good intention.

To appreciate your friend's hard work is a good intention. Protecting yourself also is a good intention. So, lying is appropriate if use with good intentions.

Essay feedback checklist

Checklist symbols:
- √+ Essay does this very well
- √ Essay does this adequately
- √– Essay does this but not always adequately
- X Essay does this poorly or not at all

I. *Response to prompt/assignment*
- √ The paper responds clearly and completely to the specific instructions in the prompt or assignment.
- √– The essay stays clearly focused on the topic throughout.

II. *Content (ideas)*
- √ The essay has a clear main idea or thesis.
- √–The thesis is well supported with several major points or arguments.
- √ The supporting points are developed with ideas from the readings, facts, or other examples from the writer's own experiences or observations.
- √– The arguments or examples are clear and logical.

 X Opposing viewpoints have been considered and responded to clearly and effectively.

III. *Use of readings*
- √ The writer has incorporated other texts into his/her essay.
- √– The writer has used summary, paraphrase, and quotations from the readings to strengthen his/her paper.
- √ The writer has mastered the mechanics of incorporating ideas from other texts, including accurate use of quotation marks and other punctuation, accurate verb tenses, appropriate identification of the author & title, and effective integration of quotations into the writer's own text.

IV. *Organization*
- √ There is a clear beginning (introduction), middle (body), and end (conclusion) to the essay.
- √ The beginning introduces the topic and clearly expresses the main idea.
- √– The body paragraphs include topic sentences which are directly tied to the main idea (thesis).
- √ Each body paragraph is well organized and includes a topic sentence, supporting details, and a summary of the ideas.

- X Coherence devices (transitions, repetition, synonyms, pronoun reference, etc.) are used effectively within and between paragraphs.
- √ The conclusion ties the ideas in the body back to the thesis and summarizes why the issue is interesting or important.

V. *Language and mechanics*

- —The paper is spell-checked (typed essays only).
- X The paper is proofread and does not have serious and frequent errors in grammar, spelling, typing, or punctuation.

Appendix 5.2 Marginal comments for Tong's essay

	Everyone have been a liar once in their life. People who lie intentionally to harm others are bad people and their lies are harmful too. However, there are lies that are done with good intention. So, there are times that lies are appropriate. A lie is either a good or bad one base upon the liar's intention. Only one person can really tell whether a lie is intended to harm or do good.	Very thoughtful introduction!
Do parents need to lie? Why not "just say no"?	Many people lie with good intention. There were times where kids were upsett that they didn't get to finish their candy. Parents are not evil. Many parents would lie that they would like to have some candy too in order to reduce the amount of candy their kid is consuming. The kid may realize that the parents may just set the candy aside and accuse them of lying, but the parent's intention was good. If the kid would continue on to finished the candy it would be bad for the kid's teeth and health. When parents lie its usually not that they are intentionally trying to harm, but to provide the kid with good teeth and health in the future.	Can you think of a different example of parents lying to protect their children?
Are people "judging others" or simply trying not to hurt their feelings?	Some people lie when judging others. In the article "Lies Are So Common Place, They Almost Seem Like The Truth," by Terry Lee Goodrich, the author points out that most guest at a dinner would never said a prepare meal was terrible. Instead, most would lie and complement the meal. Many people do so to protect the other person's feelings. The intention was not to offend a friends feelings after all the hard work he had done to get dinner ready. Sometimes it is better to lie and not hurt your friends.	Good example and good use of the reading.

	Lying can sometimes be necessary. An example is when you feel threaten by the situation that is given then lying may be the only options. There are times where you need to protect yourself and the only way to do so is by lying. No matter how bad the situation maybe majority of the people lie with good intention. If they were to told the truth they would of face serious problem. Protecting yourself is always good intentions.	This is a good argument— but it needs a specific example to make it clearer.
	Lying is such a negative word. However, if use correctly with good intentions lying can be appropriate. Wanting the best for your child is a good intention. To appreciate your friend's hard work is a good intention. Protecting yourself also is a good intention. So, lying is appropriate if use with good intentions.	Good conclusion— it sums up your arguments & restates your opinion.

Source: Adapted from Ferris (1997).

Appendix 5.3 Objective analysis scheme for teacher commentary and revision effects

A. Comment length (number of words)

1 = Short (1–5 words)
2 = Average (6–15 words)
3 = Long (16–25 words)
4 = Very long (26+ words)

B. Comment types

1 = Ask for Information/Question
   EXAMPLE: Did you work out this problem with your roommates?
2 = Suggestion/Question
   EXAMPLE: Can you provide a thesis statement here—What did you learn from this?
3 = Suggestion/Statement or Imperative
   EXAMPLE: This paragraph might be better earlier in the essay.
   EXAMPLE: Mention what Zinsser says about parental pressure.
4 = Give Information/Question or Statement
   EXAMPLE: Most states do allow a waiting period before an adoption is final—Do you feel that all such laws are wrong?
   EXAMPLE: Iowa law favors parental rights. Michigan and California consider the best interests of the child.
5 = Positive Comment/Statement or Exclamation
   EXAMPLE: A very nice start to your essay! You've done an impressive job of finding facts and quotes to support your arguments.
6 = Grammar/Mechanics Comment/Question, Statement, or Imperative
   EXAMPLES:
      *Past or present tense?
      *Your verb tenses are confusing me in this paragraph.

C. Text-specific comment

0 = Generic comment (could have been written on any paper)
   EXAMPLE: Nice Intro
1 = Text-specific comment
   EXAMPLE: Why is the American system better for children, in your opinion?

D. Effects on revision

1 Not revised
2 Positive effects (the change made the paper stronger)
3 Mixed effects (the change made the paper stronger in spots and weaker/neutral in others)
4 Negative effects (the change made the paper weaker)

Analysis chart

Comment #	Length	Type	Text-specific	Revision code (1–4)

Source: Adapted from Ferris (1997).

Writing Support in British Higher Education: An Institutional Case Study

6

John Morley

The University of Manchester is the UK's largest single-site university and was formed in 2004 following the merger of two former institutions: the Victoria University of Manchester and the University of Manchester Institute of Science and Technology, both of which were highly placed in the national research league rankings. Of a current student population of 36,000, around 7,400 are international students (representing 180 different countries), and many of these are from non-native English speaking backgrounds. Furthermore, out of the total student population, around 9,000 are postgraduates. These three broad categories of student, undergraduate, postgraduate, and international, attract different forms of writing support at the University. The patterns of this support tend to be quite variable and the form of provision is ultimately contingent on program, School, or Faculty[i] requirements, and the funding made available, as well as on the students' particular needs and circumstances. Thus a very wide-ranging and diverse program of writing support exists, and this makes an interesting case study, providing an account of a range of possible forms of writing support at tertiary level. This chapter, therefore, is a report on the various approaches to writing development available to different groups of students at Manchester. It treats writing support for international students, undergraduates, and postgraduates, separately, although there is of course some overlap between these groups since international students will also be either undergraduates or postgraduates.

The writing initiatives described here have all been developed or are run by the University Language Centre, whose specialist staff members all have Diplomas in teaching (in either ESL/EFL/English) as well as postgraduate study experience, usually in the form of an MA in Applied Linguistics/TESOL. These teachers are encouraged to attend and contribute to conferences and events held by BALEAP[ii] (the British Association of Lecturers of English for Academic Purposes) and WDHE[iii] (Writing Development in Higher Education), both of which are national bodies. For the most part, Schools and Faculties are happy to "buy in" this specialist expertise to enhance their own programs. Nevertheless, across the range of disciplines taught at Manchester, other initiatives do exist, or have existed at various times, usually at the particular program level and as a result of the efforts of individual members of staff, and these are discussed briefly toward the end of the chapter.

Writing support for international students: general versus specific

The University has provided a range of study support services specifically for this group of students since 1971, and these are currently delivered at Faculty level, School level, and also at program level. Support in academic writing stands out as the service for which there is the most demand from students and its delivery draws on a wide range of approaches in response to the varying needs of the students.

Each year the University runs around 12 classes in academic writing for international students, and these are held at different times and in different places on the campus. The classes run throughout most of semester one and the greater part of semester two, and they are delivered on a Faculty basis.

Thus, classes are offered to students in Medical and Human Sciences, Life Sciences, Humanities and Engineering and Physical Sciences. Although the materials may be broadly relevant to the students' areas of study, the material used is not "strongly" discipline- or program-specific. For example, the classes for the Faculty of Medical and Human Sciences are attended by medical students, pharmacists, psychologists, dentists and nurses, and whilst the materials all follow a health theme, they are not specific to any one of these disciplines. The syllabus essentially adopts a broadly functional approach (Hyland, 2003), covering "common core" areas such as defining terms, comparing and contrasting, describing figures and trends, with particular focus on developing awareness of sentence level and paragraph level structures. In most classes, the teaching follows a pattern of text focus, followed by analysis and practice of the linguistic forms leading to the production of a parallel text or texts. Many of the model texts used have been drawn, with permission, from students' work or from published academic papers. In addition, the classes cover a number of more general topics such as key features of academic register as well as the process of writing. A classic example of this approach, though pitched at a simpler level, is Jordan's *Academic Writing Course* (Jordan, 1980) which was originally developed at Manchester for international students.

At the same time, although the material is not specific to any one level of study, since the majority of those who attend are either on taught masters programs or following research programs, students are also introduced to some of the insights gained from genre studies of academic texts (Swales, 1981, 1990; Dudley-Evans, 1986; Hopkins and Dudley-Evans, 1988), particularly those written in the relevant disciplines relating to research. Thus the common core elements of introductions (the CARS model), literature reviews, and discussion sections of dissertations, for example, are covered in the later part of the courses, with the aim of imparting an explicit focus on how these texts are structured and on how different communicative purposes in them may be achieved linguistically. In these general classes, teachers need to be aware that these rhetorical elements may appear to be very different in different disciplines and they need to guard against being over-prescriptive, and to encourage students to be aware of alternative forms. For example, in classes offered to students in the Faculty of Engineering and Physical Sciences, when the focus is on elements of dissertations, some reference needs to be made to the fact that in Electrical Engineering, the "Literature Review" usually corresponds to a section entitled "Theory" or "Requirements of the System," the "Methods" sections as "Build and Design the System," the "Results" as "Test" and the

"Discussion" as "Evaluation." In the Faculty of Humanities, a dissertation in Law at Masters level may have the structure: "Current law," "Background," "Problems with its Implementation," "Recommendations." These examples partly illustrate the boundaries of the English for general academic purposes approach to teaching writing, and also highlight the danger of presenting certain stereotypical genre models as being universal. Nevertheless, although the texts that are analyzed in the classes may, in some cases, be some way from what certain students actually need in their own studies, they still serve the purpose of raising awareness of rhetorical form and language, and perhaps revealing insights which the students can then take forward and use to explore texts within their own disciplines. As such, this discourse consciousness raising approach does not pretend to be comprehensive in its coverage, but it does attempt to give our students insights into the typical rhetorical patterns and possibilities of academic discourse. At the very least, the work in the classes should encourage students to ask their supervisors about the rhetorical forms and conventions expected within their own subjects.

Complementing the centralized generic provision are three other forms of writing support which, funded at School and program level, are delivered on a less-centralized basis, and which are more targeted to the specific needs of the students. This may take the form of:

- fairly large programs in which up to 200 students attend a series of workshops, typically with a maximum number of 20 students in each workshop session, and with each series of workshops running over six or nine hours (e.g. Project Management, Development Policy and Management);
- weekly classes which constitute part of a large award-bearing program and is thus assessed (e.g. English Language and Research Skills for Law, counted as 5 credits);
- small group writing sessions for research students in specific research programs held over the summer period (e.g. typically around 12 students per group for research students in Pharmacy and Textiles).

These forms of provision permit the teachers to structure the teaching much more around the kind of tasks which are of immediate concern to the students (e.g. for taught postgraduates, in semester one: coursework in the literature-based discursive papers; in semester two: preparation for dissertations and research papers). These sessions permit a closer analysis of disciplinary text types and registers, and in some cases a focus on subject-specific language, but the amount that can be covered depends on the number of sessions available. The sessions with smaller groups offer greater opportunities for individual feedback as well as peer review and discussion of other students' work. More successful are the programs in which the teachers are able to collaborate closely with the subject specialists, and where the latter take an active interest in what is covered in the support classes. This is the case with the "English for Legal Studies" course in which key content and tasks dovetail with the main course, along the lines of practice outlined in Snow and Brinton's (1988) "adjunct model."

The third form of support that is available to international students is the writing consultation service. This service, which is funded by the University, allows students to book a one-to-one consultation to receive feedback on a piece of work they are writing, up to a maximum of 1,500 words. The writing is made available to the tutor one week in advance and they are able to prepare specific feedback on any aspect of the student's writing. Tutors need to be sufficiently experienced to deal with problems that may occur at any particular level of writing, whether relating to language structure, lexis and collocation, organizing information or problems to do with disciplinary conventions and subject genres. For students who make use of this service, the sessions can be extremely helpful for they offer opportunities for them to talk about their writing and to receive a significant amount of individualized formative feedback. However, there are two problems which we experience with this program: the first is that there is a tendency for some students to see it as a proofreading service; and the second is that demand tends to peak in the final weeks of semester one and semester two. So we need to work hard to encourage students to make use of the service earlier in the semesters and to see the sessions as developmental and pedagogic experiences rather than as mere proofreading opportunities. Many other British universities offer such a service, but the precise procedures differ. One institution, for example, only allows previously assessed work to be submitted for feedback; at others, proofreading on short student texts can take place but only during the face-to-face session.

Writing support for undergraduates: task, process and collaboration

Unlike universities in the US, where there is a strong tradition in incorporating Rhetoric and Composition Studies as compulsory components of first-year studies, UK universities have not seen the teaching of writing as a mainstream learning activity for undergraduates. Perhaps one reason for this has been the fact that, until recently, only a relatively small proportion of school students went on to attend university, and many of these came from the more "elite" selective grammar school or private school systems whose mission was, among other things, to prepare their more academically able students for university study.[iv] Nevertheless, against the background of an expansion of student numbers, a widening participation agenda, and in the light of a growing awareness of the fact that many students are experiencing difficulties with their writing (Davies *et al.*, 2006), this situation is beginning to change, though new developments across the sector do seem to be very patchy and "idiosyncratic" (Lea, 2006).

The University Language Centre currently runs two undergraduate course units within which writing development comprises a significant component. These are: Communication Skills, which is an assessed element of the Foundation Year Studies program (Faculty of Engineering and Physical Sciences), and Academic Literacy, which is an assessed element of the first year of the four-year M.Pharm program (School of Pharmacy, Faculty of Medical and Human Sciences). Both these courses support students in subject areas for which university preparation is unlikely to have included very much sophisticated or discursive writing.[v] The principal objective therefore is to develop students' written and spoken communication skills for general academic and also future professional purposes. As a result, the tasks and the content do not relate directly to their other current core subjects but have a more general focus. As well as covering the content in the form of lecture and class input, both courses adopt a task-based approach to developing writing, and, since they are targeted primarily at students who are native speakers (though not all), they focus much more on developing writing skills, and other academic skills, rather than on teaching language. The following areas, for example, are covered on both courses: planning, composing, drafting and editing; improving text organization; improving grammar and accuracy; writing clear and well-structured paragraphs; ensuring that texts "flow"; referring to sources, paraphrasing and summarizing; using academic conventions. In addition, the structural elements of reports, reviews and short essays are covered.

The Communication Skills course for Engineering and Physical Sciences requires students to work collaboratively on their writing tasks, specifically on a collaborative project in which groups of four or five students work together to produce a joint report (2,000 words) structured according to the Hoey (1983) functional taxonomy of background → problem → solution → evaluation. The students must write a report on an area, which they choose, and which is broadly relevant to their field of study. This collaborative dimension is a new element which we have successfully piloted following encouraging learning outcomes from other courses (see below) and which is underpinned by the theoretical principles[vi] of Vygotsky (1981) and the empirical literature on cooperative learning reported in Johnson and Johnson (1989, 2001). On this course, each student is responsible for researching and writing a particular section of the report, the subject of which is chosen by group consensus. Individuals receive formative feedback from the group tutor during the composing process at different times. In contrast to the functional/modelling approaches described in the general EAP classes for the international students, where the concern is with the language of the "target product," the emphasis on this course is on how to generate ideas, how to put them together, and on how to achieve a collaborative writing goal; in other words, writing is seen very much as a "generative and exploratory process" (Zamel, 1983: 165). In addition, and also in keeping with Vygotskyan perspectives on learning, an early version of the final written report is assessed by another group of students, who write a short evaluative report based on a given set of criteria. A strong argument for involving students in making judgements about assessment is that it helps them develop the ability to make judgements about their own work, which is not only an important academic skill, but it is a skill that students will need in their professional lives and beyond (Brown *et al.*, 1997). The literature suggests that this kind of peer assessment appears to be capable of yielding outcomes as least as good as teacher assessment, and sometimes better; furthermore, it can lead to an enhanced sense of ownership and personal responsibility and interest (Topping *et al.*, 2000).

The collaborative approach to writing has also been used very successfully on a number of undergraduate course units which have been devised for our large population of European exchange students who come to Manchester under the Erasmus student exchange scheme. Course units are available for these students in British Culture through Film, Manchester Life through Ethnographic research, and English for Academic Purposes and Creative Writing. As well as sharing a collaborative dimension, the first three courses are also enquiry-based; that is the students work collaboratively to research and report on an aspect of British film, culture or academic written practice. Thus, most of the assessed work on these award-bearing courses consists of collaborative reports and presentations. Although this kind of collaborative learning has proved to be an exciting and productive pedagogic method on all of these courses, it is not without its problems. The main challenge relates to assessment; it is just not easy to accurately gauge the relative inputs from all the group members and to reward those who have made the greatest contribution or who have produced the finest work. One partial solution that we have used is to ask one member of each group to act as "secretary" whose role it is to "log" meetings, attendance and relative inputs of all the group's members.

However, this is by no means a complete solution to the problem and we still find that it is necessary to incorporate an element of individual coursework and assessment.

Writing support for postgraduates: a subject-oriented online solution

Interestingly, in contrast to undergraduate provision, it is at the postgraduate level where writing development and support for students is beginning to be addressed in a systematic way in British universities. The recent government commissioned Roberts Review, *Set for Success* (2002), highlighted the increasing gaps in graduate training of key competencies relevant to students' future employability, and additional funds have been provided by the government to expand and enhance existing training and support provision and to develop new and innovative training schemes. Furthermore, recognition of the need for institutions to provide support and training for postgraduates is now enshrined in a number of important documents, including the Quality Assurance Agency's (QAA[vii]) *Code of Practice For Assurance of Academic Quality And Standards In Higher Education* (September 2004). Communication skills, including the ability to "write clearly and in a style appropriate to purpose" and "to construct coherent arguments and articulate ideas clearly" (*ibid.*, p. 35) are identified as one area which research students need support to develop.

This new drive to develop the written communication skills of research students has been devolved to the four Faculties at Manchester and the University Language Centre has been asked to respond in different ways. For one Faculty, we provide day-long workshops covering a range of writing topics which are typically attended by 20 students; for another, we mount lectures, each dealing with one main topic and attracting up to 100 students at a time. Running throughout the academic year, areas covered in these sessions may include combinations of the following:

- introduction to and discussion of the writing process, and a focus on the practices of experienced writers (e.g. Burnett, 1990);
- awareness of the conventions and characteristics of academic style;
- learning to write clearer and more readable texts, drawing on ideas from Turk and Kirkman (1992) and Williams (1990);
- introduction to the classic deductive paragraph,[viii] drawing on standard material found in undergraduate (Freshman) writing courses taught in US universities;

- awareness of the importance of maintaining a line of argument using cohesive devices (Halliday and Hasan, 1976);
- utilization of appropriate "given/new" information structuring to enhance textual flow (Halliday, 1976; Vande Kopple, 1991);
- reference to source texts, including referencing conventions of the Vancouver system and the Harvard system;
- exploration of key elements of common academic genres, and the typical academic phraseology associated with key textual "moves" (Swales, 1990; Dudley-Evans, 1988);
- techniques for paraphrasing and summarizing;
- common errors in writing and punctuation.

The problem with the lecture or workshop mode of delivery, however, is that not all students are able to attend at certain times, especially those research students who have laboratory commitments, and there is a limited amount that can be covered in the time available. Furthermore, because of these time limitations, opportunities for hands-on practice activities tend to be reduced. The challenge, therefore, has been how to develop and deliver an accessible program in academic writing for very busy postgraduates with fairly modest resources at our disposal. Some form of e-learning platform seemed to offer a solution.

Following a successful bid for postgraduate training funding, online writing programs for each of the Faculties have recently been developed. Delivered via a virtual learning platform, the online programs can be accessed at any time, and may be accessed from any point on the campus, even from within a research laboratory or a student residence. Access can be self-managed so that students can take responsibility for when and where they participate in the program. In addition, an e-learning program allows us to build in a needs analysis component so that students who already have a fairly well-developed level of academic literacy can be informed that they do not need to participate if they do not wish to; it also offers opportunities for students to test themselves at different stages of the work. Finally, the e-learning platform allows us to monitor the participation and progress of students in the program.

The funding obtained for this project allowed us to carry out a modest needs analysis exercise as a starting point for the new materials development. The exercise involved interviewing teachers and supervisors in the Faculties and examining samples of students' work. Only a small number of teaching staff were interviewed (n = 10) in each Faculty and these were identified as having a particular interest in the standard of writing of their postgraduate students using previously known contacts. A "snowballing" sampling technique was also employed, so that, at the end of each interview, the interviewee was asked to recommend other people who might have an interest in contributing to the project. Interviewees were asked to comment on the quality of post-graduate writing, identify particular areas of weakness, and to provide samples of their students' writing. The work that was obtained included copies of lab reports, transfer reports, and early drafts of dissertations. A review of published and online sources was also undertaken. Analysis of the interview data broadly shaped and informed the areas that we were planning to cover; it was the examination of the students' writing, however, which provided a basis for creating exercises designed to address specific problems. Other areas that are covered by the material are those already covered by the postgraduate lectures (see above).

The approach we have adopted in presenting the material to the students has been to begin with a clear, brief teaching point followed by exemplification of correct and incorrect forms. Long sections of explanatory text have been avoided. In addition, because many of our students are scientists, it was felt that few would understand complex grammatical terminology or explanations. This has meant that the explanatory texts, as far as possible, need to be couched in everyday terms and to purposely avoid metalinguistic terms. Each unit of work consists of a number of teaching points each accompanied by exemplifying material. Following the presentation stage of each unit, students then have an opportunity to work through a series of questions testing what they have learnt. All the examples of correct and incorrect forms, and the test questions, utilize content words related to the students' disciplines, so that they produce a very strong impression of authenticity and relevance for the students. The incorrect examples have been, wherever possible, taken from samples of the students' work. However, any examples taken have been simplified and transformed so that the source was rendered unidentifiable. An example of this approach can be seen in the two examples from Unit 1 on Punctuation/Common Errors (Appendix A). In other units, exemplifying texts have been modeled on content from a range of authentic published materials, such as articles in the *New Scientist*, accessible academic articles, and sections from undergraduate text books. Material from authentic research articles tended to be less useful because of the highly specialized nature of the content.

The test section requires the students to work through a series of multiple choice items in which they indicated the correct choice. This is useful as a quick way of assessing how well the students understand and learn the new material, but the multiple choice format does mean that the activity is largely one of recognition rather than production. In other words, although this is a way of checking that students could recognize correct and incorrect forms, the students are not actually required to produce text themselves. Simply being able to recognize correct forms from choices is no guarantee that students will reproduce them in their own writing. However, the advantages of the current system are that it can be completed quickly and large numbers of students can receive feedback on their performance immediately. If their first attempt is not satisfactory, then they are able to complete the unit of work a second time. Examples of two test items, following on from the teaching points mentioned above, are given in Appendix B. In other units, the choices can involve identifying in a multiple choice format: short passages which are acceptable in terms of style and/or readability, passages which "flow," correctly sequenced paragraphs, suitable paraphrases and summaries of other passages, sections of a dissertation in which typical phrase or word combinations are likely to be found, correct referencing/reporting conventions.

Evaluations have been very positive, with 100 per cent of students on a pilot study agreeing that "all postgraduates" should complete the program. In a post-trial focus group, one student commented: "*I would recommend it! Most doctors can't string two words together, that's why medical papers are so terrible to read. I wish I'd done this at the beginning of medical school.*" In a written evaluation response, another wrote: "*Personally, I've learnt more in these units than I have at my high school. I feel more confident writing.*" Perhaps more importantly, though, was the fact that students appreciated the versatility of this new form of provision: "*I think that it's good that it's on computer because it means you can do it whenever you've got time and you're not having to go somewhere, like a different building, sit down and do it!*"

The development of *Phrasebank*: a generic online resource for academic writers

The *Academic Phrasebank* (see Appendix C) is another online writing resource which the University Language Centre has recently developed. In contrast to the other resources, it has open-access and is available to all students. It is simply a collection of useful phrases for academic writers organized according to their communicative purposes. *Phrasebank* was originally designed for the University's international students and researchers. However, it has been greeted enthusiastically by many staff who also recommend it to their British students. Some members of staff at Manchester have even attested to its usefulness for their own writing, as have many academics in other countries (judging by their enthusiastic emails).

The idea for developing the resource stemmed from research I carried out into the writing experiences of a postgraduate Thai student at Manchester some years ago. The student had been recruited with low levels of written proficiency (cTOEFL 450) but still managed to complete an "excellent" PhD Dissertation in "record time." Intrigued when I heard about this, I carried out a series of interviews with the student and her supervisors to try to learn more. Pim (not her real name) explained that one of the study strategies she used was identifying useful phrases in her readings. When she read her academic papers she always highlighted or underlined English phrases which she felt she would be able to "recycle" in her own writing. She explained she was not concerned with the content when she did this, but only the usefulness and wider applicability of the phrases she found. These insights began to make sense when I read some of the work by Sinclair (1991) who, based on large-scale studies of language using very large electronic corpora, suggested that while grammar enables combinatorial possibilities, in reality much of that which is produced in language consists of semi-preconstructed phrases. He called this the principle of idiom:

> A language user has available to him or her a large number of semi-pre-reconstructed phrases that constitute single choices, even though they might appear to the analyzable into segments. (Sinclair, 1991: 110)

Sinclair's observations have been supported by Nattinger and DeCarrico (1992) and Cowie and Howarth (1996) who argued that a notable feature of the writing of academic discourse communities is the high frequency of conventional multi-word items. There is now a growing acceptance within the field of Applied Linguistics that appropriate and effective academic performance involves knowledge of a considerable stock of conventional collocations and other word combinations. Research has also shown that there is a much greater incidence of nonstandard phraseology in non-native-speaker writing, reflecting a general lack of awareness of preferred phraseological structures (Howarth, 1998). Even if they have a well-developed knowledge of English grammar and vocabulary, non-native users of English often still have a restricted repertoire of ritualized language. There are few textbooks for non-native students that incorporate sections on this very important area, and those which do tend to include a very limited range of idealized constructions (e.g. Jordan, 1980).

Linguists have classified phrase combinations in language in many different ways. For the construction of *Phrasebank*, Nattinger and DeCarrico's term "lexical phrase" was found to be useful. These are defined as commonly combined words, or collocations, which serve a pragmatic function in the discourse.

Lexical phrases can range from short fixed phrases, such as: *for the most part*, to sentence builders that provide a framework for the whole sentence and allow for the possibility of variation, such as: *one of the most important* _____ *in the recent literature is* _____ (Nattinger and DeCarrico, 1992: 165). Phrases of the latter category were felt to be particularly relevant to the development of the *Phrasebank*. Using this definition, typical phrase structures were "harvested" from an electronic corpus of 100 dissertations[ix] from a broad range of humanities, social science, life science, and physical science disciplines. Once identified, the phrases were "sifted" from their particularized subject-specific content. In other words, specialized content words were either removed or substituted for more generic items. In addition, where appropriate, the number of words was reduced for simplification. Not all content words were removed, however, since it was felt that a certain number of content items were necessary for students to see how the phrase structures operated in conjunction with other lexical items.

In order to assist the users to understand the different functions of the phrases, the content has been organized under headings reflecting the typical rhetorical moves in academic writing (see Appendix C). A move may be broadly defined as a recognizable section of text that has a particular rhetorical purpose. The identification of these moves has drawn upon earlier analyses such as those of Dudley-Evans (1986) and Swales (1990). The phrases are therefore presented under pragmatic headings that make their function within text apparent to novice writers. Examples of some of these are: (from the section on Discussions) Statement of Findings, Comparison of Findings with Previous Research, and Explaining the Findings. These headings are in turn organized into webpages that relate to the principal macro-organizational sections of academic writing, e.g. Writing Introductions; Referring to the Literature, and Discussing the Findings. Since initial identification of the ritualized language was carried out intuitively by only one native speaker writer, it was considered necessary to validate the webpages by seeking corroboration from expert writers. A further stage in the construction of the *Phrasebank*, therefore, has been to ask for comments and feedback regarding the suitability/typicality of the phrases from experienced academic writers representing a broad range of disciplines taught in the University. Feedback was sought from senior academics in the following subjects: Geography, Sociology, Psychology, Bioscience, Electrical Engineering, and Pharmacy. Each member of staff was asked to comment on and validate at least two of the pages.

The *Academic Phrasebank* is a simple and successful resource. The main page currently receives around 85,000 "hits" from over 72 countries per month.

It has a number of potentially serious limitations, however. Its simple and generic nature is one of its strengths, but it is also a weakness. Not all the phrases are suitable for all of subjects—indeed certain subjects are not well represented—and even within one subject area many of them have fairly finely tuned uses. Decisions about the appropriateness and usefulness of particular phrases are left up to the users and unless they can bring a degree of sensitivity of language use to the resource, there is a chance that inappropriate phrases will be selected. This is less of a problem with native speakers, who seem to have the necessary degree of familiarity and sensitivity, than it is with non-native speakers who often lack this. Other limitations are that the resource is not comprehensive in terms of all the possible functional moves that academic writers might wish to make, and that there may be a danger of some students becoming over-dependent on the resource.

Conclusion

The purpose of writing this chapter has not been to argue the case for a "best method" in the teaching and supporting of writing; it has been to show how different needs of students for writing instruction in higher education can best be addressed, indeed may need to be, in a variety of ways, and that writing programs at universities may be quite diverse. The method employed will ultimately depend on the resources and time available, and the needs and requirements of the students. There was no design blueprint for the current range of provision. Rather, the system has evolved, and continues to evolve as needs are identified and as new funding opportunities are made available.

At the beginning of the chapter, I mentioned that across the range of disciplines taught at Manchester, other initiatives to respond to students' writing needs do exist, or have existed at various times, within certain subject areas, and usually incorporated as part of first year Study Skills course units. Such formalized undergraduate support exists, for example, in Economics, English Language, and Nursing. Writing development only seems to represent a relatively minor part of these programs which may also cover areas such as time management, using the library, avoiding plagiarism, reading and note-taking, information technology, critical thinking, seminar technique, working in teams, and preparing for exams. On one of these courses (Law), however, the use of early formative skills essays for which large numbers of students receive coded feedback has won internal recognition in the form of a Teaching Excellence Award. A systematic survey of these kinds of responses to the study skills needs of new undergraduates has not been carried out in the new

University, and such a project is due to be undertaken shortly. The fact that Manchester is such a large institution, with four quite separate Faculties, and, within these many prestigious and well-established Schools, most with a strong sense of autonomy, partly explains the lack of a centralized and uniform approach in this area. However, there is a growing recognition of the importance and value of such courses across the institution, and this is encouraging.

In the medium and longer term, work will continue to involve identifying specific groups in need of writing support particularly at undergraduate level, and mounting level one (first year) "adjunct" courses in writing for these. Agreement for mounting such courses is typically easier where there are a high proportion of international students on the program because i) the need for writing support is more obvious and, ii) the additional income generated by large numbers of international students can more than offset the costs of mounting such courses. Many Schools also see enhanced forms of student support as being something that is attractive and advantageous in the international student marketplace, and therefore worth "investing in." However, much also depends on the importance individual members of staff attach to the need for support, and how much interest they have in this. As was stated earlier, the success of "adjunct" courses is largely contingent on the enthusiasm of one or two members of staff working within the subject area. Another area in need of development is to more fully exploit virtual learning environments to supplement and enhance existing undergraduate writing and study skills courses, but also to provide stand-alone programs for the benefit of any undergraduate student who is not able to attend face-to-face courses. Already, the Faculty of Life Sciences is working on a modified and simpler version of the postgraduate online materials for use with undergraduates.

A final, but no less important, area of future activity is in staff development, and for which teachers in the University Language Centre have recently developed two types of courses. One of these is a program of writing workshops, which includes some sessions for all members of staff, and also others specifically for academics who wish to write research articles. The former explores ways of improving clarity and flow in writing, while the latter brings some of the insights derived from genre analysis (see earlier references to Swales and Dudley-Evans) to academic articles. The second type of course is designed to sensitize academic staff to the difficulties experienced by international students in adapting to a new academic culture and in studying in a foreign language. The course also explores teaching techniques and strategies which will help to ensure that international students coming to Manchester obtain maximum possible benefit from their experience. One of the areas covered, for example, emphasizes the need for teachers to give explicit and unambiguous guidance to students on the writing tasks they are expected to complete, and also to provide clear, useful and unambiguous feedback on students' written assignments. To date, both initiatives have been received very favourably, and of course, whilst raising staff awareness in all of these areas will benefit international students, it will undoubtedly be of potential benefit to the wider student population as well.

Notes

i   The University of Manchester is divided into four Faculties, and each Faculty is divided into a number of Schools.

ii   http://baleap.org.uk/

iii   http://kn.open.ac.uk/public/index.cfm?wpid=4349

iv   In the 1960s, for example, only around 5% of under 21s attended university compared with around 34% in 2000 (DES, 2003).

v   In British high schools, in Years 11 and 12 it is not unusual for some students to do very little sophisticated writing, if , for example, they study only Maths, Physics and Chemistry at Advanced level.

vi   In Vygotsky's "social constructivist" theory, the formation of individuals and their knowledge occurs through participation in "activity systems" with others. One of the implications of this is that learning should take place as a joint activity in which individuals work toward a set of shared goals, the achievement of which depends upon collaboration.

vii   The Quality Assurance Agency (QAA) is the body responsible for maintaining standards and quality in British higher education. Quality is maintained through peer review processes where teams of academics conduct institutional audits.

viii   Surprisingly, this is an unknown concept for many British students, even at postgraduate level. This reflects that fact that teaching writing is not covered systematically, if at all, in undergraduate studies.

ix   The dissertations were obtained from British postgraduates who had recently completed their studies at Manchester, and consisted of work at Masters and at PhD level. All contributors were made aware of the aims of the project and were paid a small amount for their dissertations.

References

Brown, G., Bull, J. and Pendlebury, M. (1997), *Assessing Student Learning in Higher Education* (London: Routledge).

Burnett, R. E. (1990), *Technical Communication* (second edition) (Belmont CA: Wadsworth).

Cowie, A. P. and Howarth, P. (1996), "Phraseological competence and written proficiency," in G. Blue and R. Mitchell (eds), *Language and Education* (Clevedon: Multilingual Matters).

Davies, S., Swinburne, D. and Williams, G. (eds) (2006), *Writing Matters: The Royal Literary Fund Report on Student Writing in Higher Education* (London: Royal Literary Fund). Available online at: http://rlf.org.uk/fellowshipscheme/documents/RLFwritingmatters_000.pdf (last accessed 11 January 2007).

Department for Education and Skills (DES) (2003), *The Future of Higher Education* (London: HMSO).

Dudley-Evans, T. (1994), "Genre Analysis, An Approach to Text in ESP," in M. Coulthard (ed.), *Advances in Written Text Analysis* (pp. 219–228) (London, Routledge).

Dudley-Evans, A. (1986), "Genre analysis: an investigation of the introductions and discourse sections of MSc dissertations," in M. Coulthard (ed.), *Talking about Text* (pp. 128–145) (Birmingham: English Language Research, Birmingham University).

Halliday, M. (1976), "Theme and Information in the English Clause," in G. Kress (ed.), *System and Function in Language* (pp. 174–188) (Oxford: Oxford University Press).

Halliday, M. and Hasan,R. (1976), *Cohesion in English* (London: Longman).

Hoey, M. (1983), *On the Surface of Discourse* (London: George Allen & Unwin).

Hopkins, A. and Dudley-Evans, T. (1988), "A genre-based investigation of the discussion sections in articles and dissertations," *English for Specific Purposes*, 7, 113–121.

Howarth, P. (1998), "Phraseology and Second Language Proficiency," *Applied Linguistics*, 19(1).

Hyland, K. (2003), *Second Language Writing* (Cambridge: Cambridge University Press).

Johnson, D. W. and Johnson, R. T. (1989), *Cooperation and Competition: Theory and Research* (Edina, MN: Interaction Book Company).

Johnson, D. W. and Johnson, R. T. (2001), *An Overview of Co-operative Learning*. Available online at: http://co-operation.org/pages/overviewpaper.html (last accessed 11 January 2007).

Jordan, R. (1980), *Academic Writing Course* (London: Collins).

Kirkman, J. (1992), *Good Style; Writing for Science and Technology* (London: E & FN Spon).

Lea, M. (2006), "Writing in today's university," *Educational Developments*, SEDA, 7(4).

Nattinger, J. R. and DeCarrico, J. S. (1992), *Lexical Phrases and Language Teaching* (Oxford: Oxford University Press).

Quality Assurance Agency (2004), *Code of Practice for the Assurance of Academic Quality and Standards in Higher Education*. Available online at: http://qaa.ac.uk/academicinfrastructure/codeOfPractice/section1/default.asp (last accessed 11 January 2007).

Roberts, G. (2002), *SET for Success: The Supply of People with Science, Technology, Engineering and Mathematical Skills* (London: HM Treasury).

Sinclair, J. (1991), *Corpus, Concordance, Collocation* (Oxford: Oxford University Press).

Snow, M. A. and Brinton, D. M. (1988), "Content-based language instruction: Investigating the effectiveness of the adjunct model," *TESOL Quarterly*, 22(4), 553–574.

Swales, J. (1981), "Aspects of Article Introductions. Aston Monographs No.1," University of Aston, Language Studies Unit.

Swales, J. (1990), *Genre Analysis: English in Academic and Research Settings* (Cambridge: Cambridge University Press).

Topping, K., Smith, E., Swanson, I. and Elliot, A. (2000), "Formative peer assessment of academic writing between postgraduate students," *Assessment & Evaluation in Higher Education*, 25(2), 149–169.

Turk, C. and Kirkman, J. (1989), *Effective Writing: Improving Scientific, Technical and Business Communication* (London: E & FN Spon).

Vande Kopple, W. J. (1991), "Themes, thematic progressions, and some implications for understanding discourse," *Written Communication*, 8 (July): 311–347.

Vygotsky, L. S. (1981), "The genesis of higher mental functions," in J. V. Wertsch (ed.), *The Concept of Activity in Soviet Psychology* (Armonk, NY: Sharpe).

Williams, J. M. (1990), *Style: Toward Clarity and Grace* (Chicago: University of Chicago Press).

Zamel, V. (1983), "The composing processes of advanced ESL students: six case-studies," *TESOL Quarterly*, 17, 165–189.

Appendix A (from: Faculty of Life Sciences, Unit 1)

Common problems

- "This", "these" or "therefore" often indicates a new sentence but students often incorrectly use a comma.

Example:

–Some argue that evolution is driven by mutations, this theory is known as the neutral mutation hypothesis. *Incorrect*

–Some argue that evolution is driven by mutations. This theory is known as the neutral mutation hypothesis. *Correct*

- "whereas" and "while" are used with commas to separate two clauses within one sentence. It is incorrect to use a full stop.

Example

–Fraternal twins result from two ova, fertilised by two separate sperm. Whereas identical twins result from the separation of a single fertilised ovum. *Incorrect*

–Fraternal twins result from two ova that are fertilised by two separate sperm, whereas identical twins result from the separation of a single fertilised ovum. *Correct*

Appendix B (from: Faculty of Life Sciences, Unit 1)

Test: Which of the following is correct?

5)

a) The function of the ATPase enzyme is affected when it is reconstituted into the hydrophobic phospholipid environment. Therefore, this coupled enzyme assay can be used to determine whether reconstitution has taken place.

Correct, well done! If you use the word "Therefore" to start a new idea you must use a full stop not a comma.

b) The function of the ATPase enzyme is affected when it is reconstituted into the hydrophobic phospholipid environment, therefore, this coupled enzyme assay can be used to determine whether reconstitution has taken place.

Incorrect. If you use the word "Therefore" to start a new idea you must use a full stop not a comma.

8)

a) Gymnosperms have long narrow cells called tracheids, which transport water and provide structural support. Whereas angiosperms have two types of xylem cells, long narrow fibres for support and thin-walled vessels for water transport.

Incorrect. Read the last sentence which begins "whereas". It does not make sense by itself. This information is being contrasted with the first piece of information. If you use "whereas" to do this you must use a comma not a full stop.

b) Gymnosperms have long narrow cells called tracheids, which transport water and provide structural support, whereas angiosperms have two types of xylem cells, long narrow fibres for support and thin-walled vessels for water transport.

Correct, well done! "Whereas" is used to separate 2 clauses within a single sentence. Use a comma in long sentences.

Appendix C Excerpts from *Academic Phrasebank*

From *Writing Introductions*: Highlighting a knowledge gap in the field of study

So far, however, there has been little discussion about …
However, far too little attention has been paid to …
Most studies in X have only been carried out in a small number of areas.
The research to date has tended to focus on X rather than Y.
In addition, no research has been found that surveyed …
So far this method has only been applied to …
However, there have been no controlled studies which compare differences in …
However, few writers have been able to draw on any structured research into …
This indicates a need to understand the various perceptions of X that exist among …

From *Being Critical*: Identifying a study's weakness

the main weakness of the study is the failure to address …
the author overlooks the fact that X contributes to Y.
what Smith fails to do is to draw a distinction between …
the study fails to consider the differing categories of X that …
(However,) the research does not take into account pre-existing Xs such as …
the author offers no explanation for the distinction between X and Y.
Smith makes no attempt to differentiate between various different types of X.
Smith limited his study to only two levels of …
Smith fails to fully acknowledge the significance of …

From *Describing the Method*: Indicating sequence

Prior to commencing the study, ethical clearance was sought from …
After collection, the samples were shipped back to X in …
Once the exposures were completed, the Xs were labelled and placed in …
Once the positions *had been decided upon*, the Xs were removed from each …
On completion of X, the process of model specification and … *was carried out.*

Following this, the samples were recovered and stored overnight at …
The results were corrected for X and *then* averaged *before being* converted to …
The analysis *was* checked when initially performed and *then* checked again at the end of …
Finally, questions were asked as to the role of …

From *Discussing the Findings*: Giving explanations

A possible explanation for this might be that …
Another possible explanation for this is that …
This result may be explained by the fact that … / by a number of different factors.
It is difficult to explain this result, but it might be related to …
It seems possible that these results are due to …
The reason for this is not clear but it may have something to do with …
It may be that these students benefitted from …
The observed increase in X could be attributed to …
The observed correlation between X and Y might be explained in this way.

From *Writing Conclusions*: Recommendations for further work (research)

Further work needs to be done to establish whether …
It is recommended that further research be undertaken in the following areas:
Further experimental investigations are needed to estimate …
What is now needed is a cross-national study involving …
More broadly, research is also needed to determine …
It is suggested that the association of these factors is investigated in future studies.
Further research might explore …
Further investigation and experimentation into X is strongly recommended.
It would be interesting to assess the effects of …

Emergent Technologies and Academic Writing: Paying Attention to Rhetoric and Design

Shawn T. Casey and Cynthia L. Selfe

Academic writing represents a key focus of instruction in a variety of disciplines. Papers, lab reports, abstracts, written presentations, email, and Web content rely heavily on written discourse. Yet the meaning and methods of "teaching writing," even within composition studies, are hardly settled. The extended reach and rapid expansion of digital networks across conventional cultural, linguistic, and geopolitical borders, for example, has encouraged many teachers of English to expand their understanding of composing and to engage students in exploring multiple modalities of communicating meaning—using not only alphabetic writing as a semiotic channel, but also experimenting with moving and still images, sound, and animation, and combinations of these (Cope and Kalantzis, 2000a; Selfe and Hawisher, 2004; Wysocki *et al.*, 2004).

This chapter, while recognizing the importance of such work, suggests that the sweeping changes wrought by the global spread of electronic communication and emergent media, far from distracting our attention from writing, can be harnessed to help us explore and attend to the rhetorical and design-based materiality of the composing technologies, media, and modalities that we already use for academic communications[i]—the alphabet, books, and the printed word. The arrival of new composing technologies in the academic writing classroom (e.g. computers, networks, digital composing environments) offers teachers of academic writing the opportunity to engage in critical ways commonsense theories of disciplinary communication.

We build on a series of key assumptions here. Whether or not individual English studies teachers decide to adopt digital media in their own academic writing classrooms, academic discourses will continue to change in response to communicative practices emerging and flourishing outside the university (Brandt, 1995). Responding to such literacy practices and values, composition instruction within the academy, too, will change, moving beyond an adherence to communicative forms focused almost solely on alphabetic print and toward an increasingly broad range of media and genres that involve multiple modalities of expression (e.g. words, still and moving images, animation, sound). Indeed, evidence of such changes already exists (Yancey, 2004; Selfe and Hawisher, 2005). In response to these changes, our composition instruction, too, should be willing to change, to expand in ways that make it adequate to the task of tackling diverse forms of communication—critically and analytically—within the academy.

One way to address this set of challenges is to develop an adaptable model of analysis that can account for both the *rhetorical* and the *material design* considerations of composing tasks. Helping students to analyze the rhetorical considerations involved in communicative tasks (audience, purpose, information, and form), is well established as an approach to composing assignments. Teachers are less likely, however, to help students pay close attention to the *design considerations* of composing tasks (the technology, media, and modalities used to create messages; the material conditions under which such work is done; the historical and cultural situatedness of communication work; the creation, delivery, and circulation of communications). By treating a range of design considerations as objects of analysis in a piece of communication—and as decisions that authors need to keep in mind—both teachers and students are reminded of the material nature of *all* media and modalities: printed words, digital video and audio, and multimodal compositions.

Attending to the design dimensions of discourse, as well as to related rhetorical considerations, we believe, makes visible the values and assumptions that accompany choices of communicative technologies, media, and modalities. This attention also highlights the conceptual models we have constructed and adopted for teaching composing as a mindful set of processes. Importantly, we think, the benefits of this approach apply especially to writing instruction and are, perhaps, most valuable in this regard for contemporary English composition teachers. In the new secular universities that emerged in the US around the mid-nineteenth century and in their contemporary successors (Russell, 2002), writing assumed a role as the primary tool of communication for scholarship. From its roots in the modern secular university, writing has emerged as the primary way to record academic knowledge, and, in many instances, writing has also served as the primary tool of analysis and description that created modern academic knowledge.[ii]

Because writing has become so pervasive, such a fundamental technology underlying so many of our practices both in and out of the academy, it has become naturalized, rendered invisible or unconscious. Few composition teachers or students, for example, pause to pay attention to the choice of the alphabet as an effective technology for communication, or to print as a medium for sharing our thinking, or to the privileged position of print in the academy. These factors are taken for granted as common sense. As a result of the naturalization that surrounds writing within the academy, elements of how written discourse works, for whom, and when and where, often go unanalyzed.

Contributing to this situation is the related naturalization of conventional written genres or forms that have come to characterize the majority of assignments in academic disciplines. The standard analytic essay, for example, is a genre of written communication often assigned by habit, a routinized form marked by a conventionally derived set of rhetorical moves[iii] accepted by many teachers of English, for instance, as *the* way of communicating formal knowledge. And while, given the long history of this genre, such a situation is not surprising, it can, nevertheless, have unintended problematic consequences.

English teachers' habitual deployment of the essay as a routine genre for assignments, for instance, can serve to mask for students the important decisions and choices embodied in selecting a specific form for particular rhetorical contexts. When written essays are routinely assigned as the form for *all* assignments, for example, students may forget that the genre of the essay was developed by historical actors such as Montaigne in response to a historically situated, culturally specific set of circumstances in the eighteenth century and that these writers were making decisions about their communicative activities based on their own richly contextualized understanding of rhetorical purpose and audience, which they situated within a larger political, social, and ideological ecology.

Among the constellation of decisions made invisible in such situations were these authors' decisions to write their thoughts with a pen on paper rather delivering them as oral addresses and their decision to circulate some of these works in tracts, books, or newspapers rather than to keep them private in a personal journal. Also masked are the technological contexts of these authors' decision making: among them, the fact that mass-produced cameras had not been invented and that images were expensive to include in printed works; the fact that new technologies of paper manufacturing were emerging and making printed tracts and books less expensive and more accessible for a larger readership; and the fact that emerging forms of knowledge dissemination—newspapers and mass printing, for instance—were changing the ways in which people circulated and accumulated information.

For contemporary teachers of composition and for students in their class, the naturalization of writing and written genres has meant that we often assign writing and forms like the analytic essay as routinized or under-examined parts of our classroom assignments. An unfortunate, if unintended, consequence of this situation, is that we might inadvertently foreclose on students' opportunities to think actively and critically about the complex rhetorical decisions that *they* must make as they undertake more contemporary communicative tasks—tasks situated in very different political, cultural, social, contexts than those of the eighteenth or nineteenth centuries. Contemporary students, clearly, have different cultural and social formations shaping their lives; they must take into account different audiences and expectations; different genres are contending for their communicative attention; and new and different technologies are available for them to use in creating, exchanging, and circulating information.

With these realizations and others in mind, composition scholars, especially those influenced by digital media studies, have begun to question the naturalized status of writing and historical written forms in recent years. Changing technologies (e.g. computer networks and environments, digital video and audio), related questions about new and emerging genres (e.g. digital video essays, photographic essays, audio blogs), observations of new kinds of community-based literacy (e.g. wikis and communal blogs), and a recognition of the power associated with certain forms of discourse (e.g. podcasts and new media essays), have led these scholars to re-examine conventional forms of writing in the academy. Within this context, these scholars are asking not only *how* the forms and the nature of writing is changing within the changing context of the academy—and outside of it—but also *why* writing itself is *the* privileged form of academic communication. Within this intellectual context, scholars and teachers have begun to discover how the differences between writing and emerging modes of communication, written forms and new digital forms of communication, can help us better understand what it is we are teaching and why.

Throughout this chapter, then, our goal is to render increasingly visible many of the decisions writers make as they work at composing and communicating meaning in academic composition classes. Our goal is to provide a versatile model that can help teachers and students analyze both the rhetorical and the design considerations of a communication task—and, thus, to uncover the constructedness or enmeshment of what may at first appear transparent, or commonsense, attempts to communicate. We believe the approach we offer is heuristic in nature, that students can use it to *plan* their work with a variety of compositional modes and media, but also that it can be used reflectively and evaluatively, to work through cycles of textual drafting and revision. We hope such work will help students develop increasing critical awareness of communicative approaches, to notice the differences between conventional academic forms and emerging forms of communication and representation, both within and outside the academy. Importantly, we operate from an understanding that all texts draw on multiple modalities of expression (alphabetic, visual, aural) to make meaning and to achieve their intended purposes; that no single modality—however privileged—is wholly adequate to the task of communicating meaning by itself; and that different media and modalities of communication have "differential effects for learning" (Kress and Jewitt: 1).

In the end, we do not want to lose sight of written communication and its importance in many contemporary academic disciplines. Instead, we want to foreground writing, and examine the significance of its dominance in critical ways. Specifically, we want to challenge the "transparency" of writing as a modality, to denaturalize it, and to make it visible. In doing this work, we want students to be able to compare alphabetic writing, books, and print to other modalities of expression (visual, aural, animation) and media (screen, Web, video, radio), which, absent such close and analytical comparisons, can seem remarkable, unusual and foreign to some teachers of English.

Background: Attending to the practices of composing

Both teachers of conventional alphabetic composition and those who advocate teaching new digital and multimodal forms of composing face two common problems: how best to help students to discern "effective" communication strategies and, then, how best to help deploy these strategies within specific rhetorical contexts. These challenges are complicated by the fact that people are communicating via different media (including print, as well as screens, networks, radio), using different genres (podcasts, email, text messages), and employing different modalities (alphabetic writing, as well as still and moving images, sound, music, and animation). As educators, we want to equip students with the skills to use all the communicative technologies available in their fields in effective ways, and to provide them a critical awareness of both the affordances of various technologies, media, and modalities—their capabilities—*and* their weaknesses.

In describing this situation, scholars like Gunther Kress, Bill Cope, and Mary Kalantzis remind us that the most successful authors—authors critically aware of communicative tasks, their complexity, and their importance— engage a range of "available designs," deploying specific configurations of material elements as semiotic tools for creating and transforming meanings for specific purposes, even when using designs inherited from others and the past (New London Group: 20). Recognizing who constructs these available designs, and how they limit or enable certain kinds of meaning making, is an important part of gaining the agency to transform and redeploy those designs (Cope & Kalantzis: 203). These scholars, and others, have also pointed out that, as communicative designs are constructed within and for specific media and solidified into genres that use distinctive modalities, they are changed by individuals. Thus, new genres, modes and media are always emerging and contributing to the changing semiotic effect of messages (Kress, 2000: 184).

Such a theoretical context is useful for understanding not only new digital composing media and modalities, but also for re-examining alphabetic writing and print texts from a different analytic and rhetorical perspective. Writing, for instance, may appear to consist simply of alphabetic representations, but such texts also rely on visual elements (layout, page design, font size and type) and tactile elements (paper weight and texture, the size, weight, and material construction of a book) as well. Written texts can also be influenced by aural modalities, as when oral poetry is rendered in visual ways or when dramatic scripts are printed. As Kress notes, all communication is multimodal, even when it appears to consist of only one element.

When we pay attention to the challenges of composing in this way, we can see that the historical and contemporary privileging of writing as the primary representational mode in academic settings may also have served to limit students' sense of available design resources. Writing may have contributed to our tendency to relegate other technologies for making meaning—for example, video or audio—to a suspect status while obscuring the history and materiality of its own contested engagement with other modes of expression, such as speech, for example[iv]. Pausing to consider these factors, to explore the material, rhetorical, historical, and ideological context of alphabetic writing and print as design resources, might help both teachers and students of composition to understand the important distinction between mono and multimodal communication models. We might also come to understand the dangers, as Patricia Dunn (2001) has noted, of valuing writing as "not simply *one* way of knowing," but, as "*the* way" (p. 15).

It is this kind of close look, as Gunther Kress has noted, that helps to reveal "Our present conception of language ... as an artefact of theory and commonsense," and that prompts us to "rethink 'language' as a multimodal phenomenon" (2000: 184). Such analyses, clearly, are needed for writing just as they are needed for emerging digital modalities, perhaps more so because writing has assumed such a position of ideological privilege within the academy. In a three-year study of "non-traditional" student writers, for instance, Theresa M. Lillis found that "student academic texts are expected to be constructed in and through conventions which are often invisible to both tutors and students" (2001: 75).

Our point here is that writing as a composing modality and print as a medium of communication have become transparent features of academic communication—features understood, according to accepted commonsense, as the best way to communicate serious intellectual matters. But operating according to received common sense may not yield the most effective teaching and learning in composition classes. Failing to attend to a range of communicative modalities—including writing—to their constructedness, their conventions, their conceptual frameworks, the investments and power relations inherent in their material history, we may obscure important elements of what constitutes academic discourse.

As Kress, Lillis, and other composition and literacy researchers (Selfe, 2007; Williams, 2001; Wysocki and Johnson-Eilola, 1999) have suggested, the naturalization of conventions in print-based, alphabetic discourse—the hallmark of academic writing—takes place at many levels. Given this tendency toward naturalization, it is difficult for composition teachers and students to pay appropriate attention to alphabetic writing as one composing technology among many, and, thus, to analyze its affordances, or its weaknesses, for communicating information effectively. It is not so, difficult, however, for us to see such elements in less transparent composing media and modalities. Digital composing technologies (personal computers and PDAs), media (screens and networks), modalities (digital video and audio, animation), and genres (podcasts, websites, blogs), for example, have the attention of students, teachers, and administrators and are new enough as composing environments to help make familiar decisions about composing— both rhetorical decisions and design decisions—strange and, thus, evident. We exploit this characteristic of new communication technologies, in this chapter is to offer an approach to rhetorical and material design analysis that can help teachers and students pay attention to a wide range of communication technologies, both those that have become naturalized in the academy, like writing, and those that command our attention because of the challenges they pose to the business-as-usual model of teaching in the academy.

How multimodal composing can help us pay more attention to writing

In the very early days of the World Wide Web, Jay David Bolter noted that "our culture, in the late age of print seems inclined to accept the materiality of writing not in spite of, but because of our increasing use of electronic networked communications" (2001, p. 202, first published in 1992). The moment of transition from "the late age of print," as Bolter's work suggests, may allow us not only to engage writing as *one of many* technologies, but also to recognize it as one among many contemporary keys to the expression of disciplinary knowledge. Acknowledging the materiality of writing means no longer accepting the medium of alphabetic expression as a simple reflection of thought. And by extension, it means exploring the material relations that have contributed to the model of writing as a medium that allows students and scholars to reflect and express thought. Within this context, for instance, scholars are recognizing how the medium of print and the modality of writing contributes to the formation of disciplinary knowledge through a constellation of journals, papers, books, and reviews that comment on and, in an expanding intertextual relations, help re-inscribe the importance of written scholarship that serves as the basis for the contemporary decisions about tenure and promotion in the academy.

At the same time, however, we need to attend to how digital media themselves are subject to a similar kind of naturalization, related in kind if not specifics, to that which writing has undergone. As Anne Wysocki points out, "There is little or nothing to help composers and readers think about how the defense- and commercial-tied history of computers has shaped the logic of computer architecture and hence the logic of much computer software" (2004: 6). The history of computing and computer software is itself only one piece of a puzzle that includes complex material histories of visual, auditory, gestural, and linguistic modalities. In both situations—with both alphabetic print texts *and* with digital texts that use visual or aural modalities—students and teachers need strategies for exploring and analyzing the naturalized aspects of everyday communicative practices. This information is essential in turning the less visible assumptions and practices embedded in composing technologies to the purposes of effective and informed communication. From this perspective, the task of teaching academic writing or English composition becomes not an effort to cover every possible technological medium, or modality, but, rather, a matter of helping students learn to pay attention to, investigate, and engage the technologies they choose to use in specific material and rhetorical contexts.

According to Kress, writing, and our habitual approach to teaching and theorizing about writing, inhibits our ability to view the construction of meaning as a complex, ideologically informed, "reinforcing mesh of meaning" (2000: 189). Joan Turner, too, has identified related masking effects associated with the privileging of written discourse. Turner, recalling Street's "autonomous model of literacy," describes not only how our habitual approach to teaching writing obscures the social contexts in which writing takes place, but also "assumes that the acquisition of [written] literacy enhances cognitive abilities, facilitating reasoning and abstract thought more generally" (1999: 152). For Turner this represents a significant problem for the teaching of writing. She notes that "While the notion of academic literacy focuses on the workings of language, the taken-for-grantedness of rationality acts as a denial of [the workings of language]" (1999: 152). We assume that rational discourse leads to a certain style of clarity in language, while it is in fact that model of clarity that allows for a discourse to become rational. As a parallel example from digital media, we might assume that rational expression and the clear organization of content within a website might lead authors to develop an elegant set of site-specific navigational tools, while, in contrast, the selection and deployment of different kinds of navigational buttons might, itself, help authors organize and express Web content more clearly and rationally.

Teachers' and students' inability to view alphabetic writing as a technology, and print as a medium, enmeshed in existing and historical systems serves to reinscribe a common sense understanding of writing. It also discourages the critical exploration of other forms, or designs, of academic communication, as well as attempts to interrogate the investments of power, influence, and intention that accompany these other designs and that determine rhetorical persuasiveness in specific contexts. John Trimbur, Joan Turner, and Gary Olson (1990, 1999, and 2002, respectively), for instance, have pointed out how teachers' efforts to make academic discourse transparent, may mask, for students, a clear picture of how specific communication forms act as constructed social practices, and ultimately obscure the shaping values of a discipline. Instead of clarifying the rules for production within a certain media, for instance, teachers and students need to investigate how those rules have become operational within a given set of circumstances. While this level of critical inquiry may not always be possible in the academic writing classroom, the introduction of new media should contribute to, not distract from, the primary goal of helping students apprehend how communications technology are always historically bound, and open to change.

Adopting a multimodal approach to composing—as Cope, Kalantzis, Kress, Selfe, and many others suggest—can help call into question our disciplinary investment in writing as the sole intellectual mode of thinking and expression within the academy. This does not mean replacing writing with newer, better, alternative sets of approved technologies. Instead, emergent composing technologies, modalities, and genres can be used by teachers to demonstrate that meaning can take many forms, and that sophisticated composers must learn to acknowledge and explore the critical differences between various media, modalities, and genres—including differences based on access, privilege, power, and disciplinarity. Put more simply, the strangeness of new digital media and multimodal composing can help teachers and students pay attention—to understand that none of our communications technologies, including writing, are innocent of the effects of power, isolated from the systems within which they are situated, or free of the ideological values that shape and are shaped by them.

This is not to suggest that new digital technologies, media, or genres are immune to naturalization; they, too need to be carefully examined to show how authors use specific communications strategies to "make things happen" (Wysocki et al., 2004: 5). Indeed, the continuing trend to incorporate new digital media in composition classrooms, has been spurred by the recognition that instructing students in the social practice of communication inevitably involves a study of how multiple dimensions of meaning making, including the sensory, technological, and rhetorical, are drawn into semiosis—both in emergent and more conventional forms of composing. Yet in our academic discourse and academic writing classrooms we continue to ignore certain elements of textual production and circulation, concentrating instead on the alphabetic text as the sole location for the production and analysis of disciplinary discourse. Similarly, we often ignore how webpages incorporate images, television newscasts deploy tickers, and digital video use title and credit screens to compose and communicate meaning for readers, viewers, and listeners. In each of these instances both everyday and discipline-specific communications actively engage multiple dimensions of meaning. We move between these modalities on a daily basis, rarely noticing the differences in our composing practices, incorporating emerging technologies as they become available, convenient, or accepted.

Digital media, in other words, is as subject as writing to what John Trimbur calls "deproduction"—the transformation of composing media, modalities, genres into transparent, innocent elements that conceal their own artful nature and systematically mask their situatedness within social and cultural systems of interest and power (1990: 80). Deproduction is exacerbated by a lack of attention to the choices embedded in the creation and production of media, modalities, and genres. The NPR audio essay, for instance, has undergone deproduction as listeners lose sight of the extensive digital sound editing and narrative manipulation that characterize the creation of such stories (Solomon, 2004).

Emergent media, modalities, and genres, however—because they are often less familiar as design resources in the setting of academic writing tasks—can help teachers and students identify some of the naturalized conventions associated with more conventional communicative media, modalities and forms by forcing a new evaluation of how rhetorical tasks can be most effectively accomplished.

Opening spaces for paying attention to composing technologies, media, and modalities

Educators charged with instructing students in effective academic writing and communication will echo Alastair Pennycook's (1994) sentiment: "While on the one hand ... I need to help students meet the criteria for 'success' as they are defined within particular institutional practices, as a critical educator I need also to try to change how students understand their possibilities and I need to work towards changing those possibilities" (quoted in Harwood and Hadley, 2004: 357). Adding what can sometimes be viewed as new literacy forms and requirements to a curriculum already taxed with the need to balance practical instruction with critical engagement and proactive work to improve academic discourse can be daunting. In such situations, as Harwood and Hadley note, we risk approaching our instructional tasks either too pragmatically, as a means to ensure success for our students within a certain arena, or too critically, in which case we risk a privileging of critique rather than practice.

In the approach that follows, we suggest that "situated practice" in composing—activities that immerse students in authentic communication situations (New London Group, 2000: 31)—should be accompanied by both rhetorical and design analysis, that students need practice in thinking about *how* and *why* specific texts, produced in specific media, might use specific combinations of modalities or design resources. As students explore the possibilities of academic composing tasks and experiment with changing various elements, we believe, they will come to understand how facility with a range of semiotic recourses, including written language, makes humans "who and what we might be" (Wysocki and Johnson-Eilola, 1999: 359).

What does not work so well, we suggest, is creating academic composing assignments in which rhetorical and material design considerations are made simple and transparent for students, rather than highlighted as acts of purposeful creation, design, production, and distribution by a skillful and knowledgeable social actor who understands media, modalities, and genres as rhetorical products of complex social relations. Assignments that highlight the purposeful work of the composer include research and reflection on particular forms of composing technologies, that ask these students, for instance, to think about whether they are composing for paper or the Web and why they have chosen to do so. These assignments also occur within sequences that allow or encourage students to question the context in which specific media, modalities, and genres have arisen. Such assignments would not, for instance, ask students to "write an essay" about a particular topic. They might, however, ask students to engage in a communicative task for a specific audience and purpose, and then to decide which particular medium (print, screen, radio), or which combination of modalities (alphabetic writing, video, sound, animation), might best help them succeed at their rhetorical task. Similarly, the kind of assignment we are advocating would not simply ask students to learn a Web authoring program and then recreate the model of an effective webpage. Rather, the assignment might also ask students to decide *which* portions of the information they want to convey are best included on a website in the form of writing, which in the form of short video interviews, and which in the form of still images—as well as *why* and *how* each of these forms might work best for a certain audience, a specific rhetorical situation, and for various forms of distribution and consumption. In short, we want students to understand that rhetorical decisions and social relations can be submitted to analysis and scrutiny and brought into dialogue with the design, creation, production, and distribution of academic discourse.

To help teachers and students accomplish the goal of putting the social and rhetorical elements of communication into dialogue with concerns about materials and design resources, we have created a matrix represented, in its most basic form, in Figure 7.1. This basic matrix offers an open framework for exploring questions during assignment design, classroom discussion, or even drafting efforts, and it is capable of accommodating work in a range of technologies, media, modalities, and genres.

In suggesting this basic framework, we hope to encourage an approach to rhetorical design, composing, and evaluation that is open ended and exploratory, not limited to discrete media literacies or technologies that will inevitably shift and change. The goal of the matrix, as we envision it, is to help teachers and students explore the complex and symbiotic relationships between rhetorical considerations (purpose, audience, information content, and form) and design considerations of technology, media, modalities (material and historical resources; methods of production, delivery, and circulation) as a fundamental part of their composing processes.

In a more elaborated form, the basic matrix might include questions like the those in Figure 7.2. Such sample questions, however, are meant to be suggestive rather than exhaustive. In this more elaborated form, the matrix can provide students questions to think about as they are planning their composition, as they are drafting a text, and as they are evaluating the efficacy of their texts.

A primary goal of the matrix we have presented is to add the dimension of critical analysis, reflection, and context to composing and evaluating assignments; a secondary goal is to help both teachers and students avoid the problem of focusing on production skills that are strictly functional in nature (Selber, 2004). If we want students to become effective authors of academic texts, we need to provide them opportunities not only to attain a level of functional literacy with texts that deploy different technologies, media, and modalities, but also strategies for thinking critically about the rhetorical contexts of these texts, reflecting on the material constraints of such texts, identifying the historical and cultural provenance that resonate in such texts, and recognizing the complex systems within which such texts are created, distributed, and circulated.

	Rhetorical considerations			
Resources and considerations drawn into semiosis	Audience	Author/ purpose	Information/ content	Form/ genre
Motivating questions for rhetorical design (the rhetorical questions that need to drive design considerations)				
Material considerations (the costs of texts; their physical composition, availability, size; people's access to texts)				
Historical/cultural considerations (the affordances, provenance, cultural expectations, and history of technologies, media, modalities, texts and textual forms)				
Production, delivery, circulation (the social, cultural, and technological systems within which texts are created, delivered, circulated)				

(The leftmost vertical label reads: **Design Considerations of Technology, Medium, Modality**)

Fig. 7.1 Basic rhetorical design matrix

Although the rhetorical design matrix, for us, is best used within project-based composing assignments, which specify an authentic rhetorical context, teachers may find it useful to provide some constraints in key areas: designating a specific audience, purpose, or format, for example, or a specific composing technology, medium, or set of modalities. This allows instructors to maintain some pragmatic instructional focus while simulating typical aspects of real world communication tasks and the need to produce a text in a context that is not wholly self-determined.

We recognize that the rhetorical design matrix we offer in this chapter represents only one way to visualize the intersection of rhetorical and design constraints that composing in multiple media can highlight. It will not be adequate for all tasks, but as the breadth of the questions this matrix raises indicates, exploring any one of the intersections suggested here will lead to multiple possibilities for assignment and curriculum design. One advantage of this approach is that it allows students to contribute their own solutions and analyses while they explore various textual forms.

To illustrate the versatility of the rhetoric design matrix, we can briefly explore its use with an assignment sequence that involves students in making a persuasive case based on research, a typical focus of academic composing tasks,

Resources and considerations drawn into semiosis	Rhetorical considerations			
	Audience	Author/purpose	Information/content	Form/genre
Design Consideration of Technology, Media, Modality **Motivating questions for rhetorical design** (the rhetorical questions that should drive design considerations)	Who is the target audience(s) for this text? Why is it important to reach this specific audience at this specific time? How do the audience's expectations, practices, and resources shape the design of this text? What resources are available to shape the text's design for this audience?	What is the author(s) purpose(s) for creating, delivering, and circulating this text? How does this purpose shape the choice of communicative technology/media/modalities? Why does the author think the text important for others to read/view/listen to at this specific time and in this rhetorical context? What resources can the author(s) draw on to shape this text?	What information and content needs to be conveyed within/by/through this text? Why is this information/content important to create and convey at this specific time and in this specific context? What resources are available to shape the text's information/content?	What form should the text take to accomplish the author(s) purpose? The audience's expectations? What genre should be used? Why? What resources (technologies, media, modalities, cultural, historical) are available to the author for shaping the text's form/genre? The audience's reception, interpretation, understanding, and use of the text?

Continued

Fig. 7.2 Rhetorical design matrix with sample questions

Resources and considerations drawn into semiosis	Rhetorical considerations			
	Audience	**Author/purpose**	**Information/content**	**Form/genre**
Material considerations (costs, material/physical composition construction of text, availability of text, availability of materials, access to resources)	How will the audience *access* the text? Under what material conditions and circumstances? What material considerations and constraints will shape the audience's *interpretation, understanding, and use of this text?* How are these material considerations related to technologies/media/modalities? What material considerations and constraint will shape the *creation, delivery, and circulation of this text?* Which material factors shape the power and impact of this text for an audience? Why? How are these material considerations related to technologies/media/modalities?	What material considerations or constraints will shape the author(s) purpose in composing this text? Why? To what extent? To what production technologies/media and modalities does the author have access? Why? Where? Under what material conditions? What costs are connected with the use of these technologies/media/modalities? How do these costs shape the efforts of author(s)?	What material factors shape the information/content that can be conveyed in this text? Why? How? How will the information and content be shaped by the materiality of the technologies/media/modalities to use to create this text? Why?	How will material factors shape the final form/genre of the text? Its genre? Why? How? What material constraints and considerations will be introduced by the technologies/media/modalities used in creating the form/genre of this text? How? Why?

Historical/cultural resources (the affordances, provenance, cultural expectations, and history of technologies, media, modalities, texts and textual forms)				
What are the historical and cultural expectations of audiences for texts of this kind? How do these shape the text itself? With what cultural and historical texts/events/elements/belief systems does this text resonate for the target audience? Historically and culturally, what do audiences expect in terms of the technologies/media/modalities used to create, distribute, and circulate this text? What cultural and historical significance do the text's technologies/media/modalities have for the target audience(s)?	What historical and cultural resources can the author draw on to accomplish his/her purpose in this text? What resources have other authors drawn on in the past/in other cultural settings to accomplish similar purposes in similar texts and rhetorical situations? What technologies/media/modalities can the author draw on to accomplish his/her purpose in this text? Historically, who has designed and deployed the technologies/media/modalities used to create/distribute/circulate this kind of text? Why? For what purpose(s)? What cultural and historical meanings are inherent in the technologies/media/modalities used for this kind of text?	What are the historical and cultural resonances of the information and content of this text in this particular rhetorical context? How should/do these resonances shape the content/information that the author(s) include in this text? What historical and cultural expectations will shape the audience's reception, interpretation, understanding, and use of the content/information in this particular text? Historically and culturally, what technologies/media/modalities have authors drawn on to create the content/information in this kind of text? Why? What historical and cultural issues of ownership, authorship, cultural authority, and heritage will technologies/media/modalities raise for the inclusion of specific information/content in this particular text?	What are the historical and cultural resonances of form/genre for this kind of text? How should these resonances shape the form/genre for the author(s)? Why? Does the author want to encourage audiences to read *against* the cultural or historical grain of this form/genre? *With* it? Both? Why? Historically and culturally, what role has technology/media/modalities played in shaping the form/genre of this text? Are there cultural and historical implications for the use of specific technology/media/modalities? Expectations on the part of audiences?

Fig. 7.2 Continued

Resources and considerations drawn into semiosis	Rhetorical considerations			
	Audience	**Author/purpose**	**Information/content**	**Form/genre**
Historical/cultural resources (the affordances, provenance, cultural expectations, and history of technologies, media, modalities, texts and textual forms)	What technology/media/modalities does this specific audience consider important? Unimportant? Trustworthy or untrustworthy? Through which technology/medium/modalities does this audience derive its news? Entertainment? Information? Why? How should audience expectations, practices, needs shape the ways in which this text is to be produced, delivered, circulated? How should audience expectations, practices, needs shape the technologies/media/modalities used to create, deliver, and circulate this text?	How might the cultural and intellectual history associated with these technologies/media/modalities shape the author(s) purpose for the current text? What issues of ownership, authorship, cultural authority, and heritage should the author consider? How does the author(s) purpose for this text in these rhetorical situations shape the creation, delivery, and circulation of this text? What technologies/media/modalities will best help the author accomplish her/his purpose in creating, delivering, and circulating this text?	How might the cultural and intellectual history of these technologies/media/modalities shape the content/Information included in for the current text? How do plans for the creation, delivery, and circulation of this text in these rhetorical situations shape the content and information included in it?	What historical and cultural issues of ownership, originality, authority, and heritage might be considered in determining the form/genre of this text? What implications does the form/genre of this text have for its creation, delivery, and circulation in this rhetorical situation?

Production, delivery, circulation (the social, cultural, and technological systems within which texts are created, delivered, circulated)				
	Within what social, historical, and cultural systems will this text be created, delivered, and circulated for this audience? What implications do these systems have for audience's reception, understanding, and use of this text? What issues of access, and use could these technologies/media/modalities raise in connection with the creation, delivery, and circulation of this text for this particular audience? What constraints and possibilities might technology/media/modalities introduce for the creation, delivery, and circulation of this text for this audience?	What communicative technologies/media/modalities will the author(s) need to learn? How long will this take? What roles does the author play in the systems of creation, delivery, and circulation that serve as a context for this text? Given these roles, what issues of ownership, copyright, compensation, permission, licensing, authorship, use, etc. do these technologies/media/modalities raise in connection with the creation, delivery, and circulation of this text? What constraints and possibilities might technology/media/modalities introduce for the creation, delivery, and circulation of this text for the author?	How does the use of specific technologies/media/modalities shape the creation, delivery, and circulation of this text? How does it shape the information and content to be included in this text? What implications might these influences have for the information/content of this text in this rhetorical situation?	How do technologies/media/modalities shape/influence the systems within which this text can be created, delivered, and circulated? What constraints and possibilities might they introduce? How do these constraints and possibilities shape the form/genre of this text?

Fig. 7.2 Continued

and then employing this research to create texts of various kinds. The goals and parameters of this assignment are stated in a condensed form below:

Assignment sequence: Choose a topic of interest that has some currency in the contemporary public imagination (drug use, physical fitness, gun safety, responsible pet care, educational funding, etc.) and with which you have personal experience.

- Using the library, conduct research on this topic, employing five authoritative print sources and five authoritative online sources. Write an informative and persuasive white paper/essay (3–5 pages) for the members of a specific community organization (Rotary Club, church group, alumni organization) that takes a stand on this issue and makes a persuasive case for the members.
- Using the research information you have gathered, create an informative and persuasive public service (PSA) announcement on the issue you have chosen. Identify a specific audience for your PSA and then choose the technologies, media, and modalities that will help you accomplish your persuasive purpose with that audience.
- You might, for instance, want to focus on persuading high school seniors and decide to create a print public service announcement (PSA) about your issue, one suitable for a 24 by 30 inch poster that can be displayed in the local high school.
- Or you might want to focus on college students and decide to create a persuasive audio PSA on your issue (either 30 seconds or sixty seconds in length) suitable for airing on a college radio station.
- Or you might want to focus on teenage television viewers and decide to create a video PSA on your issue (either 30 seconds or 60 seconds in length) suitable for airing on a community television station.

For the first step of this assignment—writing an informative and persuasive white paper/essay for members of a public organization—the rhetorical design matrix may prove useful as a **drafting and peer-response aid** employed at the stage of a first-draft, peer review. In this context, the matrix could provide peer-group members with a framework for structuring their comments and providing authors additional ideas that will help them improve their white paper during revision. In the sample excerpt represented in Figure 7.3, for instance, we show one row ("Material Considerations") of a peer response from a completed matrix for the white paper/essay. Used in this way, the matrix can encourage students to reflect on multiple dimensions of a text and to provide critical feedback that extends beyond a focus on the sentence level or the functional aspects of a text.

For the second task of the sample assignment—creating a print, audio or video PSA for a specific audience—teachers may want to encourage students to use the matrix as a **planning heuristic** that helps them choose and explore a possible medium and modalities for their PSA. The excerpt represented in Figure 7.4 ("Historical and Cultural Considerations"), for example, which

Rhetorical Considerations for White Paper Assignment: Excerpt of first-draft, peer feedback

Resources and considerations drawn into semiosis	Audience	Author/purpose	Information/content	Form/genre
Material considerations (costs, material/physical composition construction of text, availability of materials, access to resources)	**How will the audience *access* the text?** This paper will be distributed to City Council members before their meeting and discussed during the meeting. **What material considerations and constraints will shape the audience's interpretation, understanding, and use of this text?** These guys are busy, so they'll probably skim this text. Better provide an abstract at the beginning and bullet the statistics you give on p. 5. Also, think about including a Table of Contents to help them find specific sections of the text. Include bold headings to make it easier for readers to skim. **How are these material considerations related to technologies/media/modalities?** If you are going to duplicate this 5 page paper for 25 city council members, you'll either need access to a high speed color copier or a high speed color printer. Both are expensive. Can you use shading for the graphs and eliminate cost of color printing/copying?	**To what production technologies/media and modalities does the author have access? Under what material circumstances?** Do you know how to create a table in MS Word? I would put those statistics on p. 2 in a table. You really need an image to show what that you're talking about on page 3. Your verbal description, by itself, doesn't work for me. Do you have access to a digital still camera? You can check one out from the Digital Media Lab or borrow one from a friend.	**What material factors shape the information/content that can be conveyed in this text? Why? How?** How will the information and content be shaped by the materiality of the technologies/media and modalities used to create this text?	**How will material factors shape the final form/genre of the text? Its genre?** Are you going to include a cover page with your contact information on it? All the formal white papers I've seen have them. These guys are probably pretty old, do you think you should increase the font size from 8 pt. to 10 pt.?

Design Consideration of Technology, Media, Modality

Fig. 7.3 Excerpt from a rhetorical design matrix used for first-draft, peer review of a white paper/essay

Rhetorical Considerations for an Audio PSA: Excerpt of author's planning heuristic

Resources and considerations drawn into semiosis	Audience	Author/purpose	Information/content	Form/genre
Historical/cultural resources (the affordances, provenance, cultural expectations, and history of technologies, media, modalities, texts and textual forms)	**What are the historical and cultural expectations of audiences for texts of this kind?** Radio audiences expect 30 second PSAs that grab their attention. Usually they're funny or take an unexpected approach. They have to both entertain and inform. Dropping out of school, though, is a serious topic, so I'll need to lighten it up a bit to engage students our age. They're tired of being lectured on this one.	**What historical and cultural resources can the author draw on to accomplish his/her purpose in this text?** The Ad Council website has lots of radio PSAs that I can study as models. I'll need music that creates the light and humorous mood I want to establish so that folks don't tune out half way through the PSA.	**What are the historical and cultural resonances of the information and content of this text in this particular rhetorical context? How should these resonances shape the content/information that the author(s) include in this text?** I've noticed that most audio PSAs include relatively little information, but a strong focused message. So, I have to focus on an attention-getting concept and choose only 1–2 facts to include about why folks shouldn't drop out.	**What are the historical and cultural resonances of form/genre for this text in this particular rhetorical context?** I have to keep my PSA right at 30 seconds because WOSU schedules 30 and 60 second gaps in their programming. I think the audience expects to be entertained by PSAs, even while they are being persuaded and informed. So I need to make this piece hip.
	Historically and culturally, what do audiences expect in terms of the technologies/media/modalities used to create, distribute, and circulate this text? Radio audiences expect professional quality audio that has undergone careful editing. But I have the advantage of the podcasting boom—students are used to listening to stuff these days, even homemade stuff.	**What technologies/media/modalities can the author draw on to accomplish his/her purpose in this text?** I have Audacity on my home machine for editing audio. I can use GarageBand, too, for editing music. So, I'm set for the audio editing part. I need a good mic for this task—radio audiences expect professional quality sound.	Also, I'll need to include a sponsoring organization to give the PSA some authority. **What historical and cultural expectations will shape the audience's reception, interpretation, understanding and use of the content/information in this text?**	**Does the author want to encourage audiences to read against the cultural or historical grain of this form/genre? With it?** Because this is my first audio PSA, think I want to follow the general conventions, but make it more hip with language and music.

Design Consideration of Technology, Media, Modality

	Historically, who has designed and deployed these technologies/media/modalities used to create/distribute/circulate this text? Why? For what purpose(s)?		**What historical and cultural issues of ownership, originality, authority, and heritage might be considered in determining the form/genre of this text?**
Most actual PSAs for the radio include some music at the beginning and the end as well as vocal commentary.	Most PSAs are produced by professional media groups with access to actors, microphones, editing decks. I'll have to create this PSA on a laptop with a borrowed mic and free, open-source software. Since I know how to do podcasts, though, so most of the production should be fairly easy. At least I won't have to learn new software.	Historically, radio PSAs have focused on serious subjects, but treated them in catchy or unexpected ways—that's what I want to do. So, I'll use some Latino music and some humor to lighten things up. My own accent should give a people a clue about the cultural audience I'm targeting with of my PSA. And the music will help, too, To reach school age latinos/latinas though, I'm going to have to get rich with the language.	Because of copyright issues, I'll have to use my own music or music licensed for commercial use on the Creative Commons website.

Fig. 7.4 Excerpt from a rhetorical design matrix used for the planning of an audio PSA on Hispanic dropout rates

Design Consideration of Technology, Media, Modality

Resources and considerations drawn into semiosis	Rhetorical Considerations for a Video PSA: Excerpt of teacher's heuristic for evaluation			
	Audience	Author/purpose	Information/content	Form/genre
	How well did the student's video PSA address the audience's historical and cultural expectations and practices? This video PSA was longer than 75 seconds, and could have benefited from focus and judicial editing. I'm afraid that a typical television audience wouldn't still for it or would see it as unprofessional.	**How successfully did the author(s)' purpose for this video PSA shape the creation, delivery, and circulation possibilities for this text?** I think the focus of this PSA—increasing the percentage of student voters—would be of interest to the Voting Registration Club, the Young Democrats, and the Young Republican groups on campus. They might be willing to air it at their registration drives.	**How successful was the author in identifying appropriate information/content for this video PSA?** Excellent job here—I think viewers of the university television station will recognize and relate to these Civil Rights images and make the connection with the need to vote in the upcoming election.	**How successful was the student in using the form/genre of video PSA?** Excellent job here, video adhered to limitations of time. It was persuasive, informative, and engaging as a PSA.
Production, delivery, circulation (the social, cultural, and technological systems within which texts are created, delivered, circulated)	**How does the student's video PSA address the audience's expectations about the technologies/media/modalities used to create, deliver, and circulate this text?** Framing and shot composition in this PSA is professionally done; sound and audio levels are clear and understandable.	**How successful was the author in using technologies/media/modalities to help accomplish her/his purpose?** This video PSA made great use of historical video clips from the Civil Rights marches, audio clips from MLK's speeches, recorded audio commentary by the author, and contemporary music to convey the importance of voting.	**How successful was the author in using specific technologies/media/modalities for use on the university television station?** I noticed that you turned in a compressed version of your video PSA. WOSU may need an uncompressed version that they can compress to their specifications. Also the letterboxing in your video will not be acceptable for most television stations.	**How successful was the student in using technologies/media/modalities to create the form/genre of this text?** I liked the fact that you used a black and white filter for all of the historical footage and that you used music of the appropriate period behind the Civil Rights video clips. This really gave viewers the sense of watching history—and, I hope—convinced them of the need to become part of it, too!
	How did the student's video PSA take advantage of the technology/media/modalities for the creation, delivery, and circulation of this text? Nice combination of music, images, and pace to create a mood of urgency in your message.			Nice job, too, of pacing the still images in time with the musical beat during the lead-in and conclusion segments.

Fig. 7.5 Excerpt from a rhetorical design matrix used for teacher's evaluation of a video PSA on exercising voting rights

refers to an audio PSA focused on lowering the school dropout rate for Hispanic high school students. As this example suggests, the use of the matrix for planning purposes can encourage student authors to focus on the range of dimensions that their choice of medium, modalities, and audiences will affect, and to make realistic plans for the work they will have to do in creating their PSA.

Teachers may also want to use the matrix as an **evaluative framework** for the texts that students produce in this assignment. The excerpt in Figure 7.5 ("Creation, Delivery, Circulation"), for example shows a teacher's evaluative comments for a video PSA on getting out youthful voters. Used in this context, the matrix provides teachers (or students themselves, in the case of self-evaluation) a rich framework for reflecting on their success in accounting for multiple rhetorical and design considerations.

Conclusion

This chapter suggests that the historical and cultural practice and instruction of academic writing should be viewed within a set of critical rhetorical and design considerations that treat questions of technology as fundamental. Our argument, here, is not based simply on the common claim that technology has transformed academic communication practices (although we believe it is in the process of doing so) or that new digital composing technologies and non-alphabetic modalities will increasingly supplement the technology of alphabetic writing and the medium of print (although we believe that communications will continue, increasingly, to take advantage of multiple semiotic modalities). Rather, we argue that emerging composing technologies and texts—because they are new and sometimes less familiar—can help teachers and students pay closer and more fruitful attention to writing, itself: not only in its rhetorical dimensions, but also in its historical and cultural dimensions, its material and design dimensions, and in the contexts where it is created, delivered, and circulated.

It is our contention that such an approach will help teachers and students pay attention to the wide range of factors that are constelled in the service of communicative tasks and the historical, social, and technological development that characterize our understanding of composing. Such historical developments will invariably continue with or without the attention of what Anne Wysocki calls "the material thinking of people who teach writing" (2004: 3) to guide them. We need to ask how contemporary choices to integrate technology into composition classrooms can function not in opposition to our understanding of writing, but in support of that understanding. It is through a careful examination of the rhetorical and design choices we make in composing with a variety of technologies, media, and modalities—and in a range of rhetorical contexts—that we can uncover our naturalized understanding of writing as a communicative tool, one invested with its own affordances, cultural interests, and historically specific features, and one that works to intercede in our ideas about who and what we are.

The opportunity that English composition teachers have right now— during a period in which a range of new technologies, media, and modalities are emerging and contesting with writing as literacy tools—is an important one, and, perhaps, short lived. It provides teachers of composition a historical moment in which the materiality of writing as a technology of influence has become denaturalized and screen-based digital media has yet to become fully naturalized. In this moment, we have a marvelous opportunity to *see* and *understand* both writing and emergent technologies from a critical perspective that lends additional depth to our study of semiosis and communication.

Susan Miller's historical overview of the relationship of writing and alphabetic literacy to rhetoric and rhetorical practice reveals how early writing assignments shifted rhetorical education at the end of the eighteenth century from a model based on the public practice of rhetorical debate to the private teacher-assessed practice of the writing assignment (1989: 160). This change from public to private assessment dramatically impacted the course of higher education for years to come. In this move, from training in a form of rhetoric that is public and performative to one that is more effectively assessed by an individual "authority" after the fact, the pedagogical choice of a new classroom technology transformed the culture of the academy. Miller relates this move to a broader "diminishment" of social participation in late eighteenth-century education. Here a change in technology, or more specifically, a change in the orientation to or "use" of an existing technology, had wide ranging social consequences. Changes such as this do not happen in the isolation of a lone classroom. While print technology and the composition textbook played an important role in the development of higher education in the US as Miller has extensively explored (1989, 1998), these changes ultimately take place as only one aspect of the larger transformations within specific cultural systems that adopt cultural and technological changes symbiotically. As writing instructors, our engagement with the materials of textual production allows us to assess and project the long-term consequences of these classroom and curricular decisions.

Exploring composing technologies, then, in our understanding of academic writing extends well beyond our ability to access, learn, and use the most current communications media. The administrative and curricular decisions now being made in relation to technology in writing classrooms may also shape the nature and direction of academic communication for years to come. Cynthia L. Selfe notes that our local, situated work with specific technologies, in specific classrooms, and at specific institutions, can also "collectively work to construct a larger vision" of the professional challenges and opportunities that integrating technology into the writing classroom represents (1999, 147). It is precisely this sense of a larger vision that we have attempted to share as an integral component to attending to the nuts and bolts of curriculum and assignment design with technology.

Notes

i   A few words of definition should clarify our use of terms in this chapter. Throughout, we use three key terms:

        technologies of composing and communication (referring to the tools of communication: the alphabet, the pen, the computer);

        media of communication (referring to vehicles used for the production and delivery of meaning: print/paper, books, screen, radio, computer networks); and

        modalities of composing (the semiotic channels that carry meaning: words, moving and still images, sound and music, animations, color).

    For these important terms and distinctions, we draw directly from the outstanding work of Gunther Kress and Theo van Leeuwen, and Bill Cope and Mary Kalantzis, and the other members of The New London Group, as represented in such books as *Multiliteracies: Literacy Learning and the Design of Social Futures* and *Multimodal Discourse: the Modes and Media of Contemporary Communication*, both of which can be found in the References.

ii   During the latter half of the nineteenth century, universities began to change in response to the rapid rise of industrial manufacturing, the explosion of scientific discoveries, and the expansion of the new country's international trade. These converging trends accumulated increasing tendential force and resulted in profound cultural transformations that placed an increasing value on specialization and professionalization, especially within the emerging middle class. Such changes required both new approaches to education and a new kind of secular university, one designed to meet the needs of individuals focused on science, commerce, and manufacturing. It was within this new collegiate context that the first departments of English were able to form, primarily by forging identities for themselves as units that educated a range of citizens occupied with business and professional affairs. In this context, departments of English focused on preparing professionals whose work, after graduation, would increasingly rely on writing, as David Russell (1991) explains—articles, reports, memoranda, and communications, "texts as objects to be silently studied, critiqued, compared, appreciated, and evaluated" (pp. 4–5). Supporting this work were technological innovations—improved printing presses, typewriters and pens, among others—that combined with innovations in business operations, efficient manufacturing techniques, and science to lend added importance to writing as a cultural code, both within the new university and outside it (Russell, 2002). The departments of English which emerged during this period focused primarily on their ability to provide instruction in written composition.

iii   For more on the premise that the academic essay has developed a set of highly conventionalized "basic moves" (p. ix), see Gerald Graff and Cathy Birkenstein's *They Say, I Say: The Moves That Matter in Academic Writing* (New York: W. W. Norton, 2006).

iv   As print assumed an increasingly privileged position in US composition classrooms during the late nineteenth century and throughout the twentieth century, aurality as an instructional tool and a composing modality was both subsumed by, and defined in opposition to, writing (Russell, 1991 and 2002; Halbritter, 2004; McCorckle, 2005; Elbow, 1994), thus, establishing and perpetuating a false binary between the two modalities of expression (Biber, 1986 and 1988; Tannen, 1982a and b), encouraging an overly narrow understanding of language and literacy (Kress), and allowing collegiate teachers of English composition to lose sight of the integrated nature of language arts. This almost single-minded focus on print in composition classrooms resulted in academic writing classes that downplayed the importance of aurality, and other composing modalities, for making meaning and understanding the world. The almost exclusive dominance of print literacy may also work against the interests of individuals whose cultures and communities have managed to maintain a value on multiple modalities of expression, multiple ways of knowing, communicating, and establishing identity (Dunn, 1995 and 2001; Gilyard, 2000; Hibbitts, 1994; Lyons, 2000; Powell, 2002; Royster, 1996, 2000).

References

Biber, D. (1986), "Spoken and written textual dimensions in English: Resolving the contradictory findings," *Language*, 62, 384–414.

——(1988), *Variation across Speech and Writing* (Cambridge: Cambridge University Press).

Brandt, D. (1995), "Accumulating literacy: writing and learning to write in the twentieth century," *College English*, 57(6), 649–668.

Booth, W. (2004), *The Rhetoric of Rhetoric* (Chicago: The University of Chicago Press).

Cope, B. and Kalantzis, M. (2000a), Multiliteracies: Literacy Learning and the Design of Social Futures (London: Routledge).

——(2000b), "Designs for social futures," in B. Cope and M. Kalantzis (eds), *Multiliteracies* (pp. 203–234).

Dunn, P. A. (1995), Learning Re-Abled: The Learning Disability Controversy and Composition Studies (Portsmouth, NH: Boynton/Cook).

——(2001), Talking, Sketching, Moving: Multiple Literacies in the Teaching of Writing (Portsmouth, NH: Boynton/Cook).

Elbow, P. (1994), "What do we mean when we talk about voice in texts?" in K. Yancey (ed.), *Voices on Voice* (pp. 1–35 (Urbana: NCTE).

Emerson, R. M., Fretz, R. L. and Shaw, L. L. (1995), *Writing Ethnographic Fieldnotes* (Chicago: University of Chicago Press).

Gilyard, K. (December 2000), "Literacy, identity, imagination, flight," *College Composition and Communication*, 52(2), 260–272.

Halbritter, S. K. (2004), Sound arguments: Aural rhetoric in multimedia composition. Unpublished dissertation, University of North Carolina at Chapel Hill. UMI 3140325.

Harwood, N. and Hadley, G. (2004), "Demystifying institutional practices: critical pragmatism and the teaching of academic writing," *English for Academic Purposes*, 23, 355–377.

Hibbitts, B. (1994), "Making sense of metaphors: visuality, aurality and the reconfiguration of American legal discourse," *Cardozo Law Review*, 16, 229. Accessed 24 September at http://law.pitt.edu/hibbitts/meta_int.htm.

Kress, G. (2000), "Design and transformation: new theories of meaning," in B. Cope and M. Kalantzis (eds), *Multiliteracies* (pp. 153–162) (New York: Routledge).

——(1999), "'English' at the crossroads: rethinking curricula of communication in the context of the turn to the visual," in G. E. Hawisher, and C. L. Selfe (eds), *Passions, Pedagogies, and Twenty-First Century Technologies* (pp. 66–87) (Logan, UT: Utah State University Press).

——(2003), *Literacy in the New Media Age* (New York: Routledge).

——and Jewitt, C. (eds) (2003), *Multimodal Literacy* (New York: Peter Lang).

——and Van Leeuwen, T. (1996), *Reading Images: The Grammar of Visual Design* (New York: Routledge).

——and Leeuwen, T. V. (2001), *Multimodal Discourse: The Modes and Media of Contemporary Communication* (London: Arnold).

Lyons, S. (February 2000), "Rhetorical sovereignty: What do American Indians want from writing?" *College Composition and Communication*, 51(3), 447–468.

McCorkle, B. (2005), "Harbingers of the printed page: Nineteenth-century theories of delivery as remediation," *Rhetoric Society Quarterly*, 35(4), 25–49.

Miller, S. (1989), *Rescuing the Subject: A Critical Introduction to Rhetoric and the Writer* (Carbondale, IL: University of Southern Illinois Press).

Miller, S. (1998), Assuming the Positions: Cultural Pedagogy and the Politics of Commonplace Writing (Pittsburgh, PA: University of Pittsburgh Press).

New London Group (2000), "A pedagogy of Multiliteracies designing social futures," in B. Cope and M. Kalantzis (eds), *Multiliteracies* (pp. 9–37) (New York: Routledge).

Olson, G. A. (2002), "Ideological critique in rhetoric and composition," in Olson (ed.), *Rhetoric and Composition as Intellectual Work* (pp. 81–91) (Carbondale, IL: Southern Illinois University Press).

Pennycook, A. (1994), The Cultural Politics of English as an International Language (London: Longman).

Powell, M. (February 2002), "Rhetorics of survivance: How American Indians use writing," *College Composition and Communication*, 53(3), 396–434.

Royster, J. J. (2000), Traces of a Stream: Literacy and Social Change among African American Women (Pittsburgh, PA: University of Pittsburgh Press).

——(1996), "When the first voice you hear is not your own", *College Composition and Communication*, 47, 29–40.

Russell, D. (1991), *Writing in the Academic Disciplines, 1870–1990: A Curricular History* (Carbondale: Southern Illinois University Press).

——(2002), "Institutionalizing English: rhetoric on the boundaries," in D. R. Shumway and C. Dionne (eds), *Disciplining English: Alternative Histories, Critical Perspectives* (pp. 39–58) (Albany: SUNY Press).

Selber, S. (2004), *Multiliteracies for a Digital Age* (Carbondale, IL: Southern Illinois University Press).

Selfe, C. L. (1999), Technology and Literacy in the Twenty-First century: The Importance of Paying Attention (Carbondale, IL: Southern Illinois University Press).

——(ed.) (forthcoming), *Teaching Multimodal Composition: Resources for Teachers* (Cresskill, NJ: Hampton Press).

——and G. E. Hawisher (2004), Literate Lives in the Information Age: Stories from the United States (Mahwah, NJ: Lawrence Erlbaum).

——and Selfe, R. J. (2002), "The intellectual work of computers and composition," in G. A. Olson (ed.), *Rhetoric and Composition as Intellectual Work* (pp. 203–220) (Carbondale, IL: Southern Illinois University Press).

Solomon, D. (31 December 2004), *Pulling Back the Curtain.* On the Media, WNYC. Accessed 13 January 2007 at http://onthemedia.org/yore/transcripts/transcripts_123104_curtain.html.

Tannen, D. (1982a), "Oral and literate strategies in spoken and written narratives," *Language,* 58, 1–21.

——(ed.) (1982b), Spoken and Written Language: Exploring Orality and Literacy (Norwood, NJ: Ablex).

Trimbur, J. (2002), "Delivering the message: typography and the materiality of writing," in G. A. Olson (ed.), *Rhetoric and Composition as Intellectual Work* (pp. 188–203) (Carbondale, IL: Southern Illinois University Press).

Trimbur, J. (1990), "Essayist literacy and the rhetoric of deproduction," *Rhetoric Review,* 9, 72–86.

Turner, J. (1999), "Academic literacy and the discourse of transparency," in Carys Jones, Joan Turner and Brian Street (eds), *Students Writing in the University: Cultural and Epistemological Issues* (pp. 149–160) (Amsterdam: John Benjamins Publishing Co.).

Wysocki, A., Johnson-Eilola, J., Selfe, C. and Sirc, G. (2004), Writing New Media: Theory and Applications for Expanding the Teaching of Composition (Logan, UT: Utah State University Press).

——and Johnson-Eilola, J. (1999), "Blinded by the letter: Why are we using literacy as a metaphor for everything?" in G. Hawisher and C. Selfe (eds), *Passions, Pedagogies, and Twenty-First Century Technologies* (pp. 349–368) (Logan, UT: Utah State University Press).

Williams, S. (2001), "Part 1: Thinking out of the pro-verbal box," *Computers and Composition,* 18(1), 21–32.

Yancey, K. (December 2004), "Made not only in words: Composition in a new key," *College Composition and Communication,* 56(2), 297–329.

"I Want to be Part of the Club": Raising Awareness of Bilingualism and Second Language Writing among Monolingual Users of English

Patricia Friedrich

Chapter Outline

Introduction

With the many advances made in the understanding of the nature of second language writing, it has become necessary to spread awareness of the challenges, accomplishment and communicative power of second language writers so as to help foster greater respect for second language use amongst monolingual users of English. This chapter will present qualitative evidence of the change of attitudes by monolingual users of English when exposed to overt instruction about both the socio and psycholinguistics of second language writing. Through an analysis of students' journal entries, I will demonstrate that it is possible to imbue in native users of a language a sense of respect and even admiration for second language use. Because this action research project took place in the southwest United States, the target second language is more typically Spanish. However, the results obtained here can possibly be used to design curricula in other areas where second language writing might be an issue.

When second language writers sit down to create a text in English, they are faced with a myriad of challenges which range from finding a voice to avoiding grammatical errors, from employing accepted rhetorical patterns to communicating abstract and complex ideas in a language other than their mother tongue. But perhaps the most pressing challenge faced by a non-native writer (NNW) is the anticipation of criticism and negative bias on the part of native writers (NW) when those writers become readers of non-native texts.

Acknowledgement of such bias is not new; it has been documented in several academic works including Amon (2000), Canagarajah (1996), and Flowerdew (2000 and 2001). It has also been a recurrent topic in works in critical applied linguistics (Pennycook, 1994) which questions traditional views of language as apolitical and acontextual, and critical contrastive rhetoric (Kubota and Lehner, 2004: 15) in which traditional approaches to contrastive analysis and the subsequent "assimilation" instructions which they generate are criticized for leading "to viewing rhetorical strategies used by ESL writers as 'violating,' 'deviant,' or 'anomalous.'"

Yet, despite such acknowledgement and many new critical perspectives in linguistics and related fields, much remains to be done to empower non-native writers and give them a voice and equal opportunity; after all, although bilingualism and multilingualism are the norm in many parts of the world, they remain unfavorably seen in parts of the west and certainly generate much controversy in the United States.

While we continue to work with bilingual and multilingual writers, asking them to question their position vis-à-vis English and challenge old assumptions about language ownership and propriety, we invest significantly less time in sensitizing native writers and readers (particularly those who are monolingual users of English) to the difficulties and the awesome accomplishments of their non-native counterparts.

The project described in this chapter aims to provide a small but meaningful contribution to the task of sensitizing native speakers to the challenges but also the many advantages of bilingualism in general and second language writing in particular. In it, college-level native writers are asked to read non-native texts, become acquainted with critical cross-cultural rhetoric, and respond to possible challenges to their position as English linguistic authority, given their condition of native users. The first part of the chapter addresses current scholarship on critical perspectives in applied linguistics, particularly contrastive rhetoric; the second links such perspectives to the rationale behind the proposed teaching initiative; the third and last presents evidence of a change in attitudes toward NNWs and their texts by English monolinguals who are explicitly instructed about the universe of second language writing.

Critical perspectives

In recent decades, research on contrastive rhetoric has taken a most welcome turn, with the incorporation of critical perspectives to discussions surrounding second language writing in general and cross-cultural issues in particular. While initial studies dating back to the very well-known 'doodles' by Kaplan (1966) were criticized for crystallizing a stereotypical view of cultures and privileging Anglo-Saxonic patterns deeming them "linear" and "direct," studies now generally acknowledge that such theorizing was a first stride in identifying communication difficulties or clashes which stemmed from levels other than the purely linguistics. Thus, thanks to works such as Kaplan's, we became aware that culture plays an important role in the shaping of texts. While Kaplan's work at that point in time hinted at the responsibility NNWs should take to correct their English to conform to native norms, many critical contrastive rhetoric academics now allude to the need to contextualize writing awarding shared responsibility for the successful establishment of written communication.

Implementing a sense of shared responsibility for written texts in English is not an easy task; culturally speaking, when it comes to English, many readers implicate the writer in any breach of communication that may occur, particularly because English seems to be associated with greater writer responsibility (Hinds, 1987). Thus, when a break in communication occurs, the writer is often held responsible for the mishap. It can be inferred that when texts are written by NNWs, the same kind of expectation exists, and as Kaplan suggested in his article, many readers will expect that those writers make the additional effort to ensure successful communication.

Texts that came after Kaplan's seminal work problematized reader/writer responsibility (Hinds, 1987) and other aspects of second language writing. Even works from other areas such as the ubiquitous management-oriented work of Hofstede (1980), conducted with IBM employees, have contributed to our understanding of cross-cultural communication. In it, Hofstede has argued that core values and beliefs (such as our desire for marked or unmarked hierarchical lines, our tolerance to uncertainty, and our greater reliance on reason as opposed to emotions) have a strong cultural component. Rhetoricians and language specialists (Connor, 1996, for example) have long utilized Hofstede's findings to explain cross-cultural differences in student texts.

More recently, however, research has questioned whether we are stereotyping second language writing too much (Kubota and Lehner, 2004) and forgetting that individuals bring their own writing personality to the texts they write. As a consequence, we now acknowledge that culture is not the only determinant of writing style and rhetorical predilections; as with other aspects of human experience, we are influenced by our gender, age, political view, professional inclination, position in the world, and our own individual preferences. As Kubota and Lehner (2004: 7) put it, "when put into practice, critical contrastive rhetoric affirms multiplicity of languages, rhetorical forms and students' identities."

Another fortuitous addition to our theoretical background has been the incorporation of a World Englishes perspective in more traditional realms of linguistic enquiry. In that respect, World Englishes scholarship has helped raise awareness of the importance and authority of varieties of English by legitimizing expressions other than the Inner Circle varieties (e.g. American and British English especially). Basically, language varieties are appreciated for their functional range and for their ability of establishing a sense of belonging and community for its users. Because of World Englishes, users of English around the world have discovered that their own varieties do not have to match native models to matter or to serve a functional purpose. They became more aware of the context and situation of communication as determiners of the appropriacy of a variety. They also became more empowered to negotiate meaning as a two-way road rather than accept it as a one way effort on the part of speaker/writer.

Very recently, Graddol (2006) has proposed that multilingualism is the linguistic equivalent of the fragmentation and complexity faced by the twenty-first-century globalized world, that is, the complexities and contradictions attributed to other areas of life extend themselves to language. Countries which have a history of portraying themselves as basically linguistic homogeneous may become entangled in a struggle to maintain such belief in homogeneity. In the United States, for example, this struggle has many times manifested itself in legislation to promote English only, to curb down bilingual education or to restrict services in other languages, particularly Spanish. Behind such efforts is the fear that cultural and linguistic heterogeneity breeds dissent and that the future should mirror a past of homogeneity.

That in the past this so-called homogeneity was in place is a myth. As I have argued elsewhere (Friedrich, 2007: 38), "behind the questionable assumption that diversity equals conflict hides the even more unrealistic assumption that the US was once homogeneous." As Crawford (2000: 3) explains, a century ago 4.5 times as many people in the US as today were non-English speaking. Despite the myth, individual states have worked on passing local laws establishing English as the official language. At this writing 50 per cent of US states specify English alone as their official state language. The results of such maneuvers have, linguistically and sociolinguistically speaking, usually been negative; educational practices, for example, have often fallen short of providing immigrant children with successful language instruction which in turn has resulted in deficient acquisition of skills in other disciplines.

On the other hand, dwelling on the assumption of homogeneity has also done little to make native users of English appreciative of the value and importance of bilingualism and multiculturalism. However, we now face the possibility of changing this picture; research in many linguistically related fields has gained momentum, acknowledgement of human rights and linguistic rights is becoming more widespread (Friedrich, 2007), and a more general awareness that we can only achieve a state of greater peace if we invest in acceptance of differences will depend on the dissemination of research, the creation of policies and laws that guarantee linguistic rights, and education at all levels, including higher education.

Rationale for the action research project

While we as researchers and teachers have invested a lot of effort in understanding and communicating new findings to NNWs and to incorporating a critical pedagogy informed by the above-described perspectives, we have devoted significantly less time to raising awareness of the challenges involved in second language writing among native speakers of target languages. In the case of English, not many monolingual native users understand and are able to sympathize with the challenges faced by their second language counterparts.

Yet, as this project has shown me, when formally introduced to the difficulties of their peers and to fundamentals of language acquisition and second language use, monolingual users show great compassion and develop much respect for the efforts of those acquiring a new language.

This action research project investigates and showcases the feedback obtained from monolingual native users of English who were overtly instruct-edabout the differences in rhetorical patterns and cultural beliefs among different groups writing in English; these students were also introduced to some basic concepts of language acquisition. Over a semester period, students enrolled in an English class (Cross-cultural Writing) were exposed to texts by NNWs of English and engaged in discussions and readings that highlighted the extent of the difficulties faced by cross-cultural writers. At first students learned that not only are second language writers acquiring a new language, but they are also discovering that rhetorical conventions (e.g. writing linearly, using digressions, leaving room for multiple interpretations) and cultural beliefs (e.g. the writer is more responsible for meaning as it happens in English as opposed to the reader being responsible as it happens in Japanese) can vary significantly across cultures. Once they were more acquainted with such ideas, they were introduced to more critical approaches to cross-cultural writing. They were asked to question concepts such as linearity, agency, language ownership, language standards, standard varieties of language, and power to review their initial understanding of cultural differences and communication clashes in light of these concepts. During all this time, students were also reading texts by NNWs, some well-known such as Amy Tan, some almost anonymous. Finally, they were asked to reflect on their findings through journal entries.

The topics for the journal entries were quite varied and remain up to the student. The only requirement was that they ground their reflections on the texts, the discussions and the lectures of the class. It is hypothesized that this kind of teaching can help monolingual writers understand and sympathize with the difficulties of NNWs. Formal classroom teaching of such rhetorical differences is paramount when it comes to cross-cultural understanding and such understanding in turn is vital in regions of the country, such as the American southwest, where virtually everyone is bound to encounter texts by second language English writers. In the southwest, this kind of practice seems even more important given that Spanish, the most common language besides English, does not enjoy the same kind of prestige that it does in other parts of the world where it serves not only as a mother tongue to millions but also as an important lingua franca.

The course

Cross-cultural Writing is a class designed to expose students to second language writings and cross-cultural expression in English. It is based on the assumption that language and culture are two of the factors that influence rhetorical patterns and that, because we live in a world where English is extensively used across cultures, these different patterns can make their way into texts in English. Unawareness of these different patterns and a lack of appreciation for the challenges of communicating in a global language can result in miscommunication and underappreciation of both the challenges and the importance of bi and multilingualism.

The structure of the course was simple: meet for three hours a week to read, write and discuss issues relating to language, rhetoric, culture and English. Activities included journaling, large group and small group discussions, group presentations, and online and in-library research. Assessment came from four journal entry submissions, a final group presentation, and a 20-page research report.

For the action research project, I read the students' journal entries specifically looking for information that would evidence any change in perspective with regards to issues of bilingualism, second language use (in particular in writing), or other cross-cultural elements. The quotations used in this text are representative of the most common themes found in the students' journals and are cited with the students' consent. These initial results can possibly motivate the design of more systematic research to investigate the extent of the impact of this pedagogy on monolingual writers.

[handwritten marginal note: "'packaging' doesn't necessarily define what's inside"]

The students

The students were college undergraduates enrolled in Cross-cultural Writing, an elective class that fulfills requirements of several majors (e.g. English, Ethnic Studies, Global Management). Most of the students were either in their third or senior year in college. Although they majored in different fields, a large number of attendees in this particular semester was majoring in humanities areas such as English, Ethnic Studies, History or Communication. A large majority of the class was composed by monolingual native speakers of English. Amongst the bilingual population only one was a user of English as a second language, while three were for the most part symmetric bilinguals. The total number in students in class was 35.

The assumptions

To design the activities and direct the discussion on the readings used in class, I departed from the following assumptions:

a) Many varieties of English exist and communication across varieties can be challenging—the expansion of English throughout the world has also meant greater distinction amongst varieties as new forms of the language are generated. While on the one hand the expansion of English results in greater communicative possibilities, on the other it may generate problems when lack of familiarity by participants of each other's varieties occurs between parties engaged in communication. Awareness of this dichotomy should be addressed in the English classroom.

b) N and NN users of English are responsible for negotiating meaning in context—as the number of NN users grows, second and foreign language users become a great force in language spread (Graddol, 1996). These new players will (it they have not already) question the authority of N users in dictating the rules of communication. Once again, this phenomenon has to be discussed in the classroom.

c) Awareness of cross-cultural issues will in turn bring a greater understanding of the role of purpose and audience in the writing process—if students can remember that purpose and audience are the two pillars of successful (in this case) written communication, they will be better equipped to make choices (linguistic, rhetorical, etc.) when they engage in communication with NNWs.

d) Greater awareness on the part of N users will result in sympathy for NN users—if N users understand the struggles of second language writing, they will be less likely to pass hurried and harsh judgement on NN users.

e) Given that two thirds of all English communication is between NN users, N norms will not always be the most appropriate—students have to be made aware of the fact that not always will written and oral communication occur in a context that involves N use. In those instances, negotiation will not be between an N and an NN variety but rather two competing and sometimes rather different and potentially barely intelligible NN varieties.

The materials

Two books served as springboard to our discussions—Connor's (1996) *Contrastive Rhetoric* and Gillespie and Becker's (2005) *Across Cultures*. For every meeting, students would read a chapter in Connor's book and a few texts by NN writers. Besides these, selected journal articles, magazine articles as well as Internet materials complemented the discussions. The students were welcome to contribute materials to our discussions and indeed a few brought texts from magazines and newspapers such as *The New York Times* and *The Economist*.

The results

What students wrote in their journals

The journals clearly showed a progression from a more self-centered view of language to a more open perspective. As students realized that cultural values and beliefs impacting language are relative, that rhetorical rules change, that however adapted they are to the second language, writers still bring their first language cultures to the text, it became easier for them to sympathize with second language writers and to find virtue in the texts of the latter. Below are some of the categories in which students demonstrated to have gained the greatest insight.

address ethnocentrism

Ethnocentrism and cultural relativism

It has always been my impression that part of the stereotyping and otherwise low level of acceptance of second language texts in English is a result of lack of exposure, lack of understanding of just what is involved in writing in a second language as well of a lack of understanding of the purpose of bilingualism. That unawareness of course applies to both oral and written texts. As a user of English as a second language myself, I have often experienced one of two reactions from a number of monolingual users of English. On learning that English is not native to me, several native users have reacted either by saying "you do not have an accent" or "you have a light hint of an accent." Neither comment, however, gets even close to the crux of the matter which to me is how effectively I have come to use a language that is not my mother tongue. On the other hand, these commentaries reflect a somewhat ethnocentric view of language, that is, the native user feels qualified to assess the use of language by a second language user and employs his or her own linguistic orientation and level of tolerance to variation as the yardstick. The variation in the level of tolerance would explain why some people can perceive me as "accent-free" while others will notice "the hint of an accent".

My understanding is that second language written texts can go under the same kind of microscopic examination; because both ESL features and possible "mistakes" differ from the typical patterns and mistakes in a native user's texts, they tend to be labeled according to their perceived value vis-à-vis native speakers' rules. Studies have questioned, for example, whether scientific and academic periodicals have a negative bias toward non-native texts (e.g. Flowerdew, 2001) which would result in the nonacceptance of articles by second and foreign language users by these media, causing then the ideas of these writers to be unavailable to a general audience (*TESOL Quarterly* has recently made the commendable move to overtly request that reviewers accept nonstandard and/or nonBritish/American as legitimate academic expression in that journal).

Despite the possibility that this kind of assessment occurs very often, I believe many native speakers are unaware of engaging in any discriminatory practice, so I decided to explicitly bring attention in the classroom to this analytical level. My hope was to make students learn to focus on purpose and audience and relativize the importance of form. In this paradigm, context and use take precedence over structure. We went about achieving these goals through a variety of tasks, some of which were particularly focused on language while others were more broadly designed to involve culture and social manifestations. Specifically, we read many of the texts provided in our book, trying to put ourselves in the position of the writer and then analyzing his/her rhetorical, linguistic and even ideological choices vis-à-vis their position in the world. In a nutshell, the class was underpinned by an attempt to make students leave their own perspectives if only for a moment and embrace someone else's. Later, I was able to attest to the fact that the students had succeeded in shifting their paradigm when I read the journals which contained excerpts like the ones below:

I

I was talking with a group of students from another class about a trip I took to Ireland last year. A fellow student interrupted me and said, "They drive on the wrong side of the road there." I explained to him that it is not the wrong side of the road; it is a different side of the road from that which Americans drive on.

II

I think that one of the concepts that has influenced me so much is ethnocentrism. I probably had a case of ethnocentrism when I walked into this class. I based most of my opinions about other cultures on my own culture, as thought my culture were superior in some way. I've learned that by embracing a more cultural relativism point of view.

III

Yet college is supposed to challenge a person's presuppositions. A person who goes into college with a certain set of beliefs should think critically of those beliefs before he graduates. When I tutored, I was younger, and I had neither the experience as a diversified student nor the exposure to the right classes to challenge my seemingly ethnocentric views. In fact, "ethnocentrism" did not necessarily apply to my situation, since I thought that good writing was an inter-cultural, universal process that did not consider the language factor.

Once the students understood the relativity of their position vis-à-vis issues of language and culture, exploring second language texts became much easier.

We were then able to start tackling issues of ethnicity, culture, language, and writing in greater depth from a multiplicity of perspectives. Students started questioning their basic values. While my idea was not necessarily to make them change their perceptive but rather question it, many students felt the need to revise some of their concepts and perceptions once the discussions were set in motion.

Culture and ethnicity

It came as a surprise to several students that the ways in which bilingualism is construed in any given society is relative and impacted by politics, ethnicity, race, class and other elements of social dynamics. Because several of the texts we read explicitly debated such issues, we had a double opportunity for analysis—both the form and the context of the texts spoke to our interest in bilingualism and cross-cultural communication. Surprisingly enough, the students' initial perception of culture and language was much too static to allow them to appreciate the real value of bi or multilinguism. It is not that the students were unwilling. Quite the contrary, they were receptive and open to a change of paradigm; they just needed exposure and the right tools.

While we explored the intricate world of ethnicity, race, and membership in multiple linguistic and cultural communities, *I* was the one surprised to discover that much as it happens with bilinguals who feel sometimes out of place and insecure about their loyalties to two (or more) languages, these students also felt deprived of membership at times and even felt a certain inferiority complex because of not being, in their words, "ethnic enough." This much became very obvious in some journal entries:

IV

So, should we claim our culture or our ethnicity? [...] Am I Caucasian or American? I am both, but how different are my ethnicity and my culture?

V

What I discovered in my quest for the novel that transcends cultures is that nothing can really transcend cultures without readers with open minds. I never would have enjoyed half the books that I love if it hadn't been for my open mind. The canon could be a great tool for people seeking good literature, but if people aren't willing to accept other ways of life, or at least have some respect for them, it is useless.

Continued

(Continued)

VI

I find it interesting that as I write these journal entries I try my very hardest to relate to the writers in the *Across Cultures* book, seeing as how I have been born and raised in the United States, and my parents are not immigrants from a foreign country. I think part of the reason for this is that I want in some way to be able to relate to these people, even if it means stretching their viewpoints and twisting their experiences to make them my own. On the other hand, I think another reason for this is that adapting culturally, be it from the United States to Korea or Virginia to Arizona, has more fundamental similarities than our American brains tend to think.

VII

The only things I know about other cultures, save one story from my father that I'll share with you later in my journal, is what I have read about. When I read Amy Tan's *The Joy Luck Club* in school a few years ago, I was fascinated. I felt like I was finally allowed into a club that I never thought I would be allowed to get into.

VIII

Is it the responsibility of the communicator to adjust to the recipient's style of writing to get their point across? Does the recipient need to understand the writer's cultural style when decoding the message? Or is there a middle ground where the cultures meet?

We cannot underestimate the effect that misnomers and too-narrowly-employed terms can have on perceptions and attitudes. Because we use words such as "ethnic" in opposition to "mainstream," for example, we can end up revalidating stereotypes which serve only to separate us; "ethnic market," "ethnic food" and even "Ethnic Studies" are often times too narrowly defined as the expressions of "the other." A less-explored side effect I came to learn from my students is that those who do not belong to an ethnic category, or "the club" as the student in VII above puts it, feel left out, and their alienation only reinforces the linguistic and cultural divide.

In writing, this divide often results in miscommunication. As we learn to see the other as an expression of ourselves, we have better chances of understanding not only the text but also the ideas that it contains. We come to appreciate our own culture(s) and start considering the possibility of learning about other cultures and other languages.

Cross-cultural writing, world Englishes, and bilingualism

Too often in language what is not standard is interpreted as a mistake, a corruption, a sign of language decay or ineffective acquisition. Students were asked to question these assumptions vis-à-vis linguistic and sociolinguistic theory. Rather than look at texts and concentrate on form alone, students were encouraged to ask questions about function, purpose and context. Because they had been introduced to concepts relating to cross-cultural writing (e.g. context and content orientation, linearity, digression, writer and reader responsibility), basic world Englishes scholarship (e.g. the concentric circles of English, varieties of English, users and uses), and bilingualism (second language acquisition and use), they were more able to gauge the relative communicative power of a text. Some of their reflections included:

> **IX**
>
> Most individuals can easily detect varieties of English through a spoken conversation, but it takes an educated eye to notice various cultural patterns in writing. I can have a telephone conversation with someone from Tonga or China and usually detect an accent or a different pattern of speech. However, one would not usually think that someone's culture would be visible through their writing. Yet, it is; culture lives in speech *and* in writing. And, it is vital for individuals, especially those training to become teachers, to become educated about different cultures' patterns for writing.
>
> **X**
>
> Although my clientele was diverse, my results were generally the same: I saw the variety of rhetorical/logical patterns these clients used as products of their personal inabilities to comprehend the sacredness of the writing process.
>
> **XI**
>
> However, entire cultural and social groups have been guilty of deviating from this norm, using their unique customs, experiences, circumstances to personalize English—and by doing so they have derived expediency from their aberration. English is merely one among many tools for expression, and sometimes many tools—say, Spanish *and* English, i.e., Spanglish—are necessary for this expression. Hence, the concept of "Englishes" is now proper, since it gives equal validity to the usages once perceived as deviant.

I wanted to finish quoting from my students by presenting a quotation which to me summarizes the idea of bringing the understanding of "the other" as equal to oneself. Our discussions came full circle when students realized that there is virtue in engaging in dialogue and becoming the other. Several students came to realize that an added value to bilingualism is the kind of understanding that can only come from first-hand experience. At a certain point in the semester, some students started to feel that by being in a position of monolingual privilege, they were actually being denied an enriching experience that language learning has to offer. Some became initially upset at this realization, as if they had been robbed of an important part of their education, but soon realized that it was up to them to turn things around.

> **XII**
>
> In last week's class discussion, there was a lot of talk regarding bilingual education in public schools across America [...] Bilingual education in the US is a good idea, but it is not truly bilingual education; it is only bilingual for those who do not already speak English [...] In order to become more culturally understanding, everyone should learn a second language, not just immigrants. Americans should make bilingual education truly bilingual.

Conclusion

I am of course only one of the many teachers making awareness to cross-cultural issues in writing a central topic in the classroom. This practice of bringing contrastive rhetoric to the forefront seems to me as one of the most powerful tools in eliminating what Riggins (1997, cited in Palfreyman, 2005: 214) refers to as othering. The former author explains that "Othering of another group typically involves maintaining social distance and making judgments about the group as a whole." When we maintain our distance, it becomes impossible to relate to "the other" at a more meaningful level. On the other hand, it is my belief that practices similar to the ones described in this text can reduce this distance and yield greater understanding of bilingualism/second language use.

The potential of higher and other levels of education to bring awareness to issues facing second language users of English needs to continue being investigated. As Morita (2004 : 573) puts it,

> Given the growing population of linguistically and culturally diverse students in North American colleges and universities, understanding how these students participate in their academic communities and acquire academic discourses in their second language (L2) has become critical.

As the world shrinks through globalization, we should pay special attention to our own linguistic communities and find ways to allow the most people possible "into the club."

References

Ammon, U. (2000), "Towards more fairness in international English: Linguistic rights of non-native speakers?" in R. Phillipson (ed.), *Rights to Language, Equity, Power, and Education* (pp. 111–116) (Mahwah, NJ: Lawrence Erlbaum).

Canagarajah, A. S. (1996), "'Nondiscursive' requirements in academic publishing, material resources of periphery scholars, and the politics of knowledge production," *Written Communication*, 13, 435–472.

Connor, U. (1996), *Contrastive Rhetoric: Cross-cultural Aspects of Second Language Writing* (Cambridge: Cambridge University Press).

Crawford, J. (2000), Anatomy of the English-only movement. http://ourworld.compuserve.com/homepages/JCRAWFORD/anatomy.htm. 4 July 2006.

Friedrich, P. (2007), *Language, Negotiation and Peace* (London: Continuum Press).

Flowerdew, J. (2000), "Discourse community, legitimate peripheral participation, and the non-native-English-speaking scholar," *TESOL Quarterly*, 34(1), 127–150.

Flowerdew, J. (2001), "Attitudes of journal editors to non-native speaker contributions," *TESOL Quarterly*, 35(1), 121–150.

Gillespie, S. and Becker, R. (2005), *Across Cultures: A Reader for Writers* (Harlow: Pearson-Longman).

Graddol, D. (1997), *The Future of English*. (London: The British Council).

Graddol, D. (2006), *English Next* (London: The British Council).

Hinds, J. (1987), "Reader versus writer responsibility: A new typology," in U. Connor and R. B. Kaplan (eds), *Writing across Languages: Analysis of L2 Text* (pp. 141–152) (Reading, MA: Addison-Wesley).

Hofstede, G. (1980), Culture's Consequences: International Differences in Work-related Values (London: Sage Publications).

Kaplan, R. (1966), "Cultural thought pattern in intercultural education," *Language Learning*, 16, 1–20.

Kubota, R. and Lehner, A. (2004), "Toward critical contrastive rhetoric," *Journal of Second Language Writing*, 13, 127–150.

Morita, N. (2004), "Negotiating participation and identity in second language academic communities," *TESOL Quarterly*, 38(4), 573–603.

Palfreyman, D. (2005), "Othering in an English language program," *TESOL Quarterly*, 39(2), 211–233.

Pennycook, A. (1994), The Cultural Politics of English as an International Language (London: Longman).

Eccentric Maps: Community-based Writing and Rhetorical Aims

Michael Stancliff

Whether we call it public or community-based writing, curriculum designed to engage students in pubic discourse is well-suited for rhetoric-based composition instruction. I keep learning this lesson even as I become less certain about the nature and quality of "the public" *per se*. Even casual analysis of how the term "public" is used indicates the diversity of stratagems, assumptions, and exclusions entailed in any invocation of the public. In my first composition courses, I required students to address public issues and urged them to take up those they felt most impacted their lives. Maybe as a graduate student with new-found freedom to pursue my own course of study, I empathically bucked the notion of imposed writing guidelines. My assumption then, one I have retained, is that people writing about matters of high interest are more engaged in their work, and thus the learning outcomes are richer. Several years passed before I developed a more methodical approach to this initial impulse to "open up" traditional modes of academic writing instruction to a diversity of public occasions and genres. In the interim, my courses were often lively and contentious, but the soapbox ethos that seemed to develop was dissatisfying. All the partisan sounding off didn't seem like the socially engaged classroom of the critical pedagogy I was reading. Further experiments in developing a rhetorical practicum instead of a process-model workshop convinced me that under the right circumstances, a teacher might more effectively help students beyond opinion—unreflective habitation of common places knowledge—to intention— a committed decision to take up writing as action.

The origins of this chapter are an effort to demonstrate the fit between community-based curricula and rhetorical aims. I submit that we should do more than ask our students to dramatize the process of public rhetorical practice; we should help them to practice outright. Orientation toward "the discovery of the available means of persuasion"—Aristotle's definition of rhetoric as invention first and foremost—should ground any community-based writing course. As college-writing instructors, we are well justified pursuing rhetorical aims. "Rhetorical Knowledge" is the first category of the Writing Program Administrator's First-Year "Outcomes Statement," a set of learning objectives that has been widely endorsed and adopted among organizations of writing teachers. Students engage socially grounded (thus rhetorically specific) contexts when they write as a function of community participation, rhetoric in the world. There are many available models for community-based writing instruction. In the pedagogical position and curricular suggestions that follow, I demonstrate that fit through a review of my own practice in two different teaching contexts. My own courses are organized as project workshops, in which self-directed student writing projects drive the study of rhetoric. I recount my own past practices of publicly situated writing instruction, the basic workshop structure of my first-year courses, and a more specific course integrated in the context of a community conference addressing immigration and "border issues." After presenting these curricula, I address some likely complications in community-based courses, confusions occurring as a result of making the shift from *practice writing* to an active practice of rhetoric. Reorienting our thinking about the risks of such teaching can turn these "problems" into curricular strengths. In my final section, I discuss the Writing Program Administrator's Outcome Statement for First-Year Writing. Using three examples of student projects, I argue that community-based writing instruction strongly supports all of these widely adopted outcomes.

I offer the following examples for their heuristic value, not as templates. Nor do I assume that this approach works well in all writing classrooms. Any number of factors, ranging from a teacher's disposition, inflexible program-wide policies and procedures, to discouraging colleagues, could reduce the positive outcomes of community-based writing instruction. I can only recommend community-based writing instruction in good conscience to teachers who welcome the challenges of a busy, labor-intensive writing workshop. This approach militates against boiler-plate curriculum and requires continuous sensitivity to the learning opportunities that emerge as students work through their project. The community-based workshop must be a reflective one, as students and instructors pay careful attention to and discuss "the available means" of rhetorical success as they present themselves across a range of self-directed student projects. The variability of such classrooms, despite its challenges, is an important ground for rhetorical instruction. Moving from the ancient premise that successful language always begins in inquiry, teachers can take the valuation "good writing" not as a prescription, but as a founding, open question.

Qualifications and friendly criticisms of community and "public" writing pedagogy

Before proceeding, some qualifications of the claims of community-based pedagogy are needed. Asking students to talk about their community life and participation admittedly courts abstraction and quite a few clichés and platitudes. Where we belong, where we are from—these positions are not self-evident. Our students as likely as anyone have given little careful thought to how they identify in the collective sense. What, after all, is meant by *community*? The problem, as Joseph Harris has pointed out, begins with the term community itself, which is used so variously that it seems almost entirely up for grabs. Harris worries that the term as used in composition studies, intended to point writing students and teachers out into the social world, is actually an "empty and sentimental word" eliding conflicts inherent in social spheres. He is critical of composition theory that "invokes the idea of community in ways at once sweeping and vague, positing discursive utopias that direct and determine the writing of their members, yet failing to state the operating rules or boundaries of these communities." Harris is only slightly less uncomfortable with the concept of "discourse communities," which has found such currency in composition theory and which does not solve the "problem ... of unspecified boundaries and hidden conflicts" (1989: 12–15). Harris concludes that the idea of "organic" social relations inherent in our thinking about community masks the social contingencies and accidents of history that account for community definition as surely as any consensus among ostensible members (at p. 20). In other words, do standard definitions of community overlook the extremely limited agency most people have to choose community? Thinking about the social world through the lens of community, might we lose focus on how often people are excluded from communities and on how community-based identities serve as the rationale for such exclusions?

Harris's concern is well-warranted. Certainly it wouldn't take long working through an Internet search engine to find several dozen public relations initiatives in which "community" is a central persuasive term. How are we "spinning" the notion of the community in our first-year courses? Two decades after Harris's 1989 critique of our disciplinary reliance on overly optimistic thinking about community, "the public" has come under similar critical fire as a as a pedagogical orientation and descriptor of social collectivity in composition studies. Paula Mathieu's *Tactics of Hope: The Public Turn in English Composition* traces what is now a relatively widespread pedagogical orientation within the field of writing instruction. What might rightly be called public writing instruction occurs in many contexts. Perhaps most straightforwardly, some teachers ask students to address social issues, writing about them in inquiry-based courses. In other departmental contexts, service learning programs partner writing classes with schools and other community organizations, partnerships in which students volunteer and write about their experience. Other public writing models position students outside academic boundaries as ethnographers in local communities. Web-based curricula seek virtual community as contexts for reading and writing. Community-based literacy projects seek to organize community member-student-faculty collaborations as resources for addressing social issues (Mathieu, 2005: 1–8). This schema of public writing pedagogies no longer sounds eccentric; these practices make up an increasingly strong current in the mainstream of composition pedagogy and curriculum. In fact, successive annual meetings of the Conference on College Composition and Communication, the largest professional organization of composition teachers, have been organized under themes of a public engagement: "Composition in the Center Spaces: Building Communities, Cultures and Coalitions" (2006); "Access, Affirmative Action and Student Success" (2005); "Making Composition Matter: Students, Citizens, Institutions, Advocacy" (2004); and "Connecting Text and the Street" (2003).[i] Mathieu and others have recently called for a more careful appraisal of the ideological assumptions of instructors crafting curriculum like those delineated in this public turn.

Reviewing theoretical interrogations of "the public sphere" and gauging the meaning of these critiques for the composition classroom, rhetoric and composition theorist Rosa Eberly questions any uncritical acceptance of the structure or quality of the public sphere, a term we use all too easily with qualification. Eberly argues that "public theorists have implicitly yet consistently suggested the rhetorical nature of publics and their formation" (1999: 167). Eberly warns that the monolithic conception of "the public" as one un-variegated and open sphere of linguistic participation obscures the more eccentric and fragmented realities of actually existing practices. I like Susan Wells' description of the public as "intensely imagined" (at p. 326). The phrase captures the strength of our ideological commitments to the idea of a popular culture of cooperation as collective agency. Teachers using public writing approaches should acknowledge the risks of "going public." Articulating her own public pedagogy, Patricia Roberts-Miller (2003) cautions against the discursive violence of civility in the supposedly "open" discourse of public exchange. For Roberts-Miller, the rhetoric of civility characterizing much public writing pedagogy should be replaced by expectations for agonistic conflict, argument in the best sense as our best hope for public problem solving. These critiques strongly echo those previously voiced by Harris, and I submit that we should be measured in optimism about the potential of public writing, not just for our students, experimenting perhaps for the first time with public address. It could be well argued that access to public forums is generally very tightly restricted. And yet assumptions about a wide-open and free communicative ethos are a part of our cultural inheritance in the United States, a nation understood to be founded on principles of "free speech" and "the marketplace of ideas." "The public," which we tend to understand as the seat of democratic power and virtue, proves to be a more labyrinthine and less populated sphere of power than perhaps we had thought.

Each of these critics offers distinct caution, it must be noted, as a *friendly* critique seeking to rehabilitate public writing as a viable approach to writing instruction in a democratic society. Criticism "on the ground" made by leery colleagues using more traditional approaches may be trenchant, or at least more uncomfortable, given the immediacy; my own experience with such resistance prompts me to dwell a bit here on some grounds of rebuttal. One complaint likely to arise is that community-based curricula fail to prepare students for success in the academia by refusing to privilege the academic essay as a primary focus. This charge, of course, assumes that traditional methods succeed routinely, when it seems evident that curricula expressly designed to teach academic modes might fail to meet this very aim for any number of reasons. The charge, in any case, is too sweeping and ignores the core *rhetorical* concerns of composition instruction. Teaching rhetoric is immediately applicable to academic writing. Across disciplines, teachers expect, reward and admire well-reasoned discourse adapted well to the moment, exactly the compositional habits community-based instructionfosters. Nor do community-based and more traditional academic methods of instruction need to be mutually exclusive. For example, I often require an annotated bibliography or research review in my community-based courses, stressing the rhetorical elements of such traditionally academic tasks. Respectfully, I submit that students who learn rhetorical habits of mind, the habit of holistically surveying the whole of a communicative situation and the options and decisions required therein, will approach academic writing situations with greater confidence and savvy, understanding academic writing as simply one possible rhetorical context.

In sum, when we overvalue consensus and civility in our writing classrooms, perhaps due to quite reasonable apprehension about the risks of public writing instruction, we channel an unexamined politics of public virtue. Millers-Robert, Wells, Eberly, Harris, Mathieu and others could be summarized together as making a trenchant call for reflective practice, focused specifically on the question of what we intend and what we assume when we ask students to "go public" with their composition. I would grant what Harris seems to dread, that community operates as "little more than a metaphor," quibbling only with his diminutive term (1989: 15). Metaphors of identity are not inconsequential, and however we name the social world in which we hope to stage writing instruction, the nomenclature will bring with it a history of assumptions and blind spots. Frankly, the hyper-earnestness and connotative cliché of the word *community* make it that much easier to take a critical turn on the concept and so to help students reflect carefully on the social situations, ways of thinking, shared fear or ambition, common history, that constitute community. Harris's is an important caution, but utopian naivety is unlikely in the rhetorical *practica* of a community-based writing course. More likely, and far more instructive, is student consternation regarding the multiple and trenchant constraints of going public and actually exercising agency as a writer. Any utopian daydreaming fades quickly as the rigor of rhetorical craft takes center stage in the classroom.

I began this chapter acknowledging my own felt sense of the democratic potential of what we now call community-based writing instruction, and even knowing what I know about the problems of "public discourse" (problems of access, or resources, accountability, and censorship) I still see my teaching work as part of this "public turn." Despite limits and complications, a community-based approach still strikes me as the best means of helping develop the conceptual resources that empower students in all the rhetorical habitations of their lives. Away from the big public of political and pedagogical imagination, vital opportunities for writing instruction await.

Community-based composition: Who brought the map?

I teach all my writing courses as *practica* in rhetoric. This is a revised version of a course description for a first-year writing course (the second semester of my university's first-year requirement). The description highlights my expectations for committed writing and emphasis on rhetorical instruction:

> This is a writing-intensive course emphasizing rhetorical invention and inquiry. Pursuing a diversity of writing, reading and research methods, each student will engage areas of high-interest, self-selected issues and problems that demand your attention, that fascinate and motivate you. As students work on self-designed projects, we will study "rhetoric," the strategies of language use that get work done in the world, or at least whatever part of the world grabs your attention, be it in the college classroom, at work, or in your "home communities," however you define them. Our course will be run as a writing and research workshop in which everyone will be expected to take responsibility for the direction of their inquiry and ultimately for producing a final project of your own design. As we all head off in our own directions, following our own interests and social commitments, we will share our challenges, struggles and successes, and this conversation will be the basis of our common pursuit to master principles of rhetorical craft.

Many students "click" almost immediately with this approach; it isn't uncommon to have students decide on a project focus in the first week or even the first day of class. This is always encouraging as it suggests a critical mass of students who arrived with rhetorical work to do, with a focus that can become an exemplar for your instruction. Others will be more reticent, unsure about the prospect of engaging "high-interest, self-selected issues," issues that "fascinate and motivate." In my experience, we can't underestimate the degree to which many students distrust advice that sounds like a mandate to "do your own thing," or "write whatever you want." Many will distrust such statements as disingenuous, and many will decide that they didn't come to college to "do whatever." It is important to be clear that the project model is a laboratory of rhetorical study, and that instruction will be rigorous and demanding.

When presented as a powerful means of problem solving, students are likely to see the value of rhetorical instruction quite readily. To structure arguments, to think carefully about audience, to examine the generic requirements of the moment, to evaluate evidence—these and other rhetorical concerns resonate with students who identify rhetoric as a widely applicable intellectual resource. One of the first barriers to this approach is that most students arriving in first-year courses have no working definition of rhetoric. This needs to be established immediately. Many textbooks offer serviceable definitions of rhetoric and multiple chapters on rhetorical invention. Teachers not departmentally bound to specific textbooks may review a range of definitions with students. As previously mentioned, Aristotle's "discovery" heuristic has the benefit of spatializing rhetorical pursuits, of suggesting a narrative in which students can see themselves participating as researchers and writing. I often offer a more academic translation here, describing rhetoric as "The research and analysis needed to understand an issue or situation and to understand the possibilities and limitations of composition within that situation."

My students' projects are consistently impressive. Students have put together slide presentations on sexual harassment in the workplace, websites speaking out against racial stereotypes, letters to a support group newsletter serving the families of soldiers deployed in Iraq, personal reflections written in defense of the conservation of Arizona's desert spaces written for an outdoor magazine, the introduction to a cookbook for single workaholics, and an article written for a school newspaper questioning the rationale for a tuition hike. There are far too many to list in this archive of engaged student work. On occasion, students have staged performances with particular rhetorical intentions. The sheer variety of scope and focus is one of the most enjoyable aspects of this teaching approach. More importantly, the variety produces continuous comparative "teaching moments." During a class discussion involving student writers pursuing their own projects, the comparison of evidentiary arguments, for example, becomes quite instructive. The student writing a review of a concert for a webzine, the one writing a workplace proposal, and the one writing a speech for his church group, can teach each other a great deal about the different levels of scrutiny audiences focus on evaluating evidence, about the forms of evidence that will be most persuasive from context to context, about expectations and conventions for documenting sources, etc. Discussions among students and regular reflective writing on their peers' work integrates this experiential cross-pollination into the rhetorical instruction of your course. Again, what students learn in this comparative mode is the lesson of context specificity, that core principle of rhetoric.

The semester runs through five phases, titled and listed here for convenience:

- Mapping Community Commitments and Choosing a Project
- Rhetorical Invention
- Drafting
- Publication (or Not).

The notion of mapping mobilizes a set of metaphors most useful in rhetorical instructions, in sum, metaphors of cartography, of surveying, of navigating terrain, of finding new destinations and home spaces. By rendering a representative map of their community participation, students locate the social spheres in their lives where rhetoric matters, that is to say, the places where they have a stake in the events and situations that constitute community. After locating project work, the pressing situation they will address in composition, students can be introduced to the strategies of research and analysis that are entailed in rhetorical invention. In other words, the choosing or rhetorical ground to navigate initiates an intensive course in rhetorical study. An exhaustive process of invention, composition and revision sustained across the course culminates in the drafts that must be assessed as acts of rhetoric, fitting for public audience.

The map metaphor: Finding community and commitment

As a means of locating student commitment, cartographic metaphors make useful heuristics. Remind students that map is a verb as well as a noun. Mapping is an active process of planning and investigation. The map, in other words, is a heuristic, a process of invention, a means of addressing larger questions and situations.

Naming communities is not always easy, as students soon find out, and as teachers should know, thinking through and discussing identity, be it collective or individual, can be tricky ethical terrain. Joseph Harris's caution is well taken on this point. But rather than trying to control the terms of community definition, or offer extensive lessons on theories of social construction, I let it go, so to speak. I place no restrictions on how students define community. In fact, evaluation of the assignment need only demand a few practical requirements. Quite randomly, I assign a minimum of ten communities.

Ten? many ask doubtfully, not imagining that their community participation is so diverse. Here is a version of the assignment description

> **You should map at least ten different communities.** Remember to be broad in your definition of community. Is the community geographic? (I'm from the Southwest.) Civic? (I'm a US citizen. I'm a Californian. I'm from the south side of Chicago. I'm from Phoenix.) Based on politics? (I'm a UAW member, a feminist, a Republican, a Democrat, a socialist, an anarchist.) Ethnic or historical? (I'm African American. I'm Israeli. I'm Mexican American. I'm Irish American. I'm Native American. I'm a Vietnam War veteran.) Religious? (I'm Catholic, Muslim, Jewish, Buddhist.) Based on gender or sexuality? (I'm a woman. I'm heterosexual.) Based on profession or vocation? (I'm a lawyer, potter, truck driver, musician.) Based on school? (I'm an ASU student, a business major, a first-year student.)

Students have done beautiful visual work, taking up the cartographic figures in earnest and composing the geo-rhetorical terrain of their lives. A mountain range marks the boundary a student sees between her work and home life. A community of staff workers is figured as an island within a hostile-looking sea representing a volatile and unpredictable workplace. Academia could be a forest or a desert, lush or barren depending on the student's perspective. I always stress, however, that the mapping heuristic is not an arts-crafts project, and that a simple list of communities works just as well for many students. A series of text boxes works well, as do flow charts and various kinds of bubble or cluster maps—whatever visual process helps students think through the idea of community participation.

The next "level of detail" required on the maps can be put in the form "issue questions." Community-based problems, I tell students, present themselves as questions when surveyed from a rhetorician's perspective. Community-based writing addresses situations that are unresolved or ongoing. As the ancients argued, rhetoric is about probability, not certainty. The challenge of posing issue questions is to capture the point of disagreement or what is at stake. Consider the map, which I take to be a successful response to the assignment. (See Figure 9.1.)

Readers will notice the eccentric definition of community suggested by this map. While "United States Citizen" claims a familiar enough national community, "Person Carrying Big Credit Card Debt" may not immediately signify the boundaries of community as traditionally construed. The intention is to show students the ways that interest and commitment frame rhetorical situation. I tell my students that communities form and fragment continually, and that even clearly defined communities such as those defined by national citizenship

Commuting student
How should we deal with road ragers?
Why can't the university be more accommodating in terms of scheduling?

United States citizen
Is the Iraq war just?
Presidential election—who to pick?
What can be done about gas prices?

Father
How do I protect my children from media influence?
How do I raise my children to be moral people?

Environmentalist
What can be done to convince the public that water is a finite resource?
Why aren't we investing more in alternative fuel sources?

Person carrying big credit card debt
What can I do about my credit record?
Should I file for personal bankruptcy?
To what degree are credit card companies to blame for the "debt epidemic"?

Divorced middle age man
Is there love after divorce and addiction?
How do I meet people now that I don't go to bars?
Can we hope to find love on the Internet?

Member of community theater
What do we do with members who don't work their volunteer hours?
Why can't we stage less mainstream productions?

Sober alcoholic
How can I stay "dry"?
How do I talk to my kids about addiction?

Caucasian
To what degree do I assume white privilege?

Fig. 9.1 Student Community Map

take on much different qualities depending on the contexts in which they are invoked. Keeping Joseph Harris's caution in mind, I always remind students that the goal is less "finding their place" than investigating the rhetorical terrain around them.

A brief look at the map included here should indicate how rich it is in directions for invention and composition. After reviewing and discussing the map with classmates, students write a reflective essay discussing the relative importance of the issues represented on the map. I dramatize this issue considerably, reminding them that with the choice of the issue, they are deciding where to direct their own rhetorical energy. The primary function of this reflection is to choose a situation for the semester's work. I ask students to explain why the situation has such pull for members of the specific community, how it became important to them personally, and how currently they hope to intervene in the situation as communicators. I make an event of these decisions, congratulating students on a major step taken.

Rhetorical invention

My typical introduction to rhetorical invention begins simply enough. This past semester, I told students to imagine this scenario. Their English teacher announces two weeks before the end of the term that he has added a thirty-page research paper to the required assignment list. The paper is due on the last day of class. How would you react? While a number of students claimed they would have accepted the addition to their workload, a greater number felt strongly that the hypothetical teacher's actions were unfair and cause for complaint or downright refusal. Given 15 minutes in small groups, students gathered a range of persuasive lines of reasoning to make objections. *Two weeks is not enough time to produce the paper. Two weeks isn't enough time to do a decent job. Little would be learned about writing and research in such a compressed space. The assignment is unfair as it isn't listed on the syllabus. The assignment puts an undue stress on students who have already scheduled big, end-of-the-term workloads.* Praising the students' ingenuity, I tell them they had just had their introduction to the theory and practice of rhetorical invention. Here is where I introduce Aristotle's maxim about the discovery of available means of persuasion. I put it in more accessible terms, explaining that the process of invention is the process of learning about all of the requirements, difficulties and opportunities in any communicative situation.

In my final section, I will be more specific about how community-based curricula support rhetorical aims. Here I offer the first stage of teaching invention, which follows closely from the mapping exercise. I ask students to pursue further mapping, this time of the communities that form around issue questions. I ask students to map *stakeholder arguments*. I use the language of stakeholders to indicate the social imperatives, thought through a rhetorical framework, that hold community together. For example, the student who put together the map shown in the previous section ultimately chose to address the issue of university course scheduling practices. Beginning with his own perception of inadequacies in the system, the student began research by listing all of the stakeholders involved in the decision-making process—administrators, instructors, students, advisors, the families of students, facilities management and others. By investigating how these various stakeholder groups thought and argued about this issue, the student began to understand his own stake and interest as existing within a complicated rhetorical situation.

The next step of the invention process challenges students to catalogue all of the arguments about the situation at hand that circulate in and among the various stakeholder groups. I tell students to think of this overall web of persuasive intention as the rhetorical terrain of their project. In a writing course focused around the academic essay, the parallel process is the consultation of experts, the survey of the relevant scholarship on the topic at hand. While this traditional academic process of articulating a position within a body of disciplinary knowledge is no less a process of invention, community-based invention challenges are more multifaceted and ultimately more challenging.

Let me briefly sketch the process of invention through which I guide my students. Again, the first step is discerning all of the relevant stakeholder groups. After listing all these groups, students must summarize the positions held within each of these groups. For example, a number of students have currently chosen the "troop surge" in Iraq as a project focus. What are the prevailing stakeholder arguments in this context? In this country there are clearly those who support and oppose the troop surge. Other, less mainstream voices call for military action even more extreme and involved than President Bush's proposed surge. European nations, some United States allies in the war and some not, have taken a range of positions on the surge. Clearly the Iraqi's fledgling government has a vested interest in United States military policy. What have other Middle Eastern leaders and commentators said about the surge? Quickly then, we can sketch major stakeholder groups, and further thought and research will reveal others. To help students discover the broadest range of prevailing arguments, we must help them go beyond the "for-and-against" paradigm that dominates less sophisticated public writing instruction. Consider for example how many different positions are taken by those opposed to the troop surge. Some oppose on tactical grounds, and of course here there are multiple perspectives. Some oppose on more purely political grounds, Democrats and Republicans for instance already thinking ahead to the 2008 Presidential election. Others oppose on humanitarian grounds. As I tell students, they most likely don't have the time and energy for an exhaustive mapping of stakeholder arguments, but that is the ideal towards which they are to work.

Once the stakeholder arguments are sufficiently catalogued, students need to take a closer look at the kinds of arguments used to forward these various positions. What are the major lines of reasoning that dominate the debate?

Which premises are generally accepted, which are hotly contested and by whom? What kinds of emotional approaches tend to be used? What experience or credentials understood to be authoritative in the context of the given situation? What historical precedents are invoked? What predictions or causal arguments are routinely made? What are the dominant modes of evidence used to support various positions? Analyzing primary texts from the rhetorical situation should be a major focus in the course. Note that this is not analysis for its own sake; it is part of the process students must undertake to find their own rhetorical grounding. Again, many textbooks have a strong enough core rhetoric to assist students with this analysis and help them think more carefully about the rhetorical moves they must make in their project drafts.

Invention in the community-based classroom requires students to situate themselves temporally in the rhetorical situation. In addition to analyzing the prevailing arguments constituting the situation, students must locate their audience in time and space and find a forum or occasion for making their work public. For example, a student trying to involve his church group in a charitable cause must find out if speaking briefly to the congregation before or at the beginning of the sermon will be allowed. Is there space in the church bulletin? Is the only available option to post a flier in the church lobby? These are not minor decisions. A student addressing the troop surge in Iraq must decide how she can reach a meaningful audience unless she has some means, perhaps web-based, to address a national or international audience. These time-and-space considerations help focus invention. For example, addressing a local audience regarding the troop surge behooves the student to pay much closer attention to the prevailing local arguments. How many troops from our state will be deployed? What have our local and state politicians said about the surge and what it means for our local communities? As I tell my students, a major factor in any persuasive act is simply locating and finding the means of reaching an audience. It seems to me that these challenges more than any other in the community-based classroom help students rethink composition as an authentic life skill as opposed to an academic exercise.

Without fail, students generate a great deal of invention writing, and this work should be central in your assessment of student success. I often require students to keep an "invention journal" in which they record their research and analysis of primary and secondary texts, their emerging project drafts, and reflections on the progress of their work. Students might also write an extended narrative of their research that charts their developing perspective on the project situation at hand. In any case, if the message we want to send students is that invention is the heart of rhetorical practice, and I do think we want to send that message, then careful assessment of their invention work is necessary.

Drafting and going public (or not)

There is no way to generalize about the drafting process in a community-based classroom. By and large, students are working in radically different contexts and composing very different kinds of texts. In all cases, drafting is not detached from the invention process, as it constitutes the arrangement of arguments, appeals, and evidence in a format most fitting for the situation at hand. My goal during the drafting process is to engage the group in dialogue, to get them learning from one another by comparison. Rhetorical principles come more clearly into focus when students see them at play across contexts. The differences of project contexts serves to highlight the common challenges of rhetorical craft generally.

I joke with my students, telling them that if I could legally force them to publish, to find access to meaningful audience, I would do so. A teacher can't demand publication or really even submission beyond the classroom in most cases. However, many students will take this final step of going public, and the results have been inspiring. Students find ingenious means of public intervention and thus demonstrating their ability to align intention, invention in the context of audience and a myriad of rhetorical constraints. Regardless of whether or not students actually engage intended audiences with their compositions, thinking carefully through the challenges of public writing extends rhetorical instruction. To work through the process of planning the occasion, choosing a forum, understanding its limitations and possibilities, requires more detailed thinking about audience, their expectations and predispositions. Some of these concerns can be quite immediate. For example, the student addressing the church group would do well to find out the topic of the sermon to be delivered on the day of his presentation to the congregation. How might this student integrate his own argument with the persuasive force of the sermon? For many students, the genre of the project doesn't come into focus until they have taken the step of placing their rhetorical intervention in time and space. All of this is to say that publication, or at the very least, publication-minded pursuit of compositional work, requires students to think more holistically through the challenges of effective communication and to experiment with a broader range of craft.

Border justice: Rhetorical instruction and the community classroom

Students can also participate in rhetorical events as members of community forums. University and college settings are often rich in opportunities, and there are likely many off-campus forums to consider. Arrange for students to attend an academic or professional conference. Participate in a local election. Take students to a commemoration or protest. The great benefit of situating writing as event-specific is the foregrounding of rhetoric, of language as contextual negotiation. In the spring of 2006, faculty, staff and students hosted the third "Border Justice" forum at the West Campus of Arizona State University where I teach. The forum, which has become a hallmark of our campus culture, featured a host of speakers, performances, workshops and films. In my course, we researched and wrote about the conglomeration of social and political issues implied when people talk about "the border." Students in this instance were self-selecting, having registered for the course knowing about the course theme. As a group, we pursued community-based invention process through analysis of policy and popular writing on the border, a review of multidisciplinary research, engagement with guest lectures, and a trip to the "migrant trails" South of Tucson.

I introduced the course as a living laboratory of rhetorical instruction, explaining that the students would make their work public for the symposium participants. One of our major assignments courted controversy but to important pedagogical ends. Students presented Wikipedia articles they composed on immigration and border-related topics at a research poster session held during the Border Justice symposium. I introduced the Wikipedia assignment as being in keeping with the community-involvement and educational intentions of the Border Justice event; although the quality of Wikipedia research was thought to be suspect in many corners, we would write for this venue with the best intentions of offering our research as a free resource for researchers. The following is from my introduction to the assignment:

> Each student will write a short article intended for publication on Wikipedia. The articles will address a key idea, event, public figure, policy, etc. associated with border issues. Writing for Wikipedia presents a useful challenge for writers because it is open to article submissions from anyone. Millions of people all around the world use Wikipedia as a source of information. Some people understand Wikipedia as a truly democratic project of grassroots knowledge making, while other see it as a dangerous example of the "blind leading the blind." At a time when other universities are prohibiting students from using Wikipedia in their research, we will take on the contradictions and confusions of this space. The challenge offers us the opportunity to think about the complicated social situation of public writing, the authority of information available to us, and the nature of knowledge itself.

At the poster session, we projected the articles on a screen for viewing, and in the spirit of Wikipedia, computer terminals offered visitors the opportunity to revise the articles. Students, of course, had final say about the content of their article, but allowing audience participation in this way was intended to impress upon students the demands of audience expectations as well as giving them another opportunity to revise their articles.

Notice that this assignment demanded students to think about the multivalent community contexts in which composition is situated, contexts in which the authority of knowledge itself is created. Requiring students to write for Wikipedia, a source much maligned for its admittedly uneven quality, forced them to think carefully about the contingency of their own authority and the attending responsibilities of the public presentation of research. If Wikipedia is notorious in many university circles, its publishing policies foreground quality as an open question requiring public adjudication. Students understood that their work could be flagged for "cleanup" or "inaccuracies," or that it might merit a warning about "quality s`tandards." The assignment concretized the ethics of public writing, as publishing at Wikipedia was to provide resources, which could immediately influence a reader's thinking about a hotly contested political issue, the stakes of which are quite high on all sides. We had instructive discussions in class imagining how readers of different political stripes would judge their work and how they might put it to use. Students had the rhetorical challenges of their work circulating well beyond contexts over which they had any control or even awareness.

To be sure, the campus event for their articles presented them with the challenge of a complex audience. Not only did faculty and students read their work, but conference goers from the surrounding community read them as well. Students had also to consider the online audience of Wikipedia users, people interested in border issues but perhaps uninformed beyond the most cursory knowledge. My task was to help students recognize and negotiate the complexity of this rhetorical challenge. This was a rich study in audience awareness. Despite our efforts to the contrary, much university instruction reduces the complexity of audience, either by reducing it to static "positions" or by listing audience attributes or "expectations" on the model of demographics research. The multivalent audiences engaging the students' Wikipedia articles at the Border Justice conference concretized the idea that audiences bring disparate interpretive practices and intentions to the task of reading and that any audience is comprised of rich variety along these lines. For example, one student's article explicated the term "coyote," the name given to guides paid to bring migrants across the Mexico–United States border. Writing her article after two months of studying border and immigration issues, she understood the many uses to which information about coyotes could be put. Would she, for example, highlight the criminality of much coyote practice? Would doing so be instructive and helpful for readers concerned about the welfare of the migrants? Would it support a primarily criminalizing perspective on border issues? Would it scapegoat a group of people who are themselves often only barely removed from the positions of vulnerability and desperation suffered by the migrants themselves?

The work of the teacher in the "community classroom" is to constantly draw the students attention to the demands of the event and thus to the rhetorical constraints of the writing situation. The Border Justice course enjoyed optimum support—technology and research support and a low enrollment of self-selecting students. Although such resources are most often not available for the great majority of those teaching composition, any forum might establish the parameters of event-focused rhetorical instruction.

Some possible challenges along the way

Several challenges likely face any instructor pursuing any model of community-based teaching. Instructed to design their own projects based on their actual interests, students can be intellectually disoriented. Standard high school curricula, in which students' writing experience is often contained to the five-paragraph essays and "creative writing," likely has not prepared most students to think holistically about the situations of rhetoric. The challenges of unfamiliarity can be effectively met, however, and in many cases constitute opportunities to further enrich rhetorical instruction.

Drawing a blank

Students will report different varieties of blankness when faced with the choice of a community-based project focus. "I don't have any commitments," some say, or, "I don't feel committed to anything." This kind of blankness is reasonable enough; many people would be hard pressed to articulate their social commitments upon demand. Another common form of blankness results from the pressure of making an important choice. Students often take the challenge to make writing matter seriously enough to struggle a bit with committing to a direction. The student writer of the map discussed above labored quite a bit in deciding what direction to take. The issues concerning his commitments as a father, as an environmentalist, and as a commuting student claimed his interest strongly, and he considered each as a possible project focus seriously before going another way.

The mapping heuristic can be quite helpful for students experiencing blankness. Ask the student to return to her or his community map. With the student, and preferably two or three other students, brainstorm situations that have impact in one or more of the communities represented on the map. Sometimes this further reflection on commitment can help a student decide on a direction for composition. Another strategy is to consider the relative difficulties of the available choices. Some project ideas are simply too ambitious for the timeframe of a typical academic semester, quarter, or period; this kind of practicality can move the decision-making process along. The aforementioned student writer was very interested in the question of "white privilege" as a systematic social problem, but initial efforts to gather relevant research (to "map stakeholder arguments" in the parlance of our course) indicated a prodigious research load across a number of disciplines, including sociology, criminal justice, and critical race studies. Given time constraints, he decided to save this course of study another time.

Collaborative invention as productive conflict

Without fail, community-based writing classrooms are topical. For every student who wants to put together a workplace proposal for new resources, one or two others will address contentious national and international situations. Here in Arizona, as I indicated, border issues are regularly a topic of disagreement, and given the vehemence of the positions people hold, disagreements can be intense. Many teachers go to great lengths to avoid such conflicts, and I submit such avoidance is a great detriment to rhetorical instructions. Rather than let issues of difference and conflict go un-remarked, we can recognize them as the actual social ground of rhetoric, and a vital site of instruction. Examining the ideological conflicts animating the rhetorical situations of students' project work concretizes what ancient Roman rhetoricians called the point of "stasis," the actual ground of dispute. Attention to the crux of ideological conflict helps students understand the distances that rhetoric must cross to persuade or to make any connection with audience. If staunch anti-immigration critics and advocates of worker-permit programs can share ideas and actually "hear" one another, they can learn a great deal about the culturally bound quality of reasoning. They can share perspectives on the relative quality of evidence, and they gain important information about how their own position is viewed across a broader political spectrum. I hope I won't be counted as overly idealistic, or, for that matter, cynical, when I say that the college classroom offers more possibilities for this kind of exchange than most other public forums in this country.

Clearly, some ground rules must be put in place to help establish a respectful forum, and as suggested above, we should not be too sanguine about the "open dialogue" of conflict models. Students won't necessarily share their positions on issues readily. Misunderstandings do not magically melt away through the mechanism of "sharing," nor do the hard feelings many students experience when conflict is engaged. I acknowledge the criticisms of the community-writing critics reviewed in the second section of this chapter. There are risks to community-based instruction. But the fact is social and rhetorical difference exists in our classrooms, even when our curricula seek to suppress them.

Students should know from the beginning of the semester that "public issues" will be discussed in class. They should understand the elements of the conflict model and that you are not simply courting controversy but promoting rhetorical awareness. Three steps can help promote productive conflict:

1 Preparation stressing respect, tolerance, open-mindedness, and good humor.
2 Structure activities to highlight rhetorical features.
3 Make time for reflection and encourage feedback.

There is no way to guarantee that students will act respectfully when studying and discussing public issues, but be clear about your expectations. I will say that in all my time teaching according to a conflict model, I have rarely encountered egregious behavior. It helps quite a bit to remind students to keep their responses focused on the *positions* articulated and not the students *articulating* them. For example, rather than saying, "You're wrong because …," or, "the problem with what you're saying is," students should address rhetorical elements. What do they think of the evidence? In what values are appeals grounded? Are precedents invoked relevant to the context? Do emotional appeals seem manipulative? Draw students' attention to the rhetorical features of the debate as often as possible. Earnestly solicit feedback on the conflict process when you are through. Encourage students to contact you if they have experienced the process as insulting or disrespectful in any way. Seek out students who seem reticent about participating, and ask them individually if they are uncomfortable with class discussions and exercises. Remind them that the goal is not "winning" an argument or "defending positions" but studying rhetorical means.

There are many ways to stage conflict-as-invention in writing courses. It can be built into instruction by simply pairing a range of arguments around an issue. Gerald Graff's well-known advice to "teach the conflicts" is worth considering as you introduce a rhetorical principle. I take a historical approach in this regard, sharing pro- and anti-slavery texts from the nineteenth century.

Still, I do not hide from conflict in the relatively safe recesses of historical controversy. In fact, I have had great success, following the "community classroom" model described above, during local elections. Most recently, I began an argumentation course around a series of ballot measures on the table during the 2006 midterm elections. I assigned students divergent positions taken by local politicians on a selection of ballot measures, and we reviewed them in class. This process, removed from positions students would have to acknowledge as "their own," helped to de-emphasize the "personal" quality of conflict. Students were forthcoming, expressing their own take on the ballot measures, but the discussion was always easily directed back to the conflicting perspectives of the lawmakers' position statements.

Assessing community-based writing

Writing instructors tightly constrain the scope of what and how students write not only out of a sense of duty to academic apprenticeship, but for practical and ideological reasons involving our own sense of authority. A class of students doing community-based writing is likely to put writing instructors in the uncomfortable position of the inexpert. How could any one teacher possibly have authoritative knowledge of the wide variety of situations students address when directed to their own home communities and interests? I was once faced with assessing a student writer's proposal to create a skate park in his city of residence. It was quite an accomplished proposal, and not the least of this architecture student's achievements was to include a sophisticated blueprint for the park design composed with a software with which I was completely unfamiliar. The truth is, teaching rhetoric, your own expertise in other "subject areas" is much less relevant. In fact, community-based writing instruction offers excellent opportunities for innovative assessment. Opening this question of "quality" to practices of self-assessment and collaborative assessment are ways to further re-enforce rhetorical principles. Here I briefly review two possible models.

In my courses, when students finish a project, they write cover letters that make an argument for the success of the work. I ask students to review the intentions of their writing and the audience or audiences for whom the work is intended. I ask them to account for the major lines of reasoning in the composition, the variety of appeals used, the quality of the evidence, choices about genre and voice, and other rhetorical considerations, and explain why the sum total of their rhetorical approaches are fitting in the context. For example, a student addressing a university's hate-speech regulations with the intention of broadening the scope of prohibited speech would have to justify her or his decision to address a student audience as opposed to administrator's in the Campus Life or Student Affairs office. The student would have to explain the choice of specific court precedents and assess his or her success in rendering complicated legal precedents accessible for a lay audience. The list of possible considerations can be quite involved, and the cover letters are often some of the most impressive documents produced all semester. Most importantly, this process extends rhetorical instruction by challenging students to think through the decisions they have made as rhetors. It is not uncommon for student cover letters to list extensive revisions needed to make the composition more effective. As I assess the rhetorical skills of mind students have developed over the semester, such a document is invaluable to my work.

My own assessment of student projects takes the self-assessing cover letter as a point of departure. I enter into dialogue with the students explaining why I am or am not persuaded by their self-assessment. This dialogic model of assessment allows teachers a more comprehensive perspective, as we are able to evaluate the success of the project as well as the students' rationale for self-assessment, which I would argue tells us something about the rhetorical habits of mind developed over the course of the term or semester. It is one thing to "write well" in a community-based context, but the ability to explain the successes and limitations of one's own work indicates a self-awareness that product assessment alone can't ascertain. Students can be asked to respond to specific criteria, or allowed to assess success in their own terms. Either way, I respond point for point to the student's self-assessment. My assessment always invites further response, asking students for further defense of the success of their work, and invites as well questions about my assessment, and, when time allows, to revise once again.

In the last few decades, there has been quite a bit of talk in composition studies about de-centering the authority of the instructor. Among the good reasons for attempting this eccentric move, doing so has the potential to enhance rhetorically focused teaching and assessment. Drawing on the knowledge of "expert readers," and thus relinquishing some of our own control as adjudicators of writing "quality" can enrich the collaborative assessment process described above. For example, I regularly have education students whose project work is to develop field-specific curriculum for their project (for which I require a pedagogical statement). In such instances, I require the student to enlist an experienced teacher in her field as an expert reader. Clearly, such expert readers can speak to elements of the newly designed curriculum, which to me would not be apparent. Such a reader would be a better judge than I of the pedagogical soundness of assignments, lesson plans, etc. This method of assessment, triangulating the interpretive frame also extends instruction regarding audience. Divergent opinions among student, instructor, and community expert teach students how radically open to interpretation their writing can be, and it can teach them how experience and intention cue audience members to read rhetorically.

In terms of assigning grades, a practice we should distinguish from assessment proper, there are options to consider. Teachers might retain outright control over assigning grades. Assigning a grade based on the persuasiveness of the student's self-assessment has the advantage of making the grading process overtly rhetorical. Students can be allowed to assign their own grades, though in the grade-driven dispensation of today's universities and colleges, this perhaps puts an undue ethical burden on students. Finally, asking students to assign themselves a grade and then doing so yourself allows you the option of averaging the grades.

Assessment and the WPA Outcome Statement for First-Year Writing

The First-Year Writing Outcomes Statement adopted by the Council of the Writing Program Administrators in 2000 has steadily grown in influence as it has been adopted by more and more writing programs.[ii] From my own pedagogical perspective, the WPA Statement is worth considering because, as I will review in this final section, it is grounded in rhetorical principles. Because my writing program recognizes the WPA Statement, I have spent time integrating those outcomes in my own teaching practice. Without a doubt, community-based curriculum is a demonstrable means of supporting the recommended outcomes of the WPA statement.

Consider the following three examples of community-based writing projects, drawn from my students' work. Through further elaboration of these three sample projects, I demonstrate the good match between community-based writing instruction and what is perhaps the most influential pedagogical document in what is a diverse and far-flung institution.

- For the mothers' group to which she belongs, a student writes a review recommending a new book on parenting, which she believes merits her peers' attention.
- A student sets up a website taking a position on national immigration policy.
- A student pursuing research in education writes a proposal for revising their test-driven curriculum.

Like all of the four major outcomes areas, the first, "rhetorical knowledge," is rather redundant in its prescriptions, offering categories with a great deal of overlap. Given the vast array of student and teacher needs and expectations to which the document must be held accountable, this emphasis-by-restatement is understandable. Taken together, the individual outcomes listed under this heading evoke a rhetorically skilled student writer.

By the end of first-year composition, students should have the following:

Rhetorical knowledge

- Focus on a purpose.
- Respond to the needs of different audiences.
- Respond appropriately to different kinds of rhetorical situations.
- Use conventions of format and structure appropriate to the rhetorical situation.
- Adopt appropriate voice, tone, and level of formality.
- Understand how genres shape reading and writing.
- Write in several genres.

To "focus on a purpose" is more difficult than it sounds on the face of it, and students find this out regardless of the curriculum. In the community-based workshop, through the function of mapping, a good deal of time is devoted not simply to focusing purpose, but conceiving it as a core rhetorical concern. Throughout the process of planning, invention, composition, reflection, and collaborative assessment, students must articulate their intentions repeatedly, refining or even redefining as they go along. The student addressing immigration policy, for example, began with a set of received commonplaces that motivated his intention to argue for a militarized border. Through the process of research and invention, he began to wonder about the advisability and efficacy of such a policy. By the time he began to draft the homepage of his website, though still a strong critic of what he saw as our "open border," the student redefined his intention, claiming now the intention to present Web visitors with several options to consider and resources to consult. Assessing his own work at semester's end, he was required to reflect on the details of his composition, for example, the core logic of his mission statement, the images he chose to illustrate the situation of the border, and his summaries of the policies he favored and his responses to those with which he disagreed. The student had to justify his compositional decisions as appropriate for his stated intention. How well had he worked through craft to achieve (or at least maximize) intentions?

The second and third categories under "Rhetorical knowledge" stress the importance of a general rhetorical orientation to composition and of the habit of thinking through the heuristic of "situation." Because the students have been responsible for "mapping" the contours of the rhetorical situation from the beginning, in other words, of undertaking that fundamental challenge of invention, discerning the availability of particular communicative means, they most often report increased ability to understand rhetorical acts as situation-bound. As the student addressing the mothers' group discovered, "purpose" leads immediately to audience and their "needs." Specialized terminology form the fields of child development psychology needed clear explanation for an audience almost entirely without this academic background. This effort to "translate" information for an audience, as many experienced writing instructors know, is a powerful exercise in rhetorical skill. Working in the unfamiliar genre of the book review, this student writer faced the challenge of balancing summary and commentary and of developing a tone and "level of formality" that was at once inviting and professional.

Critical thinking, reading, and writing

The outcomes listed under this heading cannot rightly be detached from "rhetorical knowledge." The second bulleted point focusing on "finding, evaluating, analyzing, and synthesizing" source material goes a long way toward a general description of rhetorical invention, literally of coming to terms with the features of the discourse to be navigated. By the end of first-year composition, students should:

- Use writing and reading for inquiry, learning, thinking, and communicating.
- Understand a writing assignment as a series of tasks, including finding, evaluating, analyzing, and synthesizing appropriate primary and secondary sources.
- Integrate their own ideas with those of others.
- Understand the relationships among language, knowledge, and power.

The student was convinced that the testing practices of her former high school degraded the learning experience. She articulated this conclusion with increasing degrees of clarity and persuasiveness as she consulted research in education and key statements in the policy debates of this era of "No Child Left Behind."[iii] Articulating the critique of their own local situation with these national voices required a sophisticated practice of integration. To be sure, the challenge to "integrate" one's "ideas" with "those of others" could describe at least two core rhetorical strategies: the development of ethos—aligning our position with those of other authoritative voices—and the crafting of lines of reasoning, of putting statements together as chains of premises. While it could be argued that any research assignment requires this kind of integration, a community-based approach demands greater sophistication insofar as students must reason persuasively in relation to a specific audience and a much more elaborately detailed set of context-specific constraints.

As immigration continues to take precedence as a major national issue, increasing numbers of students choose to address "border issues" in their project work. When students move beyond the commonplace stances of this media-constructed "debate," they find themselves faced with a prodigious research load. The long and complicated history of immigration in the US and the complexities of immigration politics (now as always) must be approached as a practice of multidisciplinary inquiry. Unbound by disciplinary frames, students in community-based courses approach academic disciplines as a set of resources to be applied. I take this to be a rather sophisticated approach to interdisciplinary research and writing, and surely, it evinces a strong ability to "integrate" different knowledge sets. The student writing about immigration, for example, consulted the research of political scientists, sociologists, criminologists, historians, and experts in the emerging field of "border studies."

Again, separating questions about the "relationships among language, knowledge and power" from "rhetorical knowledge" cuts against the grain of any thoroughgoing rhetorical approach. Be that as it may, community-based writing instruction foregrounds these ethical and epistemological questions. Conceiving of the rhetorical situation of the project work in terms of "stakeholders," as described above, grounds the multiple perspectives orienting any public discourse, and thus the diversity of knowledge sets that inhere in any debate, in the "interestedness" of all the stakeholders involved. One lesson all my students take away from my courses is that arguments serve the purpose of people with material interests, and that what passes as authoritative knowledge is always a contested and shifting matter, no less volatile than the political world itself. As I suggested in the above discussion of the conflict model of instruction, teaching rhetoric requires forays into matters of power politics.

Processes

Those familiar with the contemporary history of composition understand the centrality of thinking about writing process to our disciplinary identity. Community-based curricula are strongly rooted in process pedagogy. We tell students that writing is "recursive," that it follows loops of preparation, composition, revision in an on-going manner. Community-based writing instruction inspires a creative approach to revision, one that is responsive to the rhetorical situation in question. Students don't just share "drafts" but share their thinking and research from the inception of their project work and throughout the process.

By the end of first-year composition, students should:

- Be aware that it usually takes multiple drafts to create and complete a successful text.
- Develop flexible strategies for generating, revising, editing, and proofreading.
- Understand writing as an open process that permits writers to use later invention and re-thinking to revise their work.
- Understand the collaborative and social aspects of writing processes.
- Learn to critique their own and others' works.
- Learn to balance the advantages of relying on others with the responsibility of doing their part.

The community-based classroom is nothing if not the scene of poly-vocal process. Working in a group of students who are developing projects and moving through a multi-stage process, there is literally almost constant feedback. Students learn which voices offer insight and resources and which seem locked in their own perspective. I always tell students that they must adjudicate the multiple perspectives they receive. The student pursuing arguments about immigration policy was challenged by an advocate of a worker permit system that allowed for the possibility of eventual citizenship. All the students involved in the discussions of the project addressing immigration questioned one another's logic, evidence, and sometimes even one another's motives. The students writing the book review solicited feedback from members of her mothers' group before circulating the text to the group as a whole. She studied examples of the book review genre, and she received multiple readings from members of the class. In my estimation, this clearly demonstrates "flexible strategies" of composing and revising.

Knowledge of conventions

Again, a classically trained rhetorician would balk at the idea that "conventions" are anything other than rhetorical in their function. Still, these outcomes are recognizable as a group, as they seem to garner so much attention in what passes for accomplished writing.

By the end of first-year composition, students should:

- Learn common formats for different kinds of texts.
- Develop knowledge of genre conventions ranging from structure and paragraphing to tone and mechanics.

- Practice appropriate means of documenting their work.
- Control such surface features as syntax, grammar, punctuation, and spelling.

Considered as a feature of community-context, conventions, too often construed as a static set of "nuts-and-bolts" prescriptions, are revealed as entirely rhetorical in quality and function. After finally deciding to address a school board as opposed to a student audience, the student writing against the test-focused curriculum had to think through the question of genre and decide if a business letter or a formal proposal offered the most advantages set of conventions in which to work. Deciding on a proposal, the student was obliged to become conversant with the conventional rhetorical moves of this genre: articulating a problem persuasively and demonstrating the scope of the problem; detailing a feasible solution; demonstrating the likely outcome of the proposed solution; and calling attention to persuasive precedents for the recommended action. This student was sent looking for examples of proposals to examine, not as an attempt to find a template but as an act of invention, a case-specific search for available means.

Community-based approaches are particularly useful for addressing "surface features." So often, control over usage, grammar, syntax, spelling, punctuation, etc. are taken to be constitutive of "good writing." Students who struggle with control of surface features approach the issue with trepidation, seemingly with the belief that "good writers" have some comprehensive knowledge of surface conventions, which allows them to avoid errors and to produce polished prose. We can understand this to be not just misguided but pernicious if we consider the ethical stakes of naturalizing any set of linguistic standards in this way. What is the imagined subjectivity that "knows" standard written English from the "inside"? If we or our students privilege that subject of language proficiency as the subject of "good writing," do we not bracket second-language English users or users of "other" varieties of English (for example, regionally inflected English dialectics or international "world Englishes") as diminished speech?

The concretizing function of community-based writing instruction allows us to de-escalate and demystify struggles with surface conventions. A much more useful way to approach such issues is as a rhetorical consideration inseparable from the specifics of the compositional context. Grammar and the conventions of usage are contextual and audience-based, and the mix of conventional challenges faced by a group of community-based writers opens opportunities for useful instruction. Thus there is no naturalized set of conventions, a false notion often promoted by the majority of writing courses focused around the mission of training "academic writers." Taking the community standard as a guide, students must simply build more or less editing time into their writing process depending on the challenges they face. In the context of community-based writing instruction, the student grappling with sentence structure has much to learn from the student learning how to format a website. The student writing for the school board must expunge sentence fragments from his writing as surely as the website writer must organize hyperlinks in an accessible and identifiable manner. Again, this approach is only possible if an ostensible problem (students working through disparate convention sets) is reconceived as an opportunity (a comparative look at conventional constraints generally).

This kind of pedagogical reconception is the requisite mindset for experimenting with community-based curricula. Most writing teachers have never themselves experienced community-based teaching as students, and so there is often little experiential sense of how to proceed. As a concluding invitation, I offer again the abiding spatial metaphors of "mapping," navigation," and of finding "paths" as points of orientation for developing methods of community-based writing instruction. Insofar as composition and invention require a traversing of local knowledge and socially grounded perspectives on the material stakes of what are all too easily pigeonholed as "issues," community-based writing instruction is a matter of taking to the road. With our students, we are fellow travelers across these rhetorical geographies that animate our lives with meaningful language.

Notes

i   National College Teachers Association, *Conference on College Composition and Communication*, available at http://ncte.org/cccc/ .

ii   The WPA Statement includes recommendations for supporting the Outcomes through disciplinary writing, and I have taken the liberty of excising those recommendations. Rhetoric can of course be taught in a disciplinary context—writing scholarly arguments, lab reports and bibliographic entries, etc. My interest here is simply in a more expansive teaching ground.

iii   The No Child Left Behind Act of 2001 (NCLB), was signed into federal law on 8 January 2002. Ostensibly, NCLB was designed to improve performance at the primary and secondary school levels and to increase more flexibility for families to choose schools. The pedagogical basis of NCLB draws from standards-based or outcomes-based education theory, which, challenging expectations and goals set by schools, will ostensibly motivate students and teachers and drive achievement. Critics have questioned the motives and pedagogy of the NCLB. Among the criticisms of those voiced by the National Education Association, among other groups, the NCLB is seen as withholding the resources that would support increased accountability to standards. Read the full text of the NCLB at the United States Department of Education webpage: http://ed.gov/policy/elsec/leg/esea02/index.html.

References

Aristotle. *The Rhetoric and Poetics of Aristotle* (1984), trans. W. Rhys Roberts, ed. E. P. J. Corbett (New York: Random House).

Eberly, R. (1999), "From writers, audiences and communities to publics: Writing classrooms as protopublic spaces," *Rhetoric Review*, 18(1), 165–178.

Harris, J. (1989), "The idea of community in the study of writing," *College Composition and Communication*, 40(1), 11–22.

Matthieu, P. (2005), *Tactics of Hope: The Public Turn in English Composition* (Portsmouth, NH: Boynton Cook Publishers Inc.).

Roberts-Miller, P. (2003),"Discursive conflict in communities and classrooms," *College Composition and Communication*, 54(4), 536–557.

Wells, S. (1996), "Rogue cops and health care: What do we want from public writing?" *College Composition and Communication*, 47, 325–341.

Writing Program Administrator's Outcome Statement for First-Year Writing. Available at http://english.ilstu.edu/Hesse/outcomes.html.

10 Plagiarism, patchwriting and source use: Best practice in the composition classroom

Diane Pecorari

Chapter Outline

Introduction

In 2004 the British press reported the case of a student whose university determined, on the eve of his graduation, that he had plagiarized repeatedly over the course of his education, and as a result would not be awarded a degree (Baty, 2004; "Plagiarising," 2004). In response, the student acknowledged that his writing assignments contained material repeated from sources, but that he had not been aware that this constituted plagiarism. Precisely because he had been writing that way since the beginning of his studies, he argued, the university had been negligent in not telling him earlier that his work constituted plagiarism. The university countered that students were given ample information about plagiarism; according to one press account,

> a [university] spokeswoman said all students were given information about what constituted plagiarism "from day one". This was set out in a handbook from the English department and also the faculty handbook. She added that students were also encouraged to attend study skills workshops where plagiarism was explained. ("Plagiarising", 2004)

At first glance this story may seem to have something of the absurd about it: a student caught plagiarizing threatens to sue his university because they let him get away with it. Yet it raises a number of serious questions about plagiarism in student writing, including whether the student's responsibility not to plagiarize is greater than the university's responsibility to identify plagiarism when it occurs, and what constitutes sufficient information, questions which will be addressed here.

The aims of this chapter are to argue that a pedagogical response to some instances of plagiarism is more appropriate than a punitive one, and to outline how such an approach can be implemented in the composition classroom. A move away from punishment may seem an unlikely way of dealing with an act often described as an academic crime, reflecting a degree of immorality on the part of the perpetrator. Plagiarism is discussed in excoriating language. For example, an editorial in *Nature* asserted that it "is the most serious of the known crimes against scholarship" (Maddox, 1991: 13), while the editor of the *Canadian Journal of Physics* wrote that "incidents of plagiarism in science corrupt the soul of the perpetrator" (Betts, 1992: 289). Similarly, a study of university plagiarism policies found that they typically invoke language of crime and punishment, and describe the act in terms such as "academic fraud" or "nothing less than an act of theft" (Pecorari, 2001: 239).

Given this view of plagiarism, it is not surprising that the typical response to it is to punish the offender. In the study cited above, plagiarism policies of 54 universities in the US, Britain and Australia were examined. Among the policies which specified a response to the act, it was almost always punitive, ranging from lowered marks to expulsion, while only six offered a response which emphasized learning, such as attending the writing center.

Yet a body of relatively recent research into first- and second-language writing calls into question whether a punitive response is always—or indeed usually—appropriate. It has been pointed out that writing from sources is a complex act, and that new academic writers may not fully possess the necessary skills, nor be fully aware of what is expected of them when they write.

If plagiarism is caused by a lack of understanding and/or a lack of skills, then responding to it as a crime amounts to punishing students for what they have not yet learned. This would indicate a worrying mismatch between the causes of plagiarism and the responses to it. The next section argues that such a problem does indeed exist. The third section addresses the role of the composition teacher in addressing plagiarism in this problematic context.

The problem

Plagiarism is an exceedingly complex issue. This complexity contributes in no small degree to the problem of addressing it in the classroom. Space does not permit a full discussion of the complexities here (aspects of which are highlighted in Begoray, 1996; Bloch, 2001; Dettmar, 1999; and Lunsford and Ede, 1994, among others). However, three aspects which are especially relevant to the composition classroom deserve attention: the role of intention; factors which make it difficult to identify and learn about plagiarism and appropriate source use; and the difficulty of establishing what constitutes plagiarism.

Intention

The received view of plagiarism as an act of fraud implies that it is a deliberate act, an act of intentional deception. Certainly much plagiarism meets this description. When a student purchases an essay on the Internet and hands it in for a grade, that student intends to deceive. This sort of plagiarism, characterized by deliberate deception, will be referred to here as *prototypical plagiarism*.

However, a large and growing body of findings has demonstrated the existence of another form of plagiarism, one which meets typical definitions of plagiarism, for example *using language and/or ideas from a source without sufficient attribution*, but under circumstances which make it difficult to portray the writer as a prototypical plagiarist. For example, in a case study of two bilingual writers, Villalva (2006) found that one of the writers, Belinda, incorporated language from her sources into her own writing. However, Belinda did not merely copy passively; she eventually became able to use independently the academic-register words that had made their way into her text from a source initially. Copying appears to have been a stepping stone in Belinda's efforts to develop as a writer, rather than a means of sidestepping the learning process.

Some writers not only lack deceptive intent, they have an awareness of the need to *not* plagiarize that plays an important role in shaping their writing practices. Bulelwa, a writer in Angélil-Carter's (2000) study, mistrusted her ability to report ideas from her sources without distorting them, and yet was wary of plagiarizing. This placed contradictory demands on her, to depend on her sources for the sake of clarity but to be independent of them in order not to plagiarize. Her reported writing strategy was an attempt to resolve this tension: "if I want something to be clearer, sometimes I use his [the source's] words sometimes I use mine." Despite her concern about accuracy, she tried to paraphrase, saying "by paraphrasing it I don't want to plagiarize" (p. 96). Similarly, Hull and Rose found that the remedial writer they studied, Tanya, repeated language from her sources with some changes, specifically to distance herself from plagiarism: "if some parts from there I change a little bit, they know I'm not really that kind of student that would copy, 'cause another student would copy" (1989: 147).

Both the first- and the second-language writing literature contains numerous such accounts of problematic source use which differs from prototypical plagiarism in that it does not appear to be the result of the writer's attempt to deceive the reader about how sources were used (e.g. Braine, 1995; Connor and Kramer, 1995; Crocker and Shaw, 2002; Dong, 1998; Leki, 1995; McClanahan, 2005; Petrić, 2004; Prior, 1998; St. John, 1987; Shaw, 1991; Sherman, 1992; Spack, 1997, among others). Because deceptive intent is strongly implied by the word *plagiarism*, but is in fact not always involved in the act, there is a need to be able to discuss the textual aspects of plagiarism (i.e. the relationship between two texts) without entering into the question of intention. Here the term *textual plagiarism* will be used to refer to all writing which repeats the language of sources without adequate attribution, regardless of the writer's intention.

The sheer frequency of accounts of textual plagiarism suggests that it may be common in student writing. It was in part to investigate that possibility that I conducted a study of the writing of 17 postgraduate students at several British universities. Portions of the students' master's and PhD theses were compared to the sources the students reported having used. All 17 texts had some source use that could be called inappropriate, most often in the form of chunks of language from other sources included in the new texts, either verbatim or with superficial changes. However, the available evidence indicated that the writers had made an effort to understand what appropriate source use involved, and to write accordingly (Pecorari, 2003; Pecorari, 2008).

To describe this copying strategy, Rebecca Howard (1995) coined the term *patchwriting*. Patchwriting involves "copying from a source text and then deleting some words, altering grammatical structures, or plugging in one synonym for another" (Howard, 1999: xvii). Howard argues that patchwriting comes about when novice writers attempt to produce writing which resembles the texts they read, texts which have been produced by more experienced members of the academic discourse community. Because the inexperienced writers lack the skills necessary to produce that kind of writing in an autonomous way, they recycle appropriate-sounding chunks of language from their sources. Patchwriting is not the product of dishonest students who want to get a higher grade without bothering with the work. It is a rung in the ladder of the writer's development, on the way to more proficient and autonomous writing.

An analogy can be drawn between the way patchwriters lean on their sources for support and the way that novice ice skaters hold on to the railing as they make tentative circuits around a skating rink. Patchwriting is not, Howard notes (1995; 1999), acceptable in the long term, but as an interim strategy for learners it is not only understandable, it is a necessary and indeed beneficial part of the learning trajectory in much the same way that the inexperienced ice skater needs help in establishing equilibrium before being able to move on to more complicated—and independent—moves.

By highlighting the skills issue, the notion of patchwriting illustrates just how complex the task facing students really is. They are not expected merely to avoid plagiarism; that could be accomplished by simply never opening a source text, but since virtually all academic writing draws on sources, that is not a feasible approach. To avoid plagiarism a writer must possess the range of skills needed to write from sources. Warnings, handbooks, information sheets and explanations *telling* what to do and what not to do are, therefore, potentially useful but not in themselves sufficient resources, any more than the novice ice skater can become a champion simply by being told how to skate.

Another implication of the notion of patchwriting is to confer legitimacy on students' best, but still imperfect, efforts. In learning any reasonably complex skill (and writing from sources is an extremely complex one), most people get it wrong many times before they get it right. Yet beginning ice skaters are not accused of cheating—just of not being very good ice skaters yet.

The first element in the problem, then, is that many students have difficulty with an important aspect of writing, and that this writing problem—alone among a range of possible writing problems—is judged as a moral failing, putting academic careers at risk.[i]

Occlusion

Another element relates to frequency and diagnosis. Diagnosing inappropriate source use can be surprisingly difficult. For example, in Currie's (1998) study, the student, Diana, adopted during the course of an academic term the strategy of including chunks of language from the course text in her writing assignments. The course instructor noticed an improvement in Diana's language, but apparently did not notice the copying strategy. In the study of student source use referred to above, I interviewed the supervisors of nine students. None was aware of how their students had used sources until the interview, when we looked at the student texts and their sources together (Pecorari, 2003). One reason source use problems can go undetected is the fact that source use is an *occluded* feature of academic writing. Swales (1996) first used the term *occluded* to refer to genres which are read by only a small proportion of a discourse community, and are therefore seldom visible to others. I have extended the term to refer to a feature of texts which is ordinarily hidden: the relationship between a source and the way that source is incorporated in a later text (Pecorari, 2006).

This occluded relationship is a pervasive characteristic of academic writing. Most academic texts make reference to sources. Most readers have not read all of the sources cited in a given work, nor have a sufficiently vivid memory of those they have read to know whether, for example, a quotation is accurate. Readers can in principle obtain a source and check, but—for obvious reasons—most of the time they do not. Instead, they *deduce* how sources have been used, from the clues provided by a range of metatextual signals, such as quotation marks (indicating words repeated from a source), an ellipsis (missing words), a citation (identifying which source), etc.

When the writer uses these metatextual signals as the reader expects, then the reader can interpret them to understand the relationship between the new text and its sources. If this system breaks down, though, a mistaken impression can be the result. In addition, there are often no visible signs in the text to alert the reader to the breakdown. For example, the short extract from a PhD thesis in biology in (1a), includes a reference to two sources but no quotation marks. A reader is likely to conclude that the writer has reported ideas which can be found in the sources named, but has paraphrased rather than quoting directly.

> (1a) C. albicans is capable of a yeast to hyphal phase transition (dimorphic transition) and variety of high frequency phenotypic transitions, ranging from differences in colony morphology to differences in cell shape, surface and permeability. These two properties may be important in pathogenesis (Scherer and Magee, 1990; Soll, 1992).
> [Sci2]

Unless the reader has either a detailed knowledge of the sources or a reason to obtain the sources and carry out a comparison, it will not be apparent that the real relationship is closer to quotation than paraphrase, as (1b) illustrates.

> (1b) C. albicans is capable of a yeast-to-hyphal-phase transition (dimorphic transition) and a variety of high-frequency phenotypic transitions, ranging

> from differences in colony morphology to differences in cell shape, surface,
> and permeability. These two properties may be important in pathogenesis
> (119) and are of great intrinsic interest as biological processes.
> [Scherer & Magee, 1990: 226]

This is how patchwriting escapes diagnosis in the work of novice writers. The occluded relationship between texts and their sources means that readers are often unaware of an inappropriate intertextual relationship (or one which is not signaled appropriately). When the writer is a student and the reader is a teacher, the result of occlusion can be that the teacher is not able to diagnose the student's unsuccessful source use. Occlusion works in another direction as well: one way that novice writers can learn is by observing the performance of more experienced writers, i.e. reading their work. However, occlusion means that much about how the writer has used sources is hidden from the student as reader. The effect is often a missed chance to learn an important lesson.

What is plagiarism?

The final element in the problem is defining what, precisely, students are not supposed to do. What sorts of writing wrongs constitute plagiarism? Although widespread agreement exists that plagiarism is a serious violation of academic standards, when a specific case of alleged plagiarism attracts public attention, the consensus falls apart and there is inevitably debate about whether plagiarism is the right label for what has occurred.

An example of this is an episode involving a senior academic at a US university who was accused of plagiarism in the late 1990s. The reaction to this case was remarkably heterogeneous; the range of views is illustrated by comments from two academics who knew the work of the researcher involved, as reported by the *Chronicle of Higher Education*. One went on record as saying "I am convinced to my core that [the academic] is dirty," while another said "I see this as a writing error rather than some big ethics issue" (Leatherman, 1999). Over a period of several years, a panel at the researcher's university decided that she was guilty of plagiarism, another committee decided that she was not, a high-ranking university official fired her, and upon appeal, an even higher-ranking official rescinded that decision (Smallwood, 2002).

This spread of opinion is typical when a specific case of possible plagiarism is under consideration, and official policies are little help in resolving the disagreement. University plagiarism policies are in broad agreement about how to define plagiarism; this definition, from a British university, is typical: "Plagiarism is defined as the use of other people's work and the submission of it as though it were one's own work" (Pecorari, 2001: 235). However, a definition like this masks a number of specific questions involved in determining whether a writer has used other people's work as if it were his or her own. The lack of consensus on specific cases comes about because of the difficulty in arriving at satisfactory answers to those smaller questions.

One of those question is intention. The idea of using another text "as though it were one's own" implies an intention to create a misleading impression. If compelling evidence existed to show that inappropriate source use had another cause, such as bad note-taking, it would be labeled something like "sloppiness" rather than plagiarism. Intention, however, is difficult to show and the sort of evidence that can be called upon (for instance, whether a student seems to be deeply engaged in a course or simply going through the motions) is largely circumstantial.

Another question is whether the condition "the use of other people's work" has been satisfied. Plagiarism is suspected when two texts are similar, but it matters a great deal whether they are similar because one was copied from the other, or whether the similarities are coincidental, due, perhaps, to the fact that two texts on the same topic tend to use similar language. This question is difficult to answer because it requires making an inference about the writing process from the product. In extreme cases, i.e. when two texts are either entirely different or nearly identical, the inference may be made comfortably, but in the middle of the continuum it is harder to arrive at a satisfying answer. In (2), below, the presence of both similarities and differences would be likely to lead different individuals to different conclusions about whether copying had taken place. In addition, some teachers may feel that a grey area exists within which (possibly) copied language is too limited to be called plagiarism but too extensive for total comfort.

> (2a) In addition to this, some writers such as Fox and Tobias (1969) noted that historical research is a past-oriented research which seeks to throw light on current conditions and problems through an intensive study of materials and information which already exist. [from a PhD thesis from a British university]
>
> (2b) The historical approach, as has been noted before, is past-oriented research which seeks to illuminate a question of current interest by an intensive study of material that already exists.
>
> [Fox, 1969: 406]

It should be noted that these two questions—whether the writer intended to mislead the reader, and whether the relationship between two texts is a causal one—have answers; it may be difficult or indeed impossible to arrive at them, since they hinge on the writer's state of mind and processes, but the answers do exist. The situation is somewhat different with regard to a third factor: whether a given instance of source use is acceptable or not. The fact that public cases of plagiarism become sites of controversy indicates what the strong resemblance between institutional plagiarism policies tends to mask: that standards for source use are heterogeneous across the academy.

A number of factors contribute to this heterogeneity, including, quite obviously, the fact that individuals perceive and evaluate the same situation differently. In addition, academic disciplines differ in how sources are used and what sort of source use is deemed appropriate (Pecorari, 2006; Rinnert and Kobayashi, 2005). Cultural differences have also often been identified as a source of varying standards for source use (e.g. Sherman, 1992; Sowden, 2005), although others have pointed out the need for caution in drawing conclusions about the role of culture in plagiarism (e.g. Buranen, 1999; Ha, 2006). The writing context, too, is a strong factor in determining what textual features, including what type of source use, are appropriate.

The importance of context can be illustrated with the case of common knowledge. It is widely accepted that ideas or facts that are common knowledge do not need to be cited. But what counts as common knowledge? The term is often described as "what everyone knows," but even the most basic and widely shared pieces of knowledge—that a year has 365 days (usually), that apples grow on trees and that money does not—are not known to, for example, many children under the age of eighteen months. This is not the frivolous observation it may seem to be, since toddlers do not read academic writing; the point is, precisely, that the group of people who do not know those three basic facts are not part of the audience for an undergraduate essay. That essay can refer to apples growing on trees without a citation because that fact is common knowledge for anyone likely to read it. Common knowledge is, therefore, not what everyone knows, but what the writer and everyone who is likely to read the text knows. Common knowledge is the knowledge that the writer and intended readers have in common, illustrating one way in which the writing context influences what sort of source use may be appropriate. This is one of a number of factors which can make it quite difficult to determine which textual acts count as plagiarism.

This section set out to describe a problem involving plagiarism and source use in student writing. The problem can now be summarized like this:

- Many students lack the skills needed to write from sources in appropriate ways, and therefore produce texts which could be—and often are—considered to be plagiarized, even when the writers lack dishonest intention.

- Teaching and learning about how students should write from sources is complicated by the fact that teachers do not always have a clear view of how students use sources.
- Both teaching about and responding to textual plagiarism are further complicated by the difficulty (for students and teachers alike) of pinning down what plagiarism consists of.

Writing from sources is an essential skill for academic success, and yet a constellation of factors common in higher educational contexts works to the detriment of students who need to learn this skill. Inappropriate source use is often not identified at all. When it is, it is often labeled as plagiarism and punished. But the consequence for those whose inappropriate source use is not detected may well be worse: they finish the class, or indeed the degree, and go on to write in other contexts without having learned that their writing strategies are not only substandard, but actually dangerous to their future prospects.

Some solutions

The purpose of this section is to suggest approaches for dealing with patchwriting and plagiarism, and for encouraging the development of good source use skills in the composition classroom. Given the nature of the problem as described above, these approaches relate to 1) teaching about plagiarism; 2) teaching about how to use sources; 3) creating a learning environment that promotes good source use; 4) identifying inappropriate source use; and 5) responding to inappropriate source use.

Teaching about plagiarism

So far I have argued that deceptive plagiarism and patchwriting are two distinct acts, meriting different responses. As a serious violation of academic standards, plagiarism is something that all students need to know about, and the composition teacher is one important source of information. The following points are useful to keep in mind when teaching about plagiarism.

It is important to remember, and acknowledge to students, that the boundary between successful and flawed intertextuality is not always clear and uncontested. Students are aware of these complexities and grey areas, so warnings about plagiarism that suggest that it is a straightforward matter are both misleading and often skeptically received. As Barks and Watts (2001) point out, acknowledging and discussing the grey areas "may move both student and instructor beyond their personal comfort zone," but can ultimately contribute to learning about this topic (p. 254).

Care should also be taken not to make warnings excessively strong. Teachers do well to let their students understand how seriously the academic community views plagiarism, and how heavy the consequences can be. However, there is a danger that warnings about plagiarism can create a climate of anxiety in which students are unwilling to draw attention to source use problems and therefore less likely to ask questions or invite feedback on their source use.

Finally, teaching about plagiarism means teaching what not to do. Students will only be fully successful if they also have the chance to learn about what they should do when writing from sources. The next section addresses that question.

Teaching about how to use sources

For an academic writer, simply avoiding plagiarism is not enough; it is necessary to know how to write from sources appropriately. Like most other aspects of writing, this is a complex skill and one which must be refined over time. Students, in grappling with this complexity, are often understandably concerned about rather specific, concrete questions: *Do I have to cite a source for this term?* or *Can I use an example I found in a book?* However, answers to these questions depend at least as much on the specific writing context as they do on generally applicable "rules." What students really need, therefore, is not primarily an answer, but a way of finding the answers themselves, to current questions and to similar questions later on. Two key concepts, *transparency* and *purpose*, can give students a tool for finding those answers.

Transparency is closely related to the idea of source use as an occluded textual feature. The purpose of all but the most mechanical citation conventions is to lift the veil of occlusion and show the reader how sources have been used. Transparent source use means referring to sources in such a way that the reader can draw correct conclusions about the relationship between the source and the new text. All academic writers have a responsibility to report their sources transparently.

The concept of transparency suggests a ready-made counter-question to students' *can I …* and *do I have to …* questions: in which way will it be most clear to the reader what you have done? Learning to address this question enables students to find answers which are not only correct but also appropriate in the circumstances in which they are writing. To return to the example of common knowledge, one writer may have confident knowledge of a fact and state that fact without a reference, while another writer might consult a source for it, and identify the source with a citation. It is not how widely known the fact is that determines whether a reference is necessary; it is the need to acknowledge for the reader whether or not other works have had a direct influence on the new text. Transparent source use allows the reader insights into the writer's processes.

Equally important is for the writer to understand the rhetorical purpose of citation. Inexperienced academic writers are often inclined to focus on what the "rules" permit or require by way of citation. However, as Bloch and Chi have noted, "the citing of a text is not just a convention but an integral part of the writer's argument" (1995: 270). Regardless of whether transparency requires a citation for a proposition, a writer may find it advantageous to refer to one or more sources, for example to establish that a fact is widely accepted; or to show that there is disagreement on a question; or to challenge an earlier writer's mistaken assertion. In each of these cases, references are a tool that help the writer make a point. The varying purposes suggest which sources to cite, as well as the form the citation might take; references helping to make the points above might look like 3, 4 and 5, respectively.

(3) There is broad agreement that the cow jumped over the moon (Green, 2000; Jones, 1998; Smith, 2005). [claiming a proposition is widely held]
(4) It has been argued that the cow jumped over the moon (e.g. Smith, 2005), although this claim has not met with universal acceptance (Jones, 1998). [illustrating disagreement]
(5) Smith (2005) claims that the cow jumped over the moon. However, this view fails to take into account … [challenging]

With an awareness of the ways citation can contribute to their argument, and of the reader's need to understand how sources have been used, students have a better chance of avoiding textual plagiarism, and are more likely to produce strong, successful texts as well.

Creating a learning environment that promotes good source use

The right learning environment can facilitate students' efforts to write from sources effectively and appropriately. Teachers can help by keeping the following points in mind.

• *Address patchwriting proactively.* A post-hoc response may be reasonable for a problem that occurs only sporadically, but patchwriting is a common feature of the work of novice writers. It makes sense to build activities for learning about how to use sources (and how not to) into the syllabus, rather than waiting for problems to occur before addressing them.

- *Teach source use as a skill.* Writing from sources is a skill, so effective teaching cannot be exclusively in the form of instructions and prohibitions. Students need examples, opportunities for controlled practice, and feedback on their efforts.
- *Aim just high enough.* Activities should be graded to the learner's level. Asking a novice academic writer to find and synthesize half a dozen sources is unrealistic; a more reasonable task in the beginning may be to summarize or respond to a single text or to contrast what two sources say on the same topic.
- *Address reading too.* As Howard (1999) has pointed out, patchwriting is often as much a reading problem as a writing problem. An essential condition for successful paraphrasing is a good understanding of what the source says. Time spent on reading skills, and on checking that students understand assigned texts, is time well spent. (Howard, 1999: 141–145, offers useful activities.)
- *Be aware of occlusion.* Unlike many other problems which can manifest themselves in a text, source use problems often leave no immediately visible traces. As a result, it is not safe to assume that because no obvious problems leap to the eye, the source use in a text is entirely acceptable. To give students feedback, though, it is necessary to *know* how sources have been used. This is easier when assignments require students to use only a limited range of sources with which the teacher is familiar. Another approach is to ask students to submit some, at least, of their sources together with their assignment, or to bring them to a writing conference.
- *Teach by example.* A teacher who wants students to bring a measure of originality and personal investment to their writing should bring the same qualities to the task of designing writing assignments. Or, in other words, "If an assignment can be downloaded from the Internet, perhaps it should be" (Sokolik, 2000).
- *Be positive.* A direct, proactive approach to good and bad source requires open communication, and that is incompatible with suspicion and worry. If students sense that they are under suspicion, the consequences can be harmful to the learning environment (Murphy, 1990; Petrić, 2004). By treating source use problems as a common phenomenon and an opportunity for learning, teachers can enable students to be open about how they have used sources, and actively seek feedback.

Identifying inappropriate source use

Inappropriate source use needs to be diagnosed. When it takes the form of prototypical plagiarism, it should be punished; when it is patchwriting, the writers need to be aware that they have not yet mastered an important academic skill. Yet, as noted above, identifying source use problems is not always easy.

Numerous electronic plagiarism detection services and software packages are marketed as a solution to the problem. These packages either use search engines to look for students' sources on the Internet, or compare students' assignments with each other, or both. The appeal of tools like these is obvious, given how time-consuming a search for sources can be, and the reality that problems can escape detection. However, teachers considering using one of these tools should bear several caveats in mind.

First, electronic detection tools miss possible sources. They can compare student writing only to electronic sources, and however pervasive the Internet is, libraries are still full of printed materials and students still use them. In addition, the search may exclude electronic resources which require a subscription or a password (e.g. newspaper and magazine archives, electronic reference works, etc.). Both teachers and students should understand that a negative result is not a guarantee that sources have been used in an entirely appropriate way.

Another consideration is that comparison software can only quantify and describe the similarity between two texts, not decide whether the relationship is acceptable. They can be helpful by drawing teachers' attention to potential trouble areas, but the final determination about whether a problem exists must be made by the instructor, who should take more than just a quantitative measure of similarity into account.

Finally, in deciding whether to use plagiarism detection products, teachers should consider the possible effect on the classroom atmosphere. Unless the use of such tools is handled with a great deal of sensitivity, students may get the impression that their work is to be examined for potential criminality before being assessed for other characteristics, to the detriment of a climate of openness and trust which learning requires.

With or without electronic tools, the ultimate responsibility for identifying textual plagiarism lies with the teacher, and teachers bring valuable capabilities to the task which computers lack. These include an awareness of the writing context, often (though not always) familiarity with the sources students are likely to use, and knowledge of the student's capabilities. Another important and often overlooked resource in identifying source use problems is the student. Working together, teachers and students can bring the majority of problems to light.

Of course, plagiarists who are attempting to gain an unearned grade are unlikely to identify themselves, but another important group of students, those who are unsure about their writing skills but are keen to improve, are generally very willing to explain their writing processes and gain constructive criticism. However, a necessary condition for this is that the students feel confident that constructive criticism is what they will receive, and that in being asked to describe how they use sources they are not being asked to expose themselves to an accusation of plagiarism. In other words, for students to collaborate in the process of diagnosing source-use problems, they must feel comfortable that the presumption of innocence applies to them.

Responding to inappropriate source use

Intention is a key issue in distinguishing between patchwriting and prototypical plagiarism, and therefore in knowing how to respond to inappropriate source use. Unfortunately, intention can also be the most difficult aspect of textual plagiarism to establish. When problematic source use is identified, an important first step is to avoid rushing to the conclusion that intentional deception is involved. This can be difficult: when a teacher believes that he or she has provided thorough and comprehensive information about source use and plagiarism, accident or lack of awareness may not sound like plausible explanations. It is easy to conclude that, after abundant information, the student *must* have known. A variation on this theme is to assume that a student might make a legitimate mistake once, but a second instance of textual plagiarism must be evidence of dishonest intention.

However, this conclusion overlooks how very different the teacher's perspective and the student's may be. For instance, the label *plagiarism* is applied to a range of textual practices, including 1) not acknowledging the origin of an idea; 2) repeating language from a source without identifying the source; and 3) repeating language directly from a source with a citation but without quotation marks. A teacher who encountered first (2) and then (3) in successive student essays might see them collectively as repeated examples of plagiarism. The student, however, may have seen (3) as a different way of using sources, and have chosen it in order to comply with the teacher's instructions not to do (2) again.

This is one example of how directives which seem clear to the teacher may not be equally clear to the student. Another is that if teachers and their institutions create, in their warnings, an association between plagiarism and academic dishonesty, students who have no intention of cheating may assume that the warnings do not apply to them, and tune them out. The larger point is that learners very often do *not* know what their teachers think they ought. When they fail to apply general instructions accurately in a specific piece of writing, that in itself cannot be taken as evidence of a desire to cheat.

If what the student *ought* to know is not a reliable indicator of deception, how can intention be established? One very direct and effective way is to ask students what sources they have used, and where. A student who is making an attempt to use sources appropriately will welcome constructive feedback and be happy to collaborate—provided that the question is couched in a way that invites collaboration, rather than appearing to be a veiled accusation.

If a student denies using sources in a way that the teacher can demonstrate occurred, then the teacher has every reason to treat it as intentional deception and follow the disciplinary policies specified by the department or university. However, if the student participates in discussing how sources have been used, the stage is set for a productive dialogue about how the student's work meets or diverges from the teacher's expectations—precisely the type of specific feedback needed on the performance of a developing skill.

In discussing unsuccessful source use with students, it is useful not to restrict the discussion to matters of ethics and academic honesty, but to point out the effect of the source use within the text. Patchwriting not only fails to meet the transparency criterion, it generally fails at several other levels as well. Texts which are composed largely of chunks extracted from source texts, possibly with changes, are rarely coherent and seldom effective in advancing the writer's argument. Quite often, in fact, patchwritten texts lack a sense of argument or purpose; by sampling from a menu of pre-composed, fluent sentences and phrases, the writer can sidestep the need to identify a clear focus for the text. By identifying some of the problems which patchwriting creates, teachers can help students understand the real need to work actively to develop their writing skills.

At this stage in the process, the question of intention recedes somewhat in importance, since the point has been made that good source use is an important objective and one taken seriously in the course. If a too-benevolent diagnosis was made, and the writer did in fact have some degree of deceptive intent, an important message—that source-use problems are diagnosed and taken seriously—has still gone home.

Finally, it is important to see inappropriate source use, any other aspect of student writing, in proportion, and to look at problems in the context of the entire writing assignment. How successful is the text as a whole? It is equally important to comment on what has gone right, as well as what has gone wrong. Are the places where sources are cited effectively and transparently? That deserves a comment.

Conclusion

The episode which introduced this chapter was characterized by disagreement about where responsibility for the student's plagiarism should lie. The university said students were given information about plagiarism, implying that the student was therefore responsible for heeding or ignoring that information.

The student pointed out that his long-standing strategy had not attracted earlier criticism: "I always used the Internet—cutting and pasting stuff and matching it with my own points. It's a technique I've used since I started the course and I never dreamt it was a problem." The student's mother suggested that university should have been more proactive in informing the student, saying "why were they not pointing out the pitfalls and why was their head in the sand for so long?" ("Plagiarising," 2004).

The purpose of returning to this episode is not to assign blame in the case, but to illustrate a gap between institutional and student perspectives, and to highlight practices which, to the extent that the practices of this university are typical (and I contend that they are), can negatively affect a great many students. The institutional view, shared by many individual teachers, is that students can be expected to do as they are told; a failure to follow instructions can be construed as intentional refusal. Students, on the other hand, assume that their academic work will be assessed, that they will be made aware of deficiencies in it, and that the absence of criticism can be interpreted as approval. Between these two positions lies ample ground for misunderstanding.

This chapter has explained how the gap in understanding comes about. Textual plagiarism is common, but goes undiagnosed in part because inappropriate source use is often not visible on the surface of a text: it must be searched for actively. But because inappropriate source use tends to be conflated with deceptive plagiarism, it is not suspected as often as it actually occurs, and teachers who believe that their students are motivated and engaged do not routinely scrutinize their work for evidence of cheating. This has serious consequences both for the students who are punished for textual plagiarism when it is identified, and for those who are allowed to finish their education without learning that their source-use strategies are not acceptable. Against that backdrop, this chapter has argued that a pedagogical approach to source use and textual plagiarism is needed, and has suggested ways in which classroom practitioners can implement such an approach.

Addressing source use in a way that is proactive, pedagogical, effective and fair implies substantial change, both to practices and to attitudes. Attitudes are often particularly resistant to change, not least of all because of a very understandable fear that responding to patchwriting with less draconian measures amounts to encouraging and enabling deceptive plagiarism. However, responding pedagogically to plagiarism does not mean responding more leniently, but targeting the response on the real source of the problem. A pedagogical approach to source use gives students the chance to address directly an area they need to learn about—and results, ultimately, in there being much less plagiarism around to detect.

Note

i Many teachers are prepared to accept, at least in some cases, that textual plagiarism can occur without deceptive intent. However, that view is by no means universally held; nor is it, in most cases, documented in official policies, so the risk to students of using sources in unacceptable ways is real.

References

Angélil-Carter, S. (2000), *Stolen Language? Plagiarism in Writing* (London: Longman).

Barks, D. and Watts, P. (2001), "Textual borrowing strategies for graduate-level ESL writers," in D. Belcher and A. Hirvela (eds), *Linking Literacies: Perspectives on L2 Reading-Writing Connections* (pp. 246–267) (Ann Arbor: University of Michigan Press).

Baty, P. (2004), "Plagiarist student to sue university," Times Online. Retrieved 19 January 2006, from http://timesonline.co.uk/article/0,,3561-1126250,00.html.

Begoray, D. L. (1996), "The borrowers: issues in using previously composed text," *English Quarterly*, 28, 60–69.

Betts, D. D. (1992), "Retraction of an article published in the Canadian Journal of Physics," *Canadian Journal of Physics*, 70, 289.

Bloch, J. (2001), "Plagiarism and the ESL student: From printed to electronic texts", in D. Belcher and A. Hirvela (eds), *Linking Literacies: Perspectives on L2 Reading-Writing Connections* (pp. 209–228) (Ann Arbor: University of Michigan Press).

Bloch, J. and Chi, L. (1995), "A Comparison of the use of citations in Chinese and English academic discourse," in D. Belcher and G. Braine (eds), *Academic Writing in a Second Language: Essays on Research and Pedagogy* (pp. 231–274) (Norwood, NJ: Ablex).

Braine, G. (1995), "Writing in the natural sciences and engineering", in D. Belcher and G. Braine (eds), *Academic Writing in a Second Language: Essays on Research and Pedagogy* (pp. 113–134) (Norwood, NJ: Ablex).

Buranen, L. (1999), "'But I wasn't cheating': Plagiarism and cross-cultural mythology," in L. Buranen and A. M. Roy (eds), *Perspectives on Plagiarism and Intellectual Property in a Postmodern World* (pp. 63–74) (Albany: State University of New York Press).

Connor, U. M. and Kramer, M. G. (1995), "Writing from sources: case studies of graduate students in business management," in D. Belcher and G. Braine (eds), *Academic Writing in a Second Language: Essays on Research and Pedagogy* (pp. 155–182) (Norwood, NJ: Ablex).

Crocker, J. and Shaw, P. (2002), "Research student and supervisor evaluation of intertextuality practices," *Hermes*, 28, 39–58.

Currie, P. (1998), "Staying out of trouble: apparent plagiarism and academic survival," *Journal of Second Language Writing*, 7, 1–18.

Dettmar, K. J. H. (1999), "The illusion of modernist allusion and the politics of postmodern plagiarism," in L. Buranen and A. M. Roy (eds), *Perspectives on Plagiarism and Intellectual Property in a Postmodern World* (pp. 99–109) (Albany: State University of New York Press).

Dong, Y. R. (1998), "Non-native graduate students' thesis/dissertation writing in science: self-reports by students and their advisors from two US institutions," *English for Specific Purposes*, 17, 369–390.

Fox, D. J. (1969), *The Research Process in Education* (New York: Holt, Rinehart and Winston).

Ha, P. L. (2006), "Plagiarism and overseas students: stereotypes again?" *ELT Journal*, 60, 76–78.

Howard, R. M. (1995), "Plagiarisms, authorships, and the academic death penalty," *College English*, 57, 788–805.

Howard, R. M. (1999), *Standing in the Shadow of Giants* (Stamford, CT: Ablex).

Hull, G. and Rose, M. (1989), "Rethinking remediation: toward a socio-cognitive understanding of problematic reading and writing," *Written Communication*, 6, 139–154.

Leatherman, C. (1999), "At Texas A&M, conflicting charges of misconduct tear a program apart," *Chronicle of Higher Education*, 46(11), A18–A20.

Leki, I. (1995), "Coping strategies of ESL students in writing tasks across the curriculum," *TESOL Quarterly*, 29, 235–260.

Lunsford, A. and Ede, L. (1994), "Collaborative authorship and the teaching of writing," in M. Woodmansee and P. Jaszi (eds), *The Construction of Authorship: Textual Appropriation in Law and Literature* (pp. 417–438) (Durham, NC: Duke University Press).

McClanahan, K. (2005), Working through Plagiarism and Patchwriting: Three L2 Writers Navigating Intertextual Worlds. Unpublished Master's paper, University of Hawai'i at Manoa.

Maddox, J. (1991), "Another mountain from a molehill," *Nature*, 351, 13.

Murphy, R. (1990), "Anorexia: the cheating disorder," *College English*, 52, 898–903.

Pecorari, D. (2001), "Plagiarism and international students: how the English-speaking university responds," in D. Belcher and A. Hirvela (eds), *Linking Literacies: Perspectives on L2 Reading-Writing Connections* (pp. 229–245) (Ann Arbor: University of Michigan Press).

Pecorari, D. (2003), "Good and original: plagiarism and patchwriting in academic second-language writing," *Journal of Second Language Writing*, 12, 317–345.

Pecorari, D. (2006), "Visible and occluded citation features in postgraduate second-language writing," *English for Specific Purposes*, 25, 4–29.

Pecorari, D. (2008), *Academic Writing and Plagiarism: A Linguistic Analysis* (London: Continuum).

Petric, B. (2004), "A pedagogical perspective on plagiarism," *NovELTy*, 11(1), 4–18.

"Plagiarising student sues university for negligence" (2004), *Guardian Unlimited*. Retrieved 18 January 2007 from http://education.guardian.co.uk/print/0,,4934062-108229,00.html.

Prior, P. A. (1998), *Writing/Disciplinarity: A Sociohistoric Account of Literate Activity in the Academy* (Mahwah, NJ: Erlbaum).

Rinnert, C. and Kobayashi, H. (2005), "Borrowing words and ideas: Insights from Japanese L1 writers," *Journal of Asian Pacific Communication*, 15, 31–56.

St John, M. J. (1987), "Writing processes of Spanish scientists publishing in English," *English for Specific Purposes*, 6, 113–120.

Scherer, S. and Magee, P. T. (1990), "Genetics of Candida albicans," *Microbiological Reviews,* 54(3), 226–241.

Shaw, P. (1991), "Science research students' composing processes," *English for Specific Purposes,* 10, 189–206.

Sherman, J. (1992), "Your own thoughts in your own words," *ELT Journal,* 46, 190–198.

Smallwood, S. (2002), "Professor accused of plagiarism gets to keep her job," *Chronicle of Higher Education,* 48(36), at A14.

Sokolik, M. (2000), "Before the horse is out of the barn: preventing plagiarism," *Writing Across Berkeley,* 1(2). Retrieved 25 April, 2002 from http://writing.berkeley.edu/wab/1-2-before.htm.

Sowden, C. (2005), "Plagiarism and the culture of multilingual students in higher education abroad," *ELT Journal,* 59, 226–233.

Spack, R. (1997), "The acquisition of academic literacy in a second language: A longitudinal case study," *Written Communication,* 14, 3–62.

Swales, J. M. (1996), "Occluded genres in the academy: the case of the submission letter," in E. Ventola and A. Mauranen (eds), *Academic Writing: Intercultural and Textual Issues* (pp. 45–58) (Amsterdam: John Benjamins).

Villalva, K. E. (2006), "Hidden literacies and inquiry approaches of bilingual high school writers," *Written Communication,* 23, 91–129.

Index